Destruction at DAWN

The Air-Raid Coded "Bodenplatte"
Luftwaffe vs. the Allies, New Year's Day, 1945

Arthur Bishop

McGraw-Hill
Ryerson

Toronto   Montreal   New York   Burr Ridge   Bangkok   Bogotá
Caracas   Lisbon   London   Madrid   Mexico City   Milan
New Delhi   Seoul   Singapore   Sydney   Taipei

To my daughter, Diana

McGraw-Hill
Ryerson Limited

A Subsidiary of The McGraw·Hill Companies

ISBN: 0-07-560420-5

1 2 3 4 5 6 7 8 9 0   TRI   7 6 5 4 3 2 1 0 9 8
Printed and bound in Canada.

Canadian Cataloguing in Publication Data

Bishop, William Arthur, 1923–
  Destruction at dawn

Includes bibliographical references and index.
ISBN 0-07-560420-5

1. World War, 1939-1945 – Aerial operations, German. 2. Air bases – Belgium – History. 3. Air bases – France – History. 4. Air bases – Netherlands – History. 5. Germany. Luftwaffe – History – World War, 1939-1945. 6. World War, 1939-1945 – Personal narratives. I. Title.

D787.B753 1998   940.54'21   C98-932420-6

PUBLISHER: **Joan Homewood**
EDITORIAL CO-ORDINATOR: **Catherine Leek**
PRODUCTION CO-ORDINATOR: **Susanne Penny**
EDITOR: **Focus Strategic Communications (Ron and Adriana Edwards)**
INTERIOR DESIGN AND ELECTRONIC PAGE COMPOSITION: **Lynda Powell**
PHOTOS: **Courtesy Department of Defence**
COVER DESIGN: **Dianna Little**
COVER PHOTO: **Eagles at Dawn by Robert Taylor, reproduced courtesy of Military Gallery, Ojai, CA 93023**

TABLE OF CONTENTS

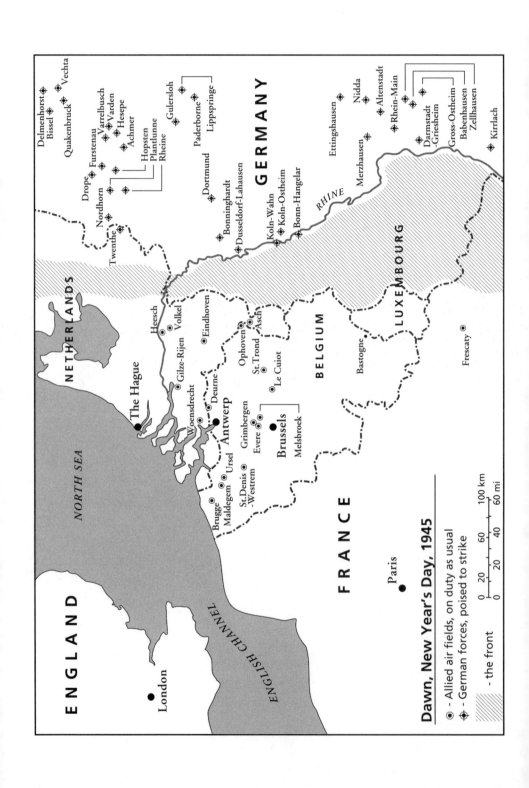

ENGLAND

NETHERLANDS

GERMANY

BELGIUM

LUXEMBOURG

FRANCE

NORTH SEA

ENGLISH CHANNEL

RHINE

London

The Hague

Antwerp

Brussels

Paris

Bastogne

Frescaty

Delmenhorst
Bissel
Vechta
Quakenbruck
Varrelbusch
Varden
Hesepe
Furstenau
Achmer
Gulersloh
Lippspringe
Paderborne
Hopsten
Plantlunne
Rheine
Drope
Nordhorn
Dortmund
Twenthe
Bonninghardt
Dusseldorf-Lahausen
Koln-Wahn
Koln-Ostheim
Bonn-Hangelar
Ettingshausen
Merzhausen
Nidda
Altenstadt
Rhein-Main
Darmstadt
-Griesheim
Gross-Ostheim
Babenhausen
Zellhausen
Kirrlach

Heesch
Volkel
Eindhoven
Ophoven
Asch
St.Trond
Le Cuiot
Gilze-Rijen
Deurne
Woensdrecht
Grimbergen
Evere
Melsbroek
Ursel
St.Denis
-Westrem
Brugge
Maldegem

Dawn, New Year's Day, 1945

⊚ - Allied air fields, on duty as usual

✦ - German forces, poised to strike

| 0 | 20 | 40 | 60 | 100 km |

| 0 | 20 | 40 | 60 mi |

░ - the front

FOREWORD

Every war has had its great battles — on the ground, at sea and in the air — battles recorded in histories and biographies of heroes and great leaders which are studied by generations of students. But many battles in our wars are scarcely recorded except in offical records. One of these was Bodenplatte.

Arthur Bishop — a former Spitfire pilot and son of one of Canada's great military heroes, Billy Bishop, high-scoring fighter ace of World War I — has focused attention on just such an epic which was, in fact, one of the most dramatic air battles of all time.

To the pilots of the Luftwaffe who had suffered undeserved ridicule from their very leaders whose decisions thrust them into a no-win situation, it was their final attempt to salvage their pride in a war already lost. It cost the Germans many of their outstanding pilots and ended an era in which they gave their best for their homeland but were blamed by their leaders for the German downfall.

For the Allied side, such as my own fighter group which was victoriously involved, this encounter was particularly spectacular for the ground crews and support personnel. For the first time, they were witness to enemy planes being shot down right over their own airfields by pilots they had, time and again, sent into combat. Before this, they could have only pictured it in their imagination.

In this comprehensive account, Arthur Bishop has provided one of the best researched narratives of those who fought and died in that remarkable air battle over Belgium, France and Holland on that New Year's Day morning in 1945. He has included their names, units and achievements — many in their own words — in this exciting and accurate story of what happened.

Robert H. Powell, Jr.
Official Historian
352nd Fighter Group Association

ACKNOWLEDGEMENTS

The old saw goes, it's better late than never. That I finally completed this compendium after more than 20 years of deliberation, fits and starts, much humming and hawing — procrastination at times, but never, ever, a loss of interest or enthusiasm — could only have been made possible through the encouragement, help and support of those who so willingly contributed in one way or another to this project. I hope my interpretation and translation of those effort properly reflect that very welcome input.

Taking it off the top, two very important women in my life go to the head of the class. Back in the mid-seventies, long before she became a noted TV journalist, my daughter Diana initiated the preliminary research and since then never lost her passion for the subject and insistently prodded me to get on with it. Then, when my ever-persistent literary agent Frances Hanna took over the controls, the project turned rapidly into venture, clearing the way for a fast take-off. *Mesdames, merci beaucoup!*

The subsequent flight path on which they had launched me led into vistas of hitherto untold first-hand reports and recollections by survivors of that notorious New Year's morning. Their memories, splendidly intact, painted as clear a picture as any chronicler could ever have asked for.

Let's begin with two veterans of the unit stationed on one of the American fighter bases in Belgium during the Luftwaffe attack that morning: Colonel Richard J. DeBruin USAF Ret, president of the 352nd Fighter Group Association, a survivor of the "Legend of Asch"; and former fighter pilot Robert H. "Punchy" Powell, the organization's official historian and chronicler, to whom I am grateful for kindly consenting to write the foreword to this book. Dick and Bob were also of tremendous help in providing the background from both the aerial and ground perspectives of that epic encounter (more about which we shall learn), as well as checking my account of this event for accuracy. Blue Skys, you guys!

It was through my old 401 Squadron mate Rod Smith that, by way of Don Lopez, Deputy Director of the National Air and Space Museum of the Smithsonian Institution (one of Claire Chennault's Flying Tigers), via William M. Butler, Historical Officer of the Air Force Historical Research Branch, that led me to Dick and Punchy.

A lot of other fighter jocks and related bods and sods also delved into their diaries, logbooks and memory banks to provide glimpses, vignettes and on-the-spot experiences from which to form a comprehensive panorama of events leading up to that fateful morning, what eventually happened and what finally resulted. Among them are: Bill Baggs, Al Bathurst (since deceased), Bill Beatty, Len Commerford, Chuck Darrow, Eric Downer, Renee Flanagan (Ed's widow), Ken Harvey, Gordon Hill, Ken Langmuir, Andy Lord, Ed MacKay, Fred Mills, George Nadon, Don Piery, Jim Prendergast, Dick Reeves, Bill Roddie, Art Sager, Ernie Savard, Ted Smith, Bob Spooner and Les Wilson. Cheers, chaps — Right on!

Many others assisted me in assorted ways: Lesley Bell and Scott Millard of the Metropolitan Toronto Reference Library; Anne Melvin, the Royal Canadian Military Institute librarian; Regimental historian John Grodzinski; Dick Malott, former Canadian War Museum curator and military consultant; and special mention to Ron Edwards for another yeoman task of editing. To all, a big thank-you!

Arthur Bishop
Toronto

DECEMBER 31, 1944

A DESTE FIDELES — In Belgium, France and the Netherlands, church bells were ringing in the New Year. The lights were going on again in London. The Stars and Stripes fluttered over most of the Philippines. The Red Army had steamrollered across the Eastern Front to the Danube where the Russians had Budapest surrounded. Hungary had turned coat to declare war on Germany, her former ally. In the West, the Americans and British still had to cross the Rhine, but that was only a matter of time. The Allies enjoyed complete air superiority everywhere. German communications, oil and transportation centres were being methodically decimated one by one through Royal Air Force and United States Army Air Forces' round-the-clock bombing. From bases in China and Saigon, American bombers were subjecting Japan to incessant air raids. Tokyo itself had been bombed five times during the month of December alone. At sea the U-boat was no longer a threat to Allied shipping in the Atlantic. In the Pacific, Japanese merchant shipping had been reduced by a half by the American submarine fleet and mine laying. It was a time for rejoicing. Tomorrow the world would be free. V for Victory!

The downside was that World War II still had over seven long, bloody months to go. Rockets and flying bombs were still falling on England, Belgium and Holland. Kamikaze suicide planes were destroying United States naval vessels by the score. Germany and Japan were fighting for their lives. The Allied terms of unconditional surrender guaranteed that they would battle to the death.

But there was no question that victory was in sight. Everywhere the Axis was reeling. And, the best news of all — on Christmas Day 1944, the first irradiated slugs of uranium had been turned out by a reactor at the atomic research centre in Hartford, Connecticut, and a month later the first plutonium was ready for shipping. Those privy to this secret sensed an elated feeling of impending triumph. The atomic bomb that would end it all was about to become a reality.

CHAPTER 1

THE WESTERN FRONT

As 1944 drew to a close, an aura of complacency had permeated the fighter, fighter-bomber, medium-bomber and night-fighter squadrons of the Allied tactical air forces on the Continent in Belgium, France and Holland, as well as the upper echelons of command. And with good reason. Thanks to their efforts, the German Ardennes offensive, the notorious Battle of the Bulge, had been blunted. Ever since the weather improved two days before Christmas, the Allies had ruled the skies over the battlefield.

Due to the strictest security on the part of the Luftwaffe, there was no inkling, no reason to suspect, that the Germans had taken great pains to prepare a surprise blow, an all-out effort to neutralise their cocky protagonists. All they needed was clear weather with unlimited visibility to launch it. And on New Year's Eve the meteorologists had forecast exactly those conditions for the following morning.

New Year's Eve, 1944
OSSINGTON FLYING TRAINING FIELD, England

Leading Aircraftwoman Renee Taylor was counting the hours. Only 12 days more and she and Ed Flanagan were going to be married. They had met at the Nottingham-based Royal Air Force Operational Training Unit, where she worked as a stenographer; he had been a student Flying Officer. Before he left to report to 440 Typhoon Squadron of the Royal Canadian Air Force at Eindhoven in Holland, he and Renee had become engaged. Ed was due to go on leave at the beginning of the second week of January. Then the couple would be wed at Golcar Parish Church in the Yorkshire town where Renee's family lived near Huddersfield.

ASCH AIRFIELD, BELGIUM

It bugged him. Call it intuition, but Lieutenant Colonel John "J.C." Meyer, acting commander of the 9th United States Tactical Air Force 352nd Fighter Group, couldn't shake a persistent, haunting premonition of impending disaster. It nagged at him, made him feel edgy, uneasy. Meyer had a hunch that with all the recent strafing, dive-bombing and rocket-firing by the Allied tactical air forces against the German Wehrmacht, some sort of retaliation beyond the normal aerial resistance on the part of the Luftwaffe just might be imminent. All the signs were there. High-flying, predatory Arado 234 twin-engine jet reconnaissance aircraft had been constantly hovering over the Allied tactical airfields, obviously reconnoitring them. On Christmas Day alone 31 of them had been counted. There was also the nightly intrusion of "Bedcheck Charlie," a German Junkers 88 twin-engine night-fighter/bomber who sprayed the field with cannon fire and dropped the odd bomb at random just after dark. He was nothing more than a bloody nuisance, really. But, perhaps an omen nevertheless?

Meyer had a theory: if "you want to beat the enemy, you have to think like the enemy." Put yourself in the others guy's flying boots. One maxim that could not be discounted was never to rule the Germans out. They were masters of surprise. The Ardennes offensive had certainly proved that. Meyer's P-51 Mustang fighters, along with the P-47 Thunderbolts of the 9th USAF 366th Fighter Group, stationed on the same field, were scheduled for a bomber-escort mission the next morning. That would leave Y-29 Airfield, as Asch was designated, virtually unprotected except for the ack-ack guns. That operation rankled Meyer, worried him even more — the last straw.

He decided on a plan of action. Pipe clenched firmly between his teeth, he picked up the telephone and put in a call to General Elwood "Pete" Quesada at 9th Tactical Air Force Headquarters to ask his permission to mount a defensive patrol of his Mustangs over the field at first light — just in case. He wanted to surprise the Germans instead of the other way around.

FURSTENAU AIRFIELD, Germany

"Ach! What kind of bullshit is this?" Oberstleutnant Josef "Pips" Priller, the pugnacious little Kommodore of the Jagdgeschwader 26, the famed Luftwaffe fighter wing recognised on both sides of the air war as the "Abbeville Boys," was livid. At 5 foot 4, with 100 victories to his credit, "Pips" Priller was not only the most diminutive of the top German aces, he was also the most vitriolic. What he lacked in size he more than made up in combativeness, and Pips had a very short fuse.

When he received his Geschwader's (wing's) orders for the long-awaited "Big Show" scheduled for the following morning, he blew his stack. The role cut out for his wing was enough to put anybody's back up. But what bridled him just as much were the restrictions laid down with the operational order — all passes cancelled, early curfew, bar closed.

Unbelievable! The idiots! No drinks? No New Year's Eve party? What do they think we are, a bunch of boy scouts? We're fighter pilots for chrissake! Don't they understand that flying, carousing and screwing around go hand in hand? The dummkopfs! When his adjutant pointed out that the instructions had arrived signed, sealed and delivered from the Jagdkorps 11 commander, Generalmajor Dietrich Peltz himself, Priller nearly had a fit.

"Just what you'd expect when you put a damned bomber pilot in charge of a fighter command," he fumed and stalked off.

BRUSSELS-MELSBROEK AIRFIELD, Belgium

Wing Commander Mike Shaw, commanding officer of 69 Squadron (night-reconnaissance) of the Royal Air Force, had a special reason for wanting an all-out New Year's Eve thrash, a complete ragtime show. Late that afternoon, on his return from Christmas leave with his family in England, he learned that he had been awarded the Distinguished Service Order for bravery, the second highest British Commonwealth decoration after the Victoria Cross.

During the celebration at the bar in the 33 Reconnaissance Wing Headquarters officers' mess — long after the "wishing-in" hour of midnight — one of Shaw's drinking companions reminded him of the promise he'd made earlier. As soon as it got light he would air test a repaired Short Sterling bomber which had been shot up and crash-landed on the field a month earlier. Since Shaw had never flown a four-engine aircraft before — 69 Squadron was equipped with twin-engine Wellingtons — his confrère subtly suggested that it might be better if he were sober when he flew the test, hinting that it was probably time to turn in. Shaw scoffed at the notion. Reaching for a fresh Scotch and soda he assured everyone within earshot: "No trouble at all. I've read the bloody pilot's manual for that crate and that's all I need to know. I can fly that son of a bitch half-pissed with one arm tied behind my back and my eyes closed." Those around him laughed but shook their heads. Shaw caught the signal. "Allright then," he conceded, gulping down his drink. "Bottoms up! But knock me up around seven, will you, so I can get a fresh start." As it turned out, all this concern couldn't have mattered less. For all the difference it would make, Shaw might as well have slept round the clock.

EINDHOVEN AIRFIELD, Holland

Like all 2nd Tactical Air Force fighter units in Europe, half the pilots of 440 Squadron were on noon-to-noon duty, while the other half had 24 hours off. Tonight, bridegroom-to-be Ed Flanagan was one of those on deck. He and his fellow Typhoon pilots had been told they were on tap for an early morning show — 0700 hours, a low-level rocket sweep in search of enemy installations and transports in the Ardennes area. These exacting attacks called for a maximum degree of concentration and precision that only came with training, practice and experience. It was dangerous work in the face of ferocious and agonisingly accurate enemy ground fire.

Fortunately the "Tiffie" was a tough old bird, built to take it, with a top speed of 400 miles an hour in level flight at low altitude, and 550 mph in a dive. The basic strategy was to pinpoint the target — tanks, bridges, trains, motor transport, installations, emplacements and others — from a safe distance, then dive to the deck and attack with rockets or bombs or both. Remaining on the deck until out of range of the ground gunners, the pilot would yank his aircraft up into a vertical climbing turn to regain height. The rocket-firing Typhoon squadrons had perfected the technique to such an extent that they were regarded as the most effective air-to-ground weapons of the entire war by all of the Allied armies.

When the weather had cleared over the Ardennes nine days earlier, US Third Army commander General George Patton had specifically requested rocket-firing support from 2nd TAF's 83 Group Typhoons because he had such confidence in them. (He was not the only one impressed. An Allied ULTRA decoding intercept quoted a 1st SS Panzer Division officer bemoaning the fact that a single direct hit by a rocket on a Panther tank would write it off completely.) Patton's request paid off handsomely for the American advance but it cost 143 Wing RCAF, of which Ed Flanagan's squadron was a part, heavily. On Christmas Eve alone the unit lost eight pilots and many more aircraft suffered severe flak damage. It was small wonder that Flanagan decided to forego the New Year's Eve party of the off-duty pilots in the small bar at the Eindhoven convent where the wing was billeted. He wanted to be alert for the morning show. After a couple of belts of schnapps he announced to the others, "I'm turning in," and hit the sack knowing he would get the wake-up call at 0500 hours next morning. He was soon joined by his squadron mates who were also scheduled for the morning patrol, among them Flying Officers Iva Gunnarson, Currie Gardner, Ted Smith, Dick Watson and Flight Lieutenant Ernie Savard. To Ed, Ossington and his fiancée Renee seemed a million miles away.

GUTERSLOH AIRFIELD, Germany

Oberleutnant Oscar Boesch looked forward to an evening of relaxation and revelry in town. During the past few weeks he and his fellow fighter pilots of Gruppe IV had been put through a particularly rough time against those "damned Fortresses" — Public Enemy Number One, the Luftwaffe fighter pilots labelled them B-17s. The American four-engine bombers were well protected by long-range P-51 Mustang fighters. But as part of Jagdgeschwader 3, named the "Udet Geschwader" after Germany's second-ranking World War I fighter ace, Ernst Udet, Boesch's Gruppe IV had been singled out for bomber-contact attacks. Ignore the American fighters and zero in on the "big birds," they were told. It was suicidal in the face of deadly cross-cover fire from the multi-armed B-17s. Those who survived — losses were horrendous — landed with their aircraft riddled. On one pass, Boesch had the perspex hood of his Focke Wulf 190 blown right off. But that evening he'd forget about all that and have some fun.

However, when he landed that evening he learned that all passes had been cancelled and the bar had been closed. An important early morning show was in the offing — orders directly from Altenkirchen, the Jagdkorps 11 Headquarters. Everything hush-hush. No details. Briefings to be held on the field at dawn. No doubt something big and important — and, most probably, goddam dangerous.

Boesch accepted these orders philosophically, though the clamp-down of station activities meant giving up a date he had with a fräulein at the brauhaus in Gutersloh which, for fear of breaching security, he couldn't even break. In any case he was in no position to object. He lacked the rank, fame, clout and nerve to resist authority à la Pips Priller. To Boesch, *befehl ist befehl* — orders are orders. Just as well. He had no way of telling that next day he would take part in one of the most memorable moments in the Udet wing's already illustrious history.

BRUSSELS-GRIMBERGEN AIRFIELD, Belgium

For a recently liberated area, there was nothing festive about B60 on this New Year's Eve. For one thing, there was hardly anybody at home. Late in the afternoon, Group Captain Alexander

Gabszewicz, along with his adjutant, had arrived by jeep from St Denis-Westram Airfield where his 131 Polish Spitfire Wing was stationed, to facilitate moving the unit to the airfield the next day. The pair spent the afternoon inspecting the facilities and making last minute arrangements for the transfer. Having finalised plans to have the three squadrons — 302, 308 and 317 — fly in the next afternoon, they celebrated the incoming year relatively unceremoniously in the officers' mess with the station personnel before turning in.

Next morning, at their leisure, they planned to double-check their preparations to make sure nothing had been over-looked. With nothing and nobody to interrupt them, they looked forward to it. And because the squadrons wouldn't be arriving until after lunch there was no great rush. They would have all the time in the world.

DELMENHORST, QUACKENBRUCK, VECHTA and BISSEL AIRFIELDS, Germany

In contrast to Pips Priller who had gone ballistic, when Jagdgeschwader 6 Kommodore, Oberstleutnant Johann Kogler received orders for New Year's Day from Jagdkorps 11 Head-quarters at noon hour, he looked upon the assignment with grim satisfaction — curfew, prohibition and all. Here was a God-given opportunity to get even for the losses sustained by his JG over the past ten days at the hands of the British RAF Tempests. From aerial reconnaissance photographs, Kogler and his Gruppe commanders knew that five squadrons of the fleet, whippet-like fighter-bombers, were based at Volkel — their intended target — which at no time were ever properly dis-persed. They had planned their attack to the nth degree days before receiving their final instructions, even to the extent of producing a table-top sand model of the target in detail.

"There's really nothing that can go wrong," asserted Gruppe III commander Major Helmut Kuhle (whose Staffeln squadrons were stationed at nearby Bissel airfield) confidently. "It's fool-proof!"[1]

VOLKEL AIRFIELD, Belgium

Back in October, B-80 became the continental home for the RAF Hawker Tempest (the successor to the Typhoon), the fastest, most modern of all of the piston-driven Allied fighter-bombers, and by far the most durable.

The Tempests had first gone into operational service in April 1944. In June they had been withdrawn from the Normandy campaign to cope with the V-1 flying bomb attacks on London. Once that threat had been overcome with the capture of the "doodlebug" launching pads when the British and Canadian Armies overran France and Belgium, the five squadrons that made up Wing Commander John Wray's 122 Wing were posted to Belgium.

On New Year's Eve, three of Wray's squadrons were scheduled for operational flying duty next morning. Leading off at 0855 hours would be two flights from Squadron Leader Jimmy Thiele's 3 Squadron on an armed reconnaissance over the Paderborn region. In quick succession they would be followed by the New Zealanders of 486 Squadron led by their CO "Spike" Umbers, and 56 Squadron led by Squadron Commander Donald Cotes-Preedy, which would join them near Hanover. The other two squadrons, 80 and 274, remained on the field.

Absent from the 3 Squadron roster was Pilot Officer Ron Pottinger who had completed a two-year tour with the squadron in which he had distinguished himself as a V-1 ace, having shot down six of the "buzz bombs" during the summer. Pottinger had just returned from a week's Christmas leave in

England that evening, more as a formality than anything else. While on furlough, orders striking him off strength had been issued; all that was left for him to do was to obtain station clearance, pack up his gear and return to the UK and await a training command posting. He had arrived back at base utterly exhausted after an arduous, circuitous trek via sea and land, anathema to any airman. But with the weather disrupting the Dakotas flying ferry service between Northolt and Eindhoven, he had no choice but to hitch a trip by Royal Naval motor torpedo boat from Dover to Ostend and then bum a ride in the back of a transport to Volkel. By the time he reached the squadron billets which were in an empty seminary at Uden, ten miles from the airfield, he was so tired, cold and dirty that all he wanted to do was to take a hot bath and climb into bed. But his confrères, intent on celebrating the New Year and commemorating the completion of his tour, were determined to deny him that. They shepherded him to the party in the mess which was well under way and, after a few straight Scotches, he quickly revived and joined in the spirit of the occasion — temporarily.

Soon after midnight Pottinger began to falter, his weariness finally catching up with him. He quietly sneaked off and staggered back to the seminary where he crawled into bed hoping he would sleep forever. Alas, it was not to be. Fate would intervene with other plans.

EINDHOVEN AIRFIELD, Holland

Jim Prendergast, a flight commander with 430 Squadron RCAF of the 39 "R" Wing, and the rest of the reconnaissance pilots couldn't wait for the morning to try out their spanking new Spitfire XIV's in action. These were especially designed for low-level fighter reconnaissance with four camera-mounting positions and armed with two 20-millimetre cannons and four

50-calibre machine-guns. Powered with 2,100-horsepower Merlin Griffin engines, they had five-bladed propellers and clipped wings, the latter to allow tighter turns at low level instead of the standard elliptical wings designed for higher altitude manoeuvrability. Eight pilots from the squadron had been assigned to support the American armies. The weather forecast for the following morning called for clear skies, a chance to put their new" kites," which they had picked up only a week earlier in England, to the purpose for which they had been built. Their assignment was low "armed recce" over the area around Xanton and Wiesel in the Rhine River area. Prendergast was chosen to lead the show. 430 Squadron not only had the best Spitfires, but, along with the other two squadrons of 39 "R" Wing, RCAF enjoyed the finest accommodation at Eindhoven, in every way. Located at the east end of the field, which in peacetime had served as a passenger-airline facility, the masonry-constructed living and messing conditions, though austere, were satisfactory and the food was at least passable. When the Germans overran Holland, the field had been mobilised as a bomber base, with concrete bombproof buildings. But the last word was the dispersal area which was hidden by pine trees brought from Germany to create a forest around the airfield. That day, three wings or 11 squadrons plus transports occupied the airfield which had one of the longest runways in Europe — 4,000 yards. It allowed for plenty of speed for take-off and ease of landing.[2]

One manifestation of the latter occurred midway through the afternoon when Flying Officer Gordon Hill of 416 Squadron based at Brussels-Evere came limping in after his Spitfire XIV was shot up by German anti-aircraft fire near Paderborn. Taxiing over to the nearest Spitfire dispersal, he was told that his aircraft could be easily repaired and it could be ready by 0900 hours next morning.[3]

A little later in the day, Flight Lieutenant George Bromfield, an official RCAF artist, one of 32 members of Canada's official war art programme, positioned himself on the west side of the airfield and began a charcoal sketch of the 143 Wing dispersal areas. The final rendering showed Typhoons neatly parked with two in the circuit orbiting, getting ready to land. Bromfield titled it *Dispersal Eindhoven, December 31, 1944.* The scene was all nice and peaceful and revealed just how totally exposed the field and its aircraft were to enemy air attack. Bromfield little realised how vividly his next drawings of the same scene would vindicate his artistic impression of that afternoon.

Before going over to the mess for dinner that evening, Paul Davoud, the officer commanding 143 Wing, looked over the flight orders for the following morning. All four squadrons were to be in the air shortly after daybreak. At 0830 hours, a flight from 439 Squadron would take off for a weather check around St Vith. At the same time a flight from 168 Squadron was to proceed on an armed reconnaissance in the same Ardennes area. At 0910 hours, 414 Squadron would take off for a three-pronged tactical sweep of the Munich and Cologne district. 440 Squadron would then take off with its objective of bombing and rocket attacks in the Ardennes. Having signed off the morning's orders, Davoud repaired to the officers' mess. After dinner he joined the others in the ante-room for the New Year's celebration. Davoud fully intended to enjoy the party to the utmost. This was his last night as Wingco flying. Tomorrow he would turn over his command to his close friend, Ernie Moncreif. Cheers Ernie. Soon it'll all be yours!

Corporal E.W.J. "Ted" Sadler, on guard duty outside the officers' mess, could hear the sounds of revelry and singing coming from inside. It was well past midnight when they were interrupted by the noise of the engine of a German Fieseler Storch spotting plane flying low across the field. By the time Sadler had levelled his Sten gun at the aircraft, it was gone. But, what the hell was it doing here anyway? He would soon find out.

FURSTENAU, NORDHORN and PLATLUNNE AIRFIELDS, Germany

Since the Battle of Britain, the "Abbeville Boys," as Jagdgeschwader 26 Schlageter was acknowledged by both sides, had built a proud tradition. Named after Albert Leo Schlageter, a World War I army officer who had been executed by the French for his opposition to the Allied occupation of the Ruhr in 1919, it was based at the mouth of the Somme and had spawned such German aces as Adolf Galland and his brother Wilhelm "Wutz" Galland, Emil "Bully" Lang and Walter "Count" Krupinski. Now it was up to its present Kommodore, the feisty, outspoken Oberstleutnant Josef "Pips" Priller, to live up to that proud heritage. He had his work cut out for him.

Priller had already expressed his indignation over the orders for the "Big Show" and their attendant disciplinary instructions he'd received from Jagdkorps Headquarters. Now he had to digest the details. It was enough to give him heartburn. They were sheer folly. The plans called for JG 26 to embark on its most ambitious, onerous and, to Priller, absolutely foolhardy venture to date. Even to the uninitiated the strategy seemed reckless. The objective was to tackle not one target, but two — the Brussels airfields of Grimbergen and Evere — and both at the same time. Nothing like splitting your forces in half! What the hell were they thinking? Priller wondered whether the planners at Jagdkorps 11 Headquarters had lost their minds altogether.

BRUSSELS-EVERE AIRFIELD, Belgium

After flying his last sortie of the day, Flight Lieutenant Dick Reeves, a flight commander with 403 RCAF "Wolf" Squadron, taxied his Spitfire over to the dispersal area and parked it along-side a row of the 16 other fighter planes in the squadron all neatly arrayed — "as if they were getting ready for a Wings Parade," Reeves would later remember ruefully. The all-Canadian 127 Wing of 83 Group, commanded by the top Allied ace Wing Commander Johnnie Johnson, was made up of four RCAF squadrons, only two of which, 403 and 416, were on the airfield at the time. The so-called "Hornet" Squadron, 443, was at No. 7 Armament Training Camp, Warmwell in the south of England on a bombing and air-firing course, where it replaced 421 Squadron after the latter unit completed its fort-night course there. The "Falcons," as they were nicknamed, had flown to Tangmere on the Sussex coast to trade their IXs in for new Spitfire XVIs before returning to Belgium. Nevertheless at Evere, according to Reeves, there were upwards of 40 Spit-fires lined up "like a flying training school" on the east side of the field. On the opposite perimeter, assorted transports were parked — Ansons, a Flying Fortress, an Auster, and a luxury VIP passenger Dakota along with Prince Bernhard of the Netherlands' private sky-blue-coloured Beechcraft.

This overcrowding was symptomatic of the way Allied Tactical Air Forces' airfields were unprepared for possible enemy air attack. But it couldn't be helped, or so the Allied TAF head-quarters seemed to want to believe. Anyway, the probability of such an assault had been virtually ruled out, if indeed it had been given any thought at all. After all, since the Normandy landings in June, except for sporadic hit-and-run raids, the tac-tical airfields had been left unscathed. Air Marshal Sir Arthur "Maori" (aka "Mary") Coningham, the New Zealand com-mander of the TAF, had only 27 airfields, spread across Bel-gium, Holland and northern France, with which to handle more than 2,000 fighters, fighter-bombers, medium-bombers and support aircraft such as transports and artillery spotters.

He was also denied adequate anti-aircraft protection. Most of the ack-ack batteries had been moved to other areas in the path of the V-1 flying bomb threat. Under these conditions any attempt to conceal aircraft by dispersal was pointless. For example, camouflage netting had been dispensed with ever since the Normandy breakthrough in August.

Johnnie Johnson's 127 Wing lived like kings in luxurious mansions in Brussels requisitioned from collaborators. And this was New Year's Eve, a time for fun and games for most. But not for Flight Lieutenant Dick Reeves, Flying Officer Mackenzie "Mac" Reeves (no relation), Flight Lieutenant Dave Harling, Pilot Officer Steve Butte, Sergeant Pilot Doug Lindsay and Flying Officer Eric Downer, to name a few. They were down for the first patrols of New Year's Day, so they decided to pass up the partying and turned in early.

However, those not on duty decided to live it up which, according to 421 Squadron Flying Officer Ken Langmuir, who had been left behind when the squadron flew to Warmwell for the air-firing course, transpired into a DCO — Duty Carried Out — with a vengeance. "We really tied one on," he recalled. It was well into the New Year by the time he and his fellow revellers closed the bar.

Earlier in the day, in the late afternoon, Flying Officer Bill Roddie of 416 had, in his own words, "nearly got my ass shot off by flying into a German flak trap." With his Spitfire "Fearless Fosdick" needing repair, his name was taken off the roster for a patrol next morning. He would be off flying until noon, though he was slated for 24-hour Orderly Officer duty that evening.[4]

Under normal circumstances Roddie would have been slotted to fly as Dave Harling's number two the next morning, part of a four-man patrol that Squadron Flight Commander Harling would lead. Ever since Harling had "shot down his first Hun in Normandy" in July, Roddie had flown as his wingman at Harling's insistence. It was a position in which Roddie felt honoured to serve because he regarded his number one as "one of the finest, most fearless leaders I ever met on my tour." Within a matter of hours he would realise that the circumstances that prevented him from being able to make one last flight in that capacity probably saved his life.

As soon as Roddie landed that afternoon, he filled in the L-17 form itemising the estimated damage to his Spit, made out his report, changed into uniform, and then took off for town. What else? It was New Year's Eve for chrissake!

In Brussels he had been far luckier than he had been over the Rhine-Munster area. During his reconnaissance of the various local bistros in town, unlike the hostile reception he'd received earlier in the unfriendly skies over Germany, on the friendly terra firma down in Belgium, Roddie was subjected to the warmest welcome anyone could ask for. This was the first New Year's in the past five that the country had been free from Nazi occupation. To the Belgians, Roddie was a hero, a liberator, and they couldn't do enough for him. This was particularly true of a pretty Brussels belle with the bright brown eyes whom he met at a dance club. *L'amour* at first sight! By the wee hours of the morning he needed no persuasion to accept her invitation to spend what was left of the night at her family's home in the suburbs, only half an hour's walking distance from the Evere airfield.

A little earlier, when the festivities wound up back at the 416 officers' mess, on behalf of the CO, Squadron Leader Jack Michner, as adjutant, signed off the month's official report in the operations record book. The final entry read:

31.12.44 Well here we are in the last day of 1944 and it hasn't been a bad year, taking everything into consideration, But (sic) we hope that we don't have every month like

December in which we lost four men. Three of our boys are down with colds, but they will probably go all out for New Year's. A Big party was held in the Billets and everyone really ushered in the New Year in true CANADIAN fashion. I wonder what the New Year holds in store for us. Let's hope we can stop sending in this report and get back to Civvy Street very shortly.

DARMSTADT-GREISHEIM, ZEILLHAUSEN and GROSS-OSTHEIM AIRFIELDS, Germany

By any measurement, Jagdgeschwader 11 was a force to be reckoned with. Three of its leaders were among the top German air aces. Between them, their one-eyed Geschwader Kommodore, Oberstleutnant Gunther Specht, Gruppe I commander Hauptmann Rudyar Kirchmayr, and Hauptmann Horst von Fassong, commanding Gruppe III, had accounted for more than 220 Allied aircraft shot down, nearly a third of them the deadly multi-armed Flying Fortresses. Added to this impressive record was the fact that, collectively, the rest of the pilots that made up the three Gruppen of the JG had been credited with another 100 victories. Make no mistake about it; the potential killing power of Specht's horde of 18 Staffeln (squadrons), numbering nearly 90 Focke Wulf 190s and Me 109s, all armed with 500-pound bombs, was not one to be taken lightly. Small wonder the Geschwader leaders looked forward with anticipation to the following morning's "duty." Tonight — early to bed. Tomorrow — *Horrido!*

ASCH AIRFIELD, Belgium

Y-29, as American fighter base was coded, home to the 366th Fighter Group of the 9th United States Air Force and the 352nd Fighter Group on loan from the 8th USAF, was swarming with Mustang and Thunderbolt fighters as well as Dakota transports. The American pilots' basic objective was aerial support for the US ground forces in the Ardennes. Specifically the Thunderbolts of the 390th and 391st Fighter Squadrons of the 366th Group, led by Captains Lowell B. Smith and Eber Simpson, respectively, were to attack ground targets by strafing, bombing and with rockets, while the Mustangs of 487th Fighter Squadron's Mustangs from Lieutenant Colonel John "J.C." Meyer's 352nd Group swept the skies above of enemy fighters.

The 352nd was a latecomer to Asch. The high-scoring group (600 victories) had been rushed into the Ardennes battle as a result of the bitter air fighting of December 23, a date in which the Luftwaffe put up its greatest effort yet — over 800 fighter aircraft — to try to ward off the incessant bomber and fighter attacks against the German ground forces. Both sides suffered heavily. That very evening, the 352nd arrived at its new home in Belgium.

After living a life of comparative luxury in their permanent quarters back at Bodney Airfield in England, the personnel were appalled at the crude accommodation that greeted them at Asch. Tents, shabby ones at that, were some comfort, but not much, from the frigid winter field conditions. The allocation of one pail of coal per day per customer didn't help much. The only shower facilities were in a nearby colliery, shared with the coal miners. The alternative was bathing by bucket. Headquarters, operations, intelligence, maintenance and supply services shared a single canvas covering, where all took turns warming their knuckles, waiting to hammer away on the lone, badly bent typewriter. The 352nd had no bar tent of its own and was in the debt of the 366th who willingly hosted their fellow officers, on a pay-cash basis, of course. For many in the newly arrived group, it was their first experience on the Continent, but they readily adapted to the local amenities in nearby Brussels and Hasselt — black market steaks and cognac, American-tasting beer, what passed off as cigarettes and, above all, *les femmes jollies.*

By December 31, only a week after their arrival, the air and ground crews of the 352nd had settled into their Spartan lodgings and accustomed themselves to their role in the Ardennes battle which, by this time, had been turned around in favour of the Allied fighters who controlled the air over the battlefield. Only their commander, Lieutenant Colonel J.C. Meyer, who by this time was the number one American fighter ace in the American Theatre of Operations with 22 enemy planes to his credit, had reservations. He couldn't shake the idea that the Luftwaffe might launch a surprise air attack on his airfield, or anybody else's for that matter, when no one was looking.

But his telephone request to General Pete Quesada, commander of the 9th Tactical Air Force, to fly an early morning patrol was refused. No dice! Strategic operations took precedence over local tactical considerations. Permission denied. The operational orders would stand as issued: Captain Eber Simpson's 391st Fighter Squadron Thunderbolts would take off shortly before 0900 hours to plaster German tanks with 500-pound bombs in the vicinity of St Vith, followed 15 minutes later by Captain Lowell Smith's 390th Squadron on an armed reconnaissance over the Ardennes. The Mustangs of the 487th would have to cool their heels until 1100 when they were scheduled to take off on an escort mission with medium-bombers attacking targets in the Kassel-Koblenz-Trier region.

While the pilots of the 366th Fighter Group squadrons were drinking in the New Year with the natives of Brussels and Hasselt, Meyer cautioned his pilots that they might very well be flying an early morning patrol the next day. Major Dick DeBruin, the 352nd Fighter Group's ground support officer, remembered: "After the evening meal, J.C. said, 'let's go over to the 366th area for one drink and then to bed.' I drove one of the jeeps and a group of us, including J.C., went for one drink. He appeared to be very calm that evening and one could imagine his thoughts were about the next morning."[5] As they bunked down in their tent cots for the night, it had begun to sleet. On the brighter side, the meteorological forecast called for it to clear overnight.

OPHOVEN AIRFIELD, Belgium

There were no such concerns of impending peril in the neighbouring British camp. At Y-32 Royal Air Force fighter field directly to the north of Asch, an all-out, no-holds-barred New Year's binge was in progress. Ophoven housed an armed reconnaissance wing made up of 41, 130, 350 (Belgium) and 610 squadrons — a total of some 120 Spitfire XIVs parked on the field. However, unlike his counterpart J.C. Meyer who was commander of the US 352nd Fighter Group, Wing Commander Frank Scott-Malden, a Battle of Britain ace, commanding 125 RAF Spitfire Wing, issued operational instructions for three of his squadrons to be airborne on extended missions by 0900 hours the following morning, without the slightest compunction that he might be exposing the airfield to enemy attack in their absence. Squadron Leader Donald Benham's 41 Squadron received orders to take off at 0820 hours on an armed reconnaissance over the Eifel, flying down the Rhine north of Koblenz looking for motorised transport. 610, led by Squadron Leader Roger Newbury, would mount a four-man patrol in the direction of Maeseych at 0850 hours. 350 Squadron which had arrived from Evere the day before where their ground crews were busily loading transports to reach the airfield by road early next morning — a route that would take them through Melsbroek

— was instructed to reconnoitre the Malmedy region. Led by Flying Officer Anton Van Wersch, three Spitfires would take off at 0900 hours.

HEESCH AIRFIELD, Holland

The most northerly of all the 2nd Tactical Air Force fields was a sorry excuse for an airfield. The personnel of 126 Spitfire Wing of the RCAF were billeted in some old wooden buildings that had once housed a regiment of the fanatical Hitler Youth. The accommodation was pretty ramshackle but at least it was better — and warmer — than living in tents. The Germans had bulldozed a single runway strip and laid down wire mesh to use it as a landing field of convenience, nothing more. Now the Canadians had turned it into an operational fighter field. The evening before taking part in the New Year's Eve festivities, Flight Lieutenant John Edison, the airfield control officer, inspected the control tower which was still being built. Satisfied that everything was in order, he then trundled over to the officers' mess where he joined Flying Officers Don Church, a member of 401 Squadron, and Al Bathurst at the bar. Both Church and Bathurst were off duty noon to noon and intended to make a real go of the evening. But Edison had to be in his tower before dawn so, after taking his fill, he bid them "Cheers and goodnight" and made for his bunk.[6]

Bathurst, who later admitted that, "I did a real number on myself," stayed on with the others. Somewhere through the haze earlier in the evening, he recalled that he had agreed to lend his kite to his squadron mate, Flight Lieutenant Donald "Chunky" Gordon," whose own Spitfire was U/S (unserviceable). A comradely gesture, it would be some time before he would be able to fly his aircraft again.

Don Church had long given up and gone to bed, but Bathurst, along with his roommate, were determined to see this New Year's Eve through to the bitter end. Long after 1945 had arrived, they closed the bar and careened their way into the night from the mess to their living billets where they flopped right into bed, asleep instantly.

BRUGES, Belgium

Pilots, Flight Lieutenants Bob Fowler and Bruce White and their navigators, Flying Officers Russ Hunter and Norm Powell, had just finished dinner in the *salle à manger* of the Cornet d'Or Hotel in the Place de Simon Stefa where they were temporarily billeted. The cuisine there was legendary — the chef could make Spam taste like Chateaubriand, the townsfolk liked to say. The four RAF Mitchell medium-bomber crews, who were in between operational tours, had been well fed indeed. Now they were ready to take on the town. However, they would have much preferred to be celebrating New Year's Eve with their mates in the RAF 2 Group Support Unit officers' mess at Fersfield in Norfolk, England, but circumstances had made that impossible.

Their job at Fersfield was to train twin-engine bomber Boston, Mitchell and Mosquito flight students. Ansons were also used as introductory trainers as well as to fly the graduated crews to the Continent to join the medium-bomber squadrons serving with RAF 2nd TAF. It was in just such a role that, shortly after noon two days earlier, the four GSU instructors found themselves, Fowler in the lead, headed towards Melsbroek-Brussels Airfield. By the time they reached the Belgian coast, it was blanketed in fog. When their Gee position-locating device told them they should be right over Melsbroek, they could see nothing. It was completely socked in, shrouded by the fog. The ground controller there advised them to proceed to Ghent which they were told was open. Shortly afterwards, as it started to turn dark, they reached the edge of the fog bank and began to let down. Ahead they could see the airfield on which a number of Spitfires were parked. Fowler told the homing controller that they had the field in sight and asked for landing clearance. There was a brief stutter of static over the radio transmitter, then silence. However, they continued their approach.

The Ansons made a sweeping left turn over Brussels to line up on the runway, a manoeuvre that put White in the lead ahead of Fowler. By now it was completely dark but with their landing lights on it was no problem getting the aircraft down onto the short perforated-steel landing strip. Turning a full 180 degrees about-face, the pilots began taxiing their aircraft one behind the other towards a barely visible control van, when suddenly White felt a sharp jolt that swung the Anson to the left and brought it to a standstill. Looking out of the cockpit, he and Powell could see that the wing-tip had been mangled by what they later learned was a huge tank trap made of rusted steel girders built by the Germans. Meanwhile, Fowler, wondering what the hell was going on when White's Anson suddenly stopped in front of him, was forced to brake sharply to avoid banging into it. When the Anson started to move forward again, Fowler, none the wiser, followed and promptly sheared off his own port wing-tip.

Having parked their aircraft, the crews and their passengers climbed out to be greeted by the airfield's orderly and engineering officers who told them that they had just landed at Maldegem, not Ghent, and were only a few miles from Bruges. The field was a maintenance depot where Spitfires, fresh from the British factories, were being modified for operational service. The engineering officer said that he thought he could trim off the Ansons' mangled wing-tips and cover them with fabric — good enough to get them back to England. But that would have to wait a few days because of the urgent demands for the Spitfires by the fighter squadrons. So much for the New Year's party at 2 GSU back in Norfolk!

The four 2 GSU instructors spent New Year's Eve doing the rounds of the cafés and small bars in Bruges. The Belgians were letting off steam after four harsh years of Nazi rule. They toasted in 1945 in high spirits and the Anson crews found themselves hosted as celebrities. It was well into the New Year before they dragged themselves back to the Cornet d'Or and tumbled into bed.

TWENTHE, DROPE and RHINE AIRFIELDS, Germany

Returning from the day's 188 sorties after some of the fiercest air fighting of the year, pilots of the Jagdgeschwader 1 "Oseau" — named after "the toughest fighter pilot in the Luftwaffe," Walter Oseau — were shocked. The sight of more than 20 twin-engine single-seater Messerschmidt 262 jet aircraft arrayed on their Gruppe I airstrip was overwhelming, to say the least. All that engine power in one spot. In a word, forbidding. What was going on? Something important must be in the wind. In fact, their very presence at this time and place was tinged with irony.

Currently the Me 262s, formed into a unit Kampfdgeschwader (Jet) 51 under Major Heinz Unrau based at Rhine, had been assigned the role of aerial reconnaissance which, though useful, was a misuse of these planes with such enormous potential. It was, however, at least a flight in the right direction. It was originally designed as the most advanced fighter in the world, one that the former chief of the Luftwaffe fighter force, Adolf Galland, had judged to be the equal of "five

Me 109s." But Hitler, who lacked even the most fundamental understanding of what air power was all about, had insisted it be employed as a "blitz" bomber to repel the Allied invasion of Europe. Of course that hadn't worked and, in any case, there had been too few of them to make any difference back in June.

Gradually however, albeit reluctantly, Der Führer had begun to see the light and came to accept the advice of his air commanders. As the Ardennes battle reached the crisis point he agreed to the use of the Me 262 as a fighter-bomber. Thus it was that on the last day of the year, all 21 of Unrau's KG(J)51 jets available for operational service stood on the line at Twenthe ready to be dispersed for duty among several of Generalmajor Dietrich Peltz's Jagdkorps 11 Geschwadern on a special assignment next morning. Located only ten miles from the German-Dutch border in the Odenzaal-Hengdo-Enschede triangle, the airfield was as an ideal assembly point for such an assignment

Where the FW 190 pilots of Hauptmann Hans-Georg Hackbarth's Gruppe I were concerned, the riddle to that role began to unravel late that afternoon when they were subjected to a pep talk, unveiling the following day's operation, from their JG Kommodore, Oberstleutnant Herbert Ihlefeld, a seasoned veteran who had first seen action during the Spanish Civil War with the Condor Legion. Ihlefeld was optimistic about the assignment, a confidence he imparted to his airmen. "You won't have to worry about anti-aircraft fire or enemy fighters," he told them jocularly, "because they will be too hung-over from celebrating the night before."

In a similar vein, Hauptmann Hermann Staiger, commander of Gruppe II, and Hauptmann Harald Moldenhauer, who had been given command of Gruppe III only the day before, briefed their FW 190 and Me 109 pilots at the adjacent air bases of Drope and Rhine, pinpointing the targets to be attacked at treetop level at dawn with the aid of tabletop sand models. Aircrews of all three JG 1 airfields were confined to quarters and an early curfew was imposed. Though they had no experience or practice with low-level attacks, they retired for the evening generally convinced that the enemy, trying to shake off the effects of celebrating New Year's Eve, would be caught flatfooted.

ST DENIS-WESTRAM AIRFIELD, Belgium

Before he and his adjutant left by transport for 131 Polish Spitfire Wing's new home at Grimbergen, to which it was scheduled to move the following afternoon, Group Captain Alexander Gabszewicz had cut orders for the next morning's operations. At 0815 hours, 308 Squadron, led by Flight Lieutenant Ignacy Olszewski, would take off on an armed reconnaissance against enemy installations near Wounstreecht. At 0835, Squadron Leader Marian Chelmecki's 317 would take to the air. Its objectives were German military targets at Werkindan on the Wahl River. Finally, 302 Squadron, commanded by Squadron Leader Maria Duryusz, had its assignment: take off at 0840 on an armed reconnaissance in the Lyons-Amersfoot-Zwell-Appledoorf region.

URSEL AIRFIELD, Belgium

It was a busy place, hectic at times. Home of No. 424 Rearming and Refuelling Unit, Ursel was, in effect, a weigh — more correctly, "way" — station. British-based fighter and fighter-bomber squadrons, and sundry other odds and sods would plonk themselves down for instant refuelling on their way to distant targets in Germany, and again on the way back. Sometimes, when there were two squadrons being rearmed and refuelled on the field at the same time, they took off simultaneously in opposite directions from either end of the elongated landing strip. It wasn't long before it had become a graveyard for pranged aircraft, including a demolished Mosquito, a shot-up Flying Fortress and a burnt-out Lancaster.

RHINE, HESEPE and ACHMER AIRFIELDS, Germany

The vicious fighting of the previous fortnight had imposed such a severe drain on Major Ludwig Franzisket's Jagdgeschwader 27 that it left his unit badly scarred and seriously shorthanded. The most aircraft Hauptmann Eberhard Schade could muster from his Gruppe I were 16 Messerschmidt 109s, not a few of which were long past due for an engine overhaul. Hauptmann Gerhard Hoyer's Gruppe II was in even worse shape. The best he could contribute was a dozen fighters.

Franzisket's other two Gruppen, III and IV, commanded by Hauptmannen Emile Clade and Hans-Heinz Dudeck, and based at Hesepe and Achmer airfields nearby, weren't much better off, but at least they were marginally up to strength. The only good news was that the JG would be bolstered by Gruppe IV's FW 190s from Oberstleutnant Hans Dortenmann's Jagdgeschwader 54 "Green Hearts," led by Major Rudolf Klemm, flying from the Vorden airstrip. It was not much help, but better than nothing. Franzisket had grave doubts about the feasibility of being able to carry out the orders he'd received from Jagdkorps 11 HQ that afternoon. To preserve morale, the veteran air fighter with 40 victories to his credit, whose fighting career went back to 1939, exercised the only two options left open to him. He decided to amalgamate his two fragmented Gruppen into one, and delay briefing his pilots on the forthcoming support operation until the very last minute the next morning.

BRUSSELS-MELSBROEK AIRFIELD, Belgium

The patched-up British Short Stirling that 69 Squadron CO Mike Shaw was scheduled to air test the following morning wasn't the only four-engine bomber to have made a "guest appearance" on the RAF reconnaissance airfield. By coincidence an American B-17 Flying Fortress had landed that afternoon after its hydraulics had been shot away by anti-aircraft fire. The aircrew signalled their base in England to send over spare parts, but that would take until the next day at the earliest.

Flight Lieutenant Hugh Tudor and his navigator Flying Officer Ian Ewing, flying Mosquitoes with 140 Squadron — a day and night reconnaissance outfit — planned to fly their wooden twin-engine fighter-bomber-recce aircraft to England next morning to pick up Tudor's father. The elder Tudor was a veteran pilot of World War I with the Royal Flying Corps who had re-enlisted for the later unpleasantness with the RAF. The Mosquito could comfortably accommodate a passenger in addition to the two-man crew and they hoped to have him as their guest at Melsbroek for a week or so.

GILZE-REIJEN AIRFIELD, Holland

Late in the afternoon, Canadian Flight Lieutenant Bill Baggs and his fellow pilots of 164 Squadron, under the command of Squadron Leader Mony Van Lierde, a Belgian, took off in line-abreast formation in their Typhoons for Gilze-Reijen from Manston on the south-east coast of England. They had just completed a two-week air-firing (in this case, rocket-firing and bombing) course at Fairwood Common in Wales on the northern coast of the Bristol Channel. It was essentially a rest assignment. They had missed the Ardennes action and were ready and eager to return to operations with gusto. However, on arrival at Gilze near dusk, things somehow didn't seem quite right. Half deserted, an eerie, tense atmosphere pervaded. They learned that two of the four squadrons that made up 123 Wing had been moved south to Chievres in Belgium to bolster the Americans, leaving only Baggs' outfit and 2 and 268 Typhoon Squadrons on the field. They also found that the airfield had been declared an emergency zone; there was a rumour of imminent German paratroop landings in the vicinity in preparation for a fresh ground offensive. What a nice way to start the New Year! That night they slept on their camp cots in the mess building, fully dressed, wearing their side arms.[7]

BABENHAUSEN, DARMSTADT-GREISHEIM and RHINE-MAIN AIRFIELDS, Germany

By a miracle, not to mention a lot of sweat and back-breaking work, the pine-tree-sheltered fighter base at Babenhausen was able to serve as the focal point of Jagdgeschwader 4 operations for a New Year's morning surprise show. But only just. At 2 o'clock on Christmas Eve afternoon, the landing strip had been left in a shambles by 120 Flying Fortresses of the US 8th Air Force, part of a massive raid to neutralise Luftwaffe airfields, during which a total of 5,025 tons of bombs had been dropped in what was one of the largest single Allied bomber strikes of the entire Second World War. Babenhausen had been completely devastated, officially described as having been rendered "one hundred per cent useless" — to all intents a *Maldandschaft* — a lunar landscape. Incredibly, however, the majority of Hauptmann Georg Schroder's Gruppe II FW 190 fighters had escaped damage and there were no casualties. And, a week later, by noon of December 31, thanks to an all-out effort by a team of labourers, including volunteers from the squadron itself, Babenhausen was once again pronounced fully serviceable.

Beginning at 1800 hours that evening, the Geschwader Kommodore, Major Gerhard Michalski, an ace with 70 victories to his credit who had made a name for himself in the skies over Malta, addressed each of his three Gruppen at Babenhausen, Darmstadt-Greisheim and Rhine-Main airfields separately on operations for the following morning at first light. His orders from Jagdkorps HQ, which he read to his pilots, were simple and explicit: "Mission — low-level attack on Le Culot Airfield. The wing is to form up over Bingen."[8] Straight to the point.

It would be a case of follow-the-leader with a converted Junkers 88 in front of the parade as a trailblazer. This at least cleared up the mystery for the Gruppe II pilots as to why the twin-engine night-fighter suddenly appeared in their midst at Babenhausen. Jabbing his thumb in the direction of the pathfinder skipper, Feldwebel Gunther Kotschote, one of them asked: "What the hell is he doing here?" Now they knew. Michalski urged tight formation flying to keep a sharp lookout for enemy fighters and avoid getting separated and lost.

Before issuing maps to the pilots, Michalski presented them with blow-ups of aerial reconnaissance photographs that showed Le Culot Airfield crowded with P-47 Thunderbolts and assorted medium-bombers. Unteroffizier Horst Thanaan, who had survived the Christmas Eve bombing at Babenhausen by taking refuge in a slit trench, noted that, at the briefings, "the fighter pilots were ardently enthusiastic about the mission — particularly those with little experience!"

But there was a downside also. The recent Allied daylight raids had taken their toll in men and machines. At Darmstadt-Griesheim, Gruppe I Kommodore, Hauptmann Wilhelm Steinmann, received the disheartening news from his ground-crew chief that he would have only ten Me 109s serviceable for the morning show. While over at Rhine-Main, although the mechanics and armourers worked through the night, only half of Hauptmann Max Laube's Gruppe IV's 40 Messerschmidts would be airworthy by dawn. These logistics failed to dampen the spirits of either Laube or Steinmann, however. If anything, they accepted the situation as just one more challenge.

ST TROND-BRUSTEM AIRFIELD, Belgium

From the air the snow-covered countryside had created the illusion, as one Luftwaffe reconnaissance observer put it, that, "all the Allied airfields looked pretty much alike. It was difficult to identify one from the other." Such was the case with St Trond and its neighbouring Le Culot a few miles away. It was hard to tell them apart.

However, the former air base was no stranger to the Luftwaffe. During the Nazi occupation of Belgium it had served as the home of Nachtjagdgeschwader 1, commanded by the famed night-fighter ace, Hauptmann Heinz-Wolfgang Schnaufer. Known as the "Ghost of St Trond," Schnaufer had posted 131 victories against RAF Bomber Command raids — nine in one 24-hour period!

Following the Allied liberation, the 48th P-47 Thunderbolt Fighter Group and the 404th P-38 Lightning Fighter Group — the latter commanded by American air ace Colonel James Johnson — of the 8th US Air Force, took up station there. Nothing else changed. The camouflage, hangars and other buildings all remained the same. Then on December 19, with the German army breakthrough in the Ardennes, Brigadier General Nugent received orders to move his 29th Tactical Air Command headquarters from a precarious front-line position back to the airfield to avoid being overrun. As a result, the defences were stiffened, making A-92 the most heavily armed and defended tactical Allied airfield in all of Continental Europe.

On the morning of the last day of the year, the American FGs encountered little Luftwaffe interference and noted the contrails of only a single high-altitude Arado 234 reconnaissance jet flying over the field. These events were in themselves cause for celebration — as if indeed any were needed. The 48th Group diarist chronicled that evening's activities:

> Officers and men of the 48th Fighter Group celebrated New Year's in a unique and novel way. From midnight until the early hours of the morn, Officers at their Club and Enlisted Men at the Fun Club could be found in various stages of inebriation at the aforementioned clubs. After drinking all there was to drink or, more appropriately, all they could hold, they wended their way on a "*beaucoup* zigzag" course home. Some managed to get there safely — others took longer routes.

MERZHAUZEN, NIDDA, ETTINGHAUSEN and ALDERNSTADT AIRFIELDS, Germany

There would be no "*beaucoup* zigzagging" for the pilots of the famed Jagdgeschwader 2 "Richthofen," baptised in the name of Germany's celebrated Red Baron. *Nein!* — no high jinx of any sort. The bar had been cut off and, soon after dark, the airmen at all four airfields were summoned to cursory briefings, at which they were told, sans details, that there would be a raid first thing next morning against a Yankee fighter base at Le Culot. Nothing more. Directly following the meetings they were confined to quarters for the rest of the evening.

Although the JG Kommodore, Oberstleutnant Kurt Buhlingen, holder of the Knight's Cross with Oak Leaves and Swords, had in his pocket a sealed envelope he had received a week earlier. It contained secret instructions specifying the exact modus operandi, the contents of which were not to be revealed to his pilots until the signal was given for Operation Bodenplatte to proceed.

Despite all this mystery, a mood of excitement mingled with relief prevailed. After weeks of tackling the powerful Allied bomber fleets and being outnumbered by their fighter escorts, here was relief and poetic justice for a change for the Luftwaffe flyers — a chance to hit the enemy where he lived.

COLOGNE-WAHN AIRFIELD, Germany

An identical atmosphere prevailed at Oberstleutnant Alfred Druschel's airstrip. Though his appointment as commander of Schlacktgerschwader 4 (support wing) would not become official until just before take-off tomorrow morning, he was scheduled to jointly lead his Gruppe III — especially equipped with the highly modified ground-assault Focke Wulf 8s, easily recognised by the bomb racks affixed to their lower main planes — in the Richthofen JG in the attack on Le Culot. Like Buhlingen, he had to wait until late that afternoon to open the sealed pouch he had received from Jagdkorps HQ earlier, which revealed the specific details of the assignment.

WOENSDRECHT AIRFIELD, Holland

Five Spitfire squadrons formed 132 Wing RAF, under Wing Commander Ronald Berg. So far, only the ground crew from the Dutch squadron 322 was on the field; the pilots had yet to arrive from England. Two of the other units, 331 and 332, both equipped with Spitfire IXs, were Norwegian squadrons. The other two, 66 and 127, which had the later Spitfire XVIs, were made up of Commonwealth flyers. Both of these latter, led by Squadron Leaders Richard Easby and Frank Sampson, respectively, were scheduled to take off next morning at 0910 hours to escort Mitchell bombers on a raid over Dasburg. No big deal, it was routine, actually. That night they would live it up as usual. Happy New Year!

ANTWERP-DEURNE AIRFIELD, Belgium

Two of the Spitfire squadrons of 146 Wing commanded by Battle of Britain veteran Wing Commander Denys Gillam, both of which were scheduled for an op the following morning, approached the coming of the New Year quite differently. 263 Squadron was scheduled for an Army support attack east of Dordrecht. The acting commanding officer, Flight Lieutenant Ronnie Sheward, recalled: "We were billeted in small houses next to the 'drome and had a rotten mess and not much to drink except plenty of advocaat! ... I remember getting the lads to bed early as we were on first thing next morning."[9]

By contrast, 193 Squadron which had the assignment of putting the Vianen bridge south of Utrecht out of business, had a real piss-up in town, ensuring "a few hangovers by dawn," as Flight Lieutenant Jimmy Simpson, one of the flight commanders, put it.

It didn't much matter how the rest of the units stationed at B-70, as the field was designated, celebrated the evening. None of them, neither the other two Typhoon squadrons, 257 and 266, nor the four Spitfire squadrons from 145 Wing, were scheduled for operations until later in the day. Besides the Spitfires and Typhoons, a flight of Dakota transports and a lone Flying Fortress also sat on the field.

DORTMUND, BONNINGHARDT and DUSSELDORF-LOHAUSEN AIRFIELDS, Germany

When Knight's Cross holder Major Erich Leie landed his Messerschmidt on the airstrip shortly before noon to take over the Herzas — "Red Hearts" — from the severely wounded Major Johannes Wiese, he was under no illusions that his new assignment would be a smooth ride. He knew he had inherited a headache with a capital H. Lately the beleaguered Jagdgeschwader 77 had been suffering more than its share of woes.

One of the Luftwaffe's most venerable fighter wings, it had been the only German fighter unit to take part in Exercise Weser, the occupation of Denmark and Norway in 1940. And since then it had participated in nearly every major operation, from the Battle of Britain through North Africa and Normandy. It had also seen action in the abortive Allied airborne Arnhem assault the previous September, in which the unit had been badly crippled, losing 19 pilots in four days. Like all German home defence fighter groups in the fall of 1944, JG 77 suffered from the malaise of heavy losses compounded by inexperienced, untrained replacements.

Oberst Johannes "Macky" Steinhoff, erstwhile Kommodore of the "Red Hearts" at the time, put his finger on the problem when he said:

> We were assigned young pilots who were timid, inexperienced and scared ... [and] not yet ready for combat. It was hard enough leading and keeping a large combat formation of experienced fighter pilots; with youngsters it was hopeless. They were just windy. They were expected to fly in precise formation, stuck in the middle of an enormous unit made up of more than a hundred fighters, keeping distance, height and spacing constant. They were supposed to watch their airspace and not let themselves be lured into dogfights with enemy fighters (they had absolutely no experience in aerial combat), and when the formation attacked the bomber armada they were told they must keep in position — come what may. It could never work...

Bearing him out, at Arnhem on September 29 in one engagement alone against 30 Me 109s and FW 190s, 12 Spitfire pilots of Squadron Leader Rod Smith's 401 Squadron RCAF were able to destroy nine enemy aircraft and damage five others. "It was like swatting them with a tennis racket," Smith recalled. "I had never seen so many aircraft hit the ground in so short a time."[10]

Things had not improved for the German fighter forces since then. In fact, they had deteriorated to such an extent that the wounded were being sent back into battle. One of these was Leutnant Armin Fritzer, a pilot with Gruppe III of JG 77 flying out of Dusseldorf-Lohausen Airfield, who lost his life on Christmas Eve. During that frantic mêlée with Canadian Spitfires and British Tempests over the Eifel, the Geschwader lost 13 of its Messerschmidt 109s, with eight pilots killed and one missing. In the same battle the Kommodore, Major Johannes Wiese, came off second best in a duel with a Canadian Spitfire pilot and was forced to bail out near Euskirchen. However, his parachute failed to open properly and he hit the ground so hard that his injuries brought his career as CO of the Herzas to an end.

A week later his successor had not only flown into the midst of a maelstrom of flagging leadership, sagging morale and an acute shortage of pilots and planes, but he was also met with orders from upstairs to prepare a maximum effort for the following morning. However, Erich Leie, his Knight's Cross testimony to his 118 victories in the air, was not one to be easily rattled by such obstacles. These he summarily shoved aside in search of a ready solution.

After appraising the task ahead, Leie decided on a positive course of action. To all personnel of his new command, Gruppen commanders, Staffeln leaders, pilots, ground crews as well as the auxiliary staff ranging from chefs to mess stewards, he presented the forthcoming dawn raid on the RAF fighter-bomber base — Y-70 at Antwerp-Deurne — as a God-sent opportunity. A fortuitous twist of fate allowed the famed "Red Hearts" to continue their glorious tradition.

The appeal to pride worked. At every level, despite a ban on alcohol and an early curfew for the pilots (the ground crews worked all-night), there was a marked improvement in enthusiasm and *esprit de corps.* The most outward manifestation of this metamorphosis was seen in the almost miraculous ability of the mechanics and armourers on all three airfields — Dortmund, Bonninghardt and Dusseldorf-Lohausen — to have a collective complement of nearly 100 Me 109s serviceable and combat-ready by early light the next morning. Quite an effort.

METZ-FRASTACY AIRFIELD, France

Although the Ardennes offensive had been brunted, the Allies had learned through the ULTRA interception service of Hitler's preparations to launch a fresh attack — Operation Northland — against the Americans, this time in Alsace. General Hoyt Vandenberg, commander of the 9th US Air Force, was taking no chances. He had transferred his 9th Tactical Air Force units, which had been positioned close to the front line, to less vulnerable bases in the rear. These included Colonel Ray Stecker's 365th Fighter Group, the "Hells Hawks." Four days earlier, on December 27, it had been moved from Mons in Belgium to Metz-Frastacy (Y-34), the only Allied Tactical Air Force airfield in all of France. By New Year's Eve the group had finally settled in and the pilots were looking forward to better flying weather than they had been experiencing in fog-bound Belgium. They were delighted to learn that for the morrow the forecast was for bright, clear conditions. But this boded both good and bad for either side. Wireless interception works two ways. While ULTRA had tipped off the Allies to the coming of a new offensive, German intelligence had been closely following the moves of Stecker's 365th due to sloppy radio security, in the air as well as on the ground. Unbeknown to the Americans who were intent on toasting in the New Year in tried-and-true fighter-pilot fashion, neutralising the Thunderbolts at Metz had become a Luftwaffe priority.

MALMSHEIM, KIRRLACH and ST ECHTERDINGEN AIRFIELDS, Germany

There were no current photographs of the target available; the only ones at hand were left over from the Nazi occupation of France. Nonetheless, vigilant radio intelligence gathered over the past four days had enabled the "Pik As" (Ace of Spades) Jagdgeschwader 53, under seasoned air-fighter Oberstleutnant Helmut Bennemann, with 92 planes shot down, to plot the attack of Metz-Frastacy Airfield to a fare thee well. They had the projected scenario covered to a T.

Hauptmann Karl Luckenbach's Gruppe III had been assigned to take out the anti-aircraft defences in and around the field, while the other two Gruppen, II and IV, led by Hauptmannen Julius Meimberg and Heinz Muer, were to hit the parked P-47 Thunderbolts of the American 365th Fighter Group's three squadrons in a series of at least three low-level passes. The planes were to come in on the deck, strafe the field, then, pulling up in stall turns, whip around and repeat the performance from the opposite direction, in a very professional, perfectly co-ordinated attack. Even the unbloodied novices were gung-ho.

THE PHILIPS BUILDING, EINDHOVEN, Holland

The former head office for the giant Dutch electronics manufacturer, Philips, had been requisitioned by the British Army four weeks earlier as living quarters for the commanding officer of 83 Group of the 2nd Tactical Air Force, Air Vice Marshal Harry Broadhurst and his staff. Each morning, after a cup of tea, the former fighter ace would either drive or fly over in his captured German Fieseler Storch touring plane, which he kept parked on the golf course next to the building, to his office at Group Headquarters on the airfield, arriving between 0730 and 0800 hours, as regularly as clockwork.

Just because it was New Year's "Broady" saw no reason to change his routine. There'd been no party that evening at Philips. He and his staff had celebrated the event two days earlier by holding their own soirée following a meeting at Group HQ. So, 1945 or no 1945, it was carry on as usual.

Coincidentally, the protagonist who was about to upset the AVM's morning schedule had caught him with his pants down on two previous occasions. In August 1942 during the Desert Campaign, Broady had flown to Cairo to attend a staff meeting. In his absence, one of Generalmajor Dietrich Peltz's bomber squadrons had taken the opportunity to raid his base. By the time Broadhurst returned in his Spitfire it was too late to do anything. The bombers had gone, leaving the field in smouldering ruins. Later, in Sicily, Peltz had again got the better of the then group commander, under similar circumstances, and that was not to be the last time.

ALTENKIRCHEN, JAGDKORPS 11 HEADQUARTERS, Germany

In the directives marked SECRET that had been drawn up and issued to the Jagdgeschwader 11 commanders detailing target objectives for the individual attacks at dawn on New Year's Day, each of them had been painstakingly custom-tailored to specify details applying to the particular wing involved. But each contained instructions common to all units to be impressed upon the pilots under their commands in no uncertain terms.

Because these operations would be carried out over hostile territory, unlike home defence sorties, new rules of conduct applied. A shot-down pilot, if he were lucky enough to survive, faced the likelihood of being taken prisoner. Under the provisions of the Geneva Convention, a prisoner of war was not obliged to provide his captors with anything more than name, rank and serial number. The new instructions stressed that – Name, Rank, Serial Number, Period! Any deviation from this could be regarded as a breach of military discipline or treason or both. Punishable by court martial, it could mean a dishonourable discharge from the service, life imprisonment or death by the firing squad.

As an added security measure, the pilots were ordered to empty their pockets of all personal belongings — everything except their escape rations — before taking off. If the slightest clue — a theatre ticket stub, address, phone number, picture, memento, no matter how seemingly trivial — fell into enemy hands it just might provide them with that missing piece of information they needed to complete a mosaic of gathered intelligence.

It is rumoured that another note, of unknown origin, had filtered down from Generalmajor Peltz's Jagdkorps 11 offices: "If the missions do not succeed, you'll damn well be sent out again to make sure you finish the job." Pass the word!

MUNSTER-HANDORF AIRFIELD, Germany

The crews of the four twin-engine Arado 234 jets, led by their Einsatzstaffel III Kampfdgeschwader (Jet) 51 Kommodore, Hauptmann Diether Lukesch, ushered in the New Year with black coffee approximately 20,000 feet above the Dutch-German border. Ostensibly, their mission was to scout weather conditions for the forthcoming low-level air raids against the Allied tactical airfields, but they had, in fact, taken the liberty of loading up with bombs before take-off. Well, you never know. In any event, Happy New Year!

Endnotes

1 Werner Gerbig, *Six Months to Oblivion*, p. 96.

2 Jim Prendergast, interviews and correspondence, March to November 1997.

3 Gordon Hill, correspondence, July 20, 1996.

4 Bill Roddie, correspondence, July 8, 1996.

5 Colonel Richard DeBruin, correspondence, October 14, 1996.

6 John Edison, interviews, 1984.

7 Bill Baggs, interviews and correspondence, May 7 and 8, 1997.

8 Werner Gerbig, *Six Months to Oblivion,* p. 93.

9 Danny S. Parker, *To Win the Winter Skies*, p. 429.

10 Dave McIntosh, *High Blue Battle,* p. 178.

Scene at Eindhoven, New Year's Day 1945 early in the raid.
(Department of Defence)

One of many typhoons stationed at Eindhoven, 438 Squadron.
(Department of Defence)

CHAPTER 2

THE STAGE IS SET

For the Allies the defeat of the Luftwaffe did not evolve easily. To the very last, the German air force resisted resolutely and stubbornly. Although Anglo-American aerial strategy and strength overwhelmed the enemy air force, its eventual demise rested in no small measure on the fundamental ignorance of the use of air power on the part of the Nazi hierarchy. This, in turn, led to inept leadership, miscalculation and misjudgement, poor planning and execution and, finally, inescapably, unjustified and unwarranted lack of confidence in the aircrews themselves. Beginning with the Battle of Britain in the summer of 1940, through to the Battle of the Bulge during the winter of 1944, the inevitable result was the steady erosion of that mighty aerial armada.

The pilots of the Luftwaffe displayed a courage in combat and a defiance in the face of adversity and danger for which they received nothing but disdain from the one responsible for sending them back into battle time and time again — Hermann Goering.

January 27, 1943
20,000 FEET OVER THE WILHELMSHAVEN NAVAL BASE, Germany

At a quarter to eleven in clear, sunny morning skies above East Friesland, 55 B-17 four-engine Flying Fortresses, part of Major General Ira Eaker's British-based 8th United States Air Force, began dropping their bombs on German warships berthed at that northern seaport. It was the first time that American planes had appeared over a German city. Although unescorted, the bombers managed to shoot down 22 enemy fighters without suffering a single loss themselves. While that gave the American bomber leaders the erroneous impression that such forays were a piece of cake, that initial penetration of enemy air space by US marauders in broad daylight was, nevertheless, an ominous portent of things to come for the Third Reich in general and the Luftwaffe in particular.

May 4, 1943
ANTWERP, Belgium

Three months later, on May 4, Flying Fortresses, this time accompanied by four-engine B-24 Liberator bombers, were escorted by American P-47 Thunderbolt fighters in a daylight raid on the Antwerp docks in Holland. The predictable significance of this event was not lost on Generalleutnant Adolf Galland, General der Jagdflieger, the commander of the Luftwaffe Fighter Arm. He foresaw that the day was not far off when such fighter-escorted American missions would reach the German industrial Ruhr — and beyond. The forewarning was enough to infuriate Reichsmarchall Hermann Goering. The chief of the Luftwaffe had, early in the war, boasted that "if any enemy bomber penetrates to Germany, my name is no longer Hermann Goering. You can call me Meir."[1] Der Dicke — the Fat One — as he was popularly known to the public, had long since been forced to swallow those words; in fact he was in danger of choking on them. But, pugnacious as ever, Goering vowed that his fighter force, which he designed as an offensive weapon, would never be wasted in a defensive role, not if he, Hermann Goering, had anything to say about it. But the fact of the matter was that he hadn't anything to say about it, not a damn thing. His own fate and that of the Luftwaffe rested in the hands of the British-American air forces.

Goering, however, obstinately refused to recognise the inevitable — even though the Thunderbolts, now affixed with long range drop-tanks, could bring the Fortresses to the Ruhr and other targets inside the German border. He also chose to ignore out of hand Galland's prescient pronouncement:[2]

> Outside [enemy] fighter range our pursuit and night-fighter operations are successful. If we gave up any serious attempt to engage on the peripheries and pulled our fighters right back, we should, in logic, at the same time, be able to use them in high concentration at key points.

Generalfeldmarschall Erhard Milch, the German Air Minister, under whose guidance the aircraft factories were turning out over 1,000 planes a month, underscored the issue of defence. After inspecting the destruction in the Ruhr wrought by the Allied air forces, he recommended doubling German fighter production. But on both these accounts Goering remained steadfastly and pig-headedly unmoved. However, at the end of July, an incident of horrific proportions took place that caused him to make an abrupt about-face.

July 28 - August 2, 1943
HAMBURG, Germany

In a devastating series of day and night incendiary raids, nearly 2,000 Anglo-American bombers systematically set the ancient Schleswig-Holstein port ablaze, creating the first-ever "firestorm." Whole blocks of buildings, streets and all were enveloped in flames as the conflagration sucked in the surrounding oxygen, causing hurricane-force winds to fan the fire and spread it racing through the city. Bombing accuracy was intensified with the introduction of the "window" by the RAF — strips of metal foil were dropped from the aircraft to confuse enemy radar defences by giving off false echoes. Civilian casualties totalled some 50,000 killed and as many wounded, while 800,000 people were rendered homeless. A week later the charred remains of 26,000 victims were still stretched out amid the ruins waiting to be buried.

Adolf Hitler went ballistic. "An outrage!" he raved. Humiliating! A disgrace! How could the Luftwaffe let such a catastrophe happen? He demanded an immediate explanation for the blunder. Goering hastily convened an emergency meeting of his top brass. To a man, the assembly — among them General Hans Jeschonnek, Chief of the Air Staff, Generalmajor Dietrich Peltz, in charge of bombers, Milch and Galland — all agreed, as did the Reichsmarschall himself, that the focus from then on had to be on defence against the Allied intruders. That meant more fighter production, at the expense of anything and everything else. "Never before," Galland would later recall, "did I witness such determination and agreement ... only the one common will to do everything in this critical hour for the defence of the Reich."[3] It remained only for Goering to obtain Der Führer's OK. Brimming with exuberance and enthusiasm he set off for a one-on-one conference with Hitler in Der

Wolfschanze (the Wolf's Lair), the German Chancellor's headquarters in East Prussia.

August 6, 1943
DER WOLFSCHANZE, EAST PRUSSIA, Germany

To say that Goering received an icy reception would be putting it mildly. His proposal for a radical change in the approach to the war in the air was greeted with scorn, denounced as defeatist and stonily rejected. No room for argument. Hitler then told Goering that he had lost complete confidence and faith in him, that the Luftwaffe had let him down once too often. A switch about from offensive to defensive was absolutely, unequivocally out of the question and, above all, was cowardly. Only through ruthless retaliation could the enemy be taught a lesson and be stopped once and for all.

Goering was stunned, shattered, but on leaving the Wolf's Lair he quickly recovered his composure. To Galland and Peltz he confided, almost apologetically: "The Führer has made me realise our mistake — the Führer is always right. We must deal such mighty blows to our enemy in the West that he will never dare to risk another raid like Hamburg."[4] Galland and Peltz were flabbergasted. (Goering's cynical obeisance to his master, even coping with Hitler's most irrational moods and behaviour, seemingly knew no bounds — play it safe, follow the leader.) Always on the lookout for a scapegoat, Goering turned to Peltz, "I hereby appoint you assault leader against England."[5] Hitler's will be done. Ever the faithful minion, Peltz loyally complied. But, predictably, the "mini-blitz" on London was a failure and a costly one too — 57 bombers and their crews were lost within the first week.

August 17-18, 1943
The Day and Night Skies over the Fatherland:
SCHWEINFURT, REGENSBURG and PEENEMUNDE, Germany

The Commander-in-Chief of all American air forces in Europe, General Carl "Tooey" Spaatz, would later describe the twin-pronged 8th USAF attack on the Schweinfurt ball-bearing plants in South Huringia and the Messerschmidt fighter factories at Regensburg in South Bavaria as "a bold strategic concept, one of the most significant and remarkable air battles of the Second World War."[6]

It was all of that and then some because it demonstrated that, no matter how distant the target, although German fighters could wreak a horrendous toll on unescorted bomber formations in broad daylight, they could not stop them. This was the deepest American penetration into Germany so far. From the airdromes in southern East Anglia, where the 8th US bombardment groups were based, the flying distance to Regensburg was 500 miles and 400 to Schweinfurt. Even with long-range fuel tanks, American Thunderbolt and Commonwealth Spitfire fighters were limited to escorting the 376 Flying Fortresses only as far as the German border — a distance of only 100 miles. Beyond that, the bombers were on their own. And a harrowing trip it was. The bomber crews soon caught sight of the contrails in the wake of Luftwaffe Focke Wulf 190 and Messerschmidt 109 fighters waiting like vultures to pounce on their prey.

To and from the Dutch border to the target the 1st Air Division, assigned to bombing Schweinfurt, was besieged by enemy fighter attacks without let-up for six solid hours. The 3rd Division, which attacked Regensburg, was at least spared the agony of having to fight their way home. Knowing that the extended range of their objective would leave them without enough fuel to return to Britain, the crews had been instructed that on completing their bomb run they were to head due south to airfields in North Africa. Thus the Schweinfurt-Regensburg raid became catalogued as the first "shuttle mission."

It was also one of the fiercest, most savage air battles of all time. The Germans threw everything at the American invaders — "terror bombers," as they called them. Luftwaffe fighter Staffeln (squadrons) were mobilised from all over Europe — Norway, Denmark, Holland, France, Belgium, Germany, Austria and Italy — and thrown into the fray. Everything available was hurled at the marauding forces — anti-aircraft shelling, machine-gun and cannon fire as well as rockets. Fighters dropped bombs onto the Fortresses from above. Converted twin-engine Junkers 88 night-fighters were equipped with grappling irons to drag through the formations. One overly zealous squadron commander told his pilots, that if all else fails, they should sacrifice themselves by ramming the enemy machines.

USAF losses amounted to 20 per cent of the attacking force — 24 bombers on the Regensburg strike, 36 on the raid on Schweinfurt — an unacceptably high ratio which could not be sustained on a regular basis. It clearly underlined the absolute need for long-range fighter protection. That was already in the works. The single-engine P-51 Mustang, which had originally been designed and built in the United States to British specifications as a low-level army-Cooperation (reconnaissance) aircraft, was being modified as a fighter by incorporating the high-altitude British Merlin engine while increasing its fuel capacity with built-in wing tanks.

Despite the high casualty rate, the Schweinfurt-Regensburg raid set a pattern for daylight missions to come. The Americans could take consolation in the fact that the reported loss of over 100 German fighters had created consternation in the highest echelons of the Third Reich. And there was even more bad news for "Hitler and his gang," to quote Churchill, on the darkening horizon.

That night, 600 RAF and RCAF bombers struck Peenemunde, the German rocket research centre conveniently hidden on the Baltic sea coast. However, an alert British photo interpreter spotted a black smudge on one of the runways at Peenemunde while examining a reconnaissance photograph which, after further investigation, revealed itself to be the V-1 flying bomb. While the Americans used the precision technique earlier that day for the strike on the research establishment, the British employed the area bombing system. This called for a steady stream of bombers stretching for hundreds of miles and guided by pathfinder flares, to drop their payloads on the targeted area over a period of several hours. Despite a diversionary raid on Berlin by British and Canadian twin-engine Mosquito intruders to siphon off the German night-fighters, 44 bombers were shot down. However, the damage to the installation was substantial. In addition to equipment, facilities and stockpiles destroyed, more than 700 key personnel — scientists, technicians and military advisers — were killed or wounded, setting the rocket programme back several months.

The telephone lines between the German Chancellor's Spartan Wolfschanze headquarters and the Reichschmarschall's palatial Karinhall baronial estate bristled with wrath throughout the early morning darkness.

Ruthlessly, Goering deliberately picked the handiest, most logical victim for the twin fiascos — General Hans Jeschonnek. At dawn, in despair, his loyal chief of air staff blew his brains out, a suicide that left the head of the Luftwaffe characteristically and singularly unmoved. All that counted was that his vengeful Führer was mollified, for the time being at least. Beyond that, Goering knew he had to come up with an answer to the hated American bombers.

October 9, 1943
MAIRIENBERG AIRCRAFT FACTORY, Germany

Plant officials were busy getting ready to roll out the red carpet to welcome the Luftwaffe chief who was scheduled to dedicate at an opening ceremony the recently completed runway on which he would land the very next day around noon. With the appearance of Flying Fortresses overhead to accomplish what General Eaker described as "a classic example of precision bombing," however, those plans had to be postponed indefinitely.[7]

This incident infuriated Goering but at the same time, through some strange alchemy, it also fired his imagination. The following morning, on a flight to Obersalzburg, as he gazed out the window of his Dornier transport, Goering decided, for some reason which even he did not understand, that he had to give the Americans a bloody nose to keep Der Führer out of his hair, at least temporarily.

The Luftwaffe chief envisaged himself as a Fortress airgunner. What is it, apart from being killed, that will render that individual totally defenceless? The answer was obvious: lack of ammunition. With his ammo gone, the gunner is as useless as a fifth wheel. This can be achieved Goering reasoned, and his fighter chief Galland wholeheartedly agreed, by exposing the bombers to unceasing attacks. Unlike the desperate measures employed during the Schweinfurt-Regensberg raid where the fighters were thrown into the battle willy-nilly, these fighter attacks would be precisely organised, timed and coordinated to ensure that the Fortress airgunners would use up their ammunition in the shortest possible time. Thus, robbed of their self-defences and without fighter escort, they would become sitting ducks. The strategy would be for the fighters to attack in waves, land at airfields across the country, refuel, take off and attack again, three, four times, or more if necessary. Three days later, a God-given opportunity presented itself that was beyond Galland's and Goering's wildest dreams.

October 14, 1943
To and from SCHWEINFURT, Germany
by Flying Fortress

Mission 115, a return visit to the Schweinfurt ball-bearing plant, got off to a poor start and things did not improve as the operation progressed. Although the 1st and 3rd Divisions of Flying Fortress were able to assemble over East Anglia, poor weather conditions prevented the 2nd Division, made up of Liberators, from joining them. This left only 219 unescorted B-17s to proceed to the target at the mercy of German fighters for at least five hours. As they crossed the German border over Aachen, Galland's Staffeln were waiting for them. The first formation lunged down from 12 o'clock high to take the bombers head-on while succeeding squadrons struck from the rear and from either side. As Goering had planned, the German fighters landed at airfields all over Germany, refuelled and took off again. They repeated this procedure over and over until the two battered American bomber divisions were picked up on the way home by their fighter escorts at the Dutch border.

Goering's most ambitious hopes had come to fruition. The mission was a total shambles for the Americans. The Germans claimed a whopping 121 bombers shot down while losing only 14 of their own fighters. Other bombers were badly damaged with dead and wounded aboard. One group, the 306th, lost 13 of its 16 bombers before it even reached the target. As one

Fortress captain remarked incredulously, on alighting from his aircraft, "You could walk to Berlin on those parachutes."[8] This terrible sacrifice of some 1,000 aircrew killed, missing, wounded or taken prisoner was all the more tragic because the mission itself was a total failure. Bombing results on the Schweinfurt plant were so pitifully poor that ball-bearing output, so essential to the German war effort, was almost completely unaffected. Moreover, due to their heavy losses, the Americans were compelled to refrain from further unescorted missions into Germany, at least for the time being. This seriously limited the range of daylight bombing effectiveness. However, the most significant outcome was that the exercise convinced Galland that in the very near future, if Germany were to maintain air superiority or, even parity, over the homeland, an extension of this strategy was the only correct one. His worst fears were about to be realised.

December 13, 1943
KIEL, Germany

For the first time the new model of the Mustang fighters with their high-altitude Merlin engines and extra fuel capacity made their appearance over Germany as escort to Flying Fortresses bombing German warships at Kiel harbour on the north-eastern Schleswig-Holstein coast. Their initial appearance in the European Theatre took place two weeks earlier on a fighter sweep over Belgium. Both missions were uneventful; there was a noticeable absence of German fighters. But the latter event marked a turning point that transformed the war in the air over Hitler's Third Reich. Equipped with long range drop-tanks adding to the increased fuel capacity of their wing tanks, the new American fighters could now escort the bombers anywhere in Germany. The Luftwaffe no longer had a free shot at American bombers. Furthermore, the Mustangs could not only protect the bombers, as hunters they could sweep the skies clear of enemy fighters in all directions.

That this particular metamorphosis took place at this juncture in the war is of paramount importance in the general renaissance of the Allied approach to air power. Its ramifications would lead to the eventual destruction of the Luftwaffe, in a way that not even the most prescient of leaders could possibly have foreseen.

By the beginning of 1944 plans were well underway for the Allied invasion of Europe. The success of this venture would rely heavily on aerial support. It was fortuitous that the Deputy Supreme Commander of the Allied Expeditionary Forces was none other than Air Chief Marshal Sir Arthur Tedder. It was Tedder who, in October 1941, as Air Officer Commanding RAF Mediterranean Air Command, established the formula for tactical air support in the desert war against General Erwin Rommel's Afrika Korps. Prior to launching Operation Crusader, an attempt to relieve the besieged port of Tobruk and capture Libya, what became known as "The Desert Air Force," gained air superiority over the Axis. Hurricane and Tomahawk fighters swept over enemy territory (in place of the customary standing patrols) along with strafing attacks on enemy airfields and supply routes. Blenheim and Maryland twin-engine medium- and Wellington heavy-bombers struck at Axis storage dumps, shipping and oil depots. Once the ground attack got under way, the fighters took out enemy positions and pursued retreating enemy troops while the bombers continued to hammer at communications centres behind enemy lines.

All this was the result of Tedder's innovative leadership and attention to detail. He also insisted on proper equipment, such as forward radar units, maintenance facilities and operations control centres, and proper training, planning and practice.

Operation Crusader failed, but not because of the tactical air support. It would have succeeded had the British troops not been withdrawn to bolster the defences against the Japanese in Malaya, Burma and India.

A year later, on November 1-2, 1942 at El Alamein, it was exactly this type of air support, but on a much expanded scale, that was generally credited with turning the tide of the battle. Rommel later wrote, "British air superiority threw to the winds all our operational and tactical rules.... The strength of the Anglo-American Air Force was, in all the battles to come, the deciding factor."

By this time the Royal Air Force Middle East Command had been reinforced with bomber squadrons from the 10th United States Army Air Force (which later became the 9th USAF) under the command of Major General Louis Brereton. Though his B-17 Flying Fortress and B-25 Mitchell crews had been trained in the customary strategical role, at El Alamein, they were committed to tactical strikes against enemy transport and supplies. Subsequently, the 9th was reassigned as a tactical unit, which was to have emphatic implications later in the war.

By mid-1943 the lessons learned in the desert, and subsequently in Sicily and Italy, were being applied to organise tactical air support for the coming invasion of Europe. Under Air Vice Marshal Sir Arthur Coningham, who had distinguished himself as a fighter commander in the Mediterranean, the Second Tactical Air Force (RAF) was formed. It consisted of: two fighter groups equipped with Spitfires and Typhoons; a light- (or medium-) bomber group composed of Bostons, Mitchells and Mosquitoes; a reconnaissance group of Mosquitoes, Mustangs and Spitfires; and an additional support group of Mosquito night-fighters and Walrus air-sea-rescue amphibians.

Also under Coningham's realm at his Advance Operations Headquarters in Hillingdon, Sussex, was Louis Brereton's 9th

USAF (later to be commanded by General Hoyt Vandenberg). This was made up of three tactical air commands equipped with Lightning, Mustang and Thunderbolt fighters, Lightning reconnaissance planes, as well as Black Widow and Havoc night-fighters. In addition, a bomber command consisted of Havocs and Marauders, while a troop carrier command was composed entirely of Dakota transports.

The tactical air support concept which was daily growing in size and gaining in importance was eventually to play a pivotal role in the last crisis of World War II. After some indecision it would be linked to strategic bombing, upon which for the time being, the sole responsibility in crushing German industry and its air force wholly rested.

January 11, 1944
MISSION TO OSCHERSLEBEN AIRCRAFT FACTORY, Germany

While "Tooey" Spaatz, now commanding general of the US Strategic Air Force, disagreed with his RAF counterpart Air Chief Marshal Sir Arthur "Bomber" Harris, chief of Bomber Command, that area bombing of German civilians would break the enemy, he firmly believed that precision bombing of specific manufacturing targets and war production would finally bring the Germans to their knees. "If the German leaders," he proclaimed, "begin to realise they cannot count on an aircraft factory at Gotha or a tank plant in Berlin for replacements because of our bombing, then their morale will break."[9] This was wishful thinking by both Spaatz and Harris. Neither method alone could ever force a German surrender. The terms of unconditional surrender laid down at the Casablanca Conference in January 1943, made such a pipe dream so much smoke. But both Spaatz and Harris agreed that petroleum refineries and aircraft manufacturing plants should be made priority targets. With the long-range Mustang fighters at his disposal, General Jimmy Doolittle, the new commander of the 8th USAF, was in a position to implement this precision bombing strategy anywhere in Germany.

Out of 238 Flying Fortresses assigned to the Oschersleben mission, a mere 90 miles from Berlin, 64 bombers were lost. But on this, the very first major confrontation between the Luftwaffe Fighter Arm and the long-range Mustang escorts, 40 German planes were brought down and the aircraft plant was absolutely wasted. The cost was worth the candle — destruction of both producer and progeny in the same blow. And this was but a hint of what was to come during the following month. Adolf Galland's worst fears were quickly being realised.

February 20-27, 1944
"BIG WEEK"

With the 8th US and Bomber Command flying out of Great Britain and Major General Nathan Twining's 15th USAF from Italy, during February, Allied bombers unloaded a hefty total of 35,600 tons of explosives on the German aircraft industry. Berlin factories absorbed most of the RAF attacks but plants in Leipzig, Stuttgart and Schweinfurt also came in for a fair share of night-bombardment punishment. During "Big Week" itself, the American strategic air forces launched attacks on plants in Augsberg, Bernberg, Brunswick, Furth, Gotha, Leipzig, Stuttgart and Regensberg. On February 20 alone, the Americans dispatched an armada of 940 bombers escorted by a massive formation of 700 fighters. Only 21 bombers were lost while the Mustangs claimed upwards of 100 German fighters. Meanwhile 2nd TAF went to work. Medium-bombers from the 9th USAF dropped 4,800 tons of bombs on V-1 flying bomb sites in France and Belgium.

For the German air force "Big Week" was a disaster. Over and above fighter losses in the air, production was halted at the Leipzig and Bernberg factories which were responsible for 30 per cent of single- and twin-engine fighter output. Brunswick assembly plants were put out of business for four months. Total German aircraft output in March fell to below that of August 1942 and April production was lower still. In the words of General Henry "Hap" Arnold, US Chief of Air Staff, "Those five days changed the history of the air war."[10]

March 30-31, 1944
NUREMBERG, Germany

The month of March saw an intensification of Allied strategic bombing of Germany. Between them, the RAF and the USAF dropped 57,000 tons of bombs on oil refinery and aircraft manufacturing targets at Berlin, Brunswick, Essen, Frankfurt, Friedrichshafen, Nuremberg and Stuttgart. In preparation for Operation Overlord, the invasion of France, they also struck at French airfields and rail centres. In addition, the V-1 sites were also attacked.

On the 6th of the month, the Americans raided Berlin for the first time. Out of 660 bombers, 69 were lost along with 14 of the 800 escorting fighters. This performance was repeated two days later in which 50 out of a force of 580 bombers were shot down.

On the night of March 30-31, in an attack on Nuremberg, the RAF sustained its largest single loss of the entire war. Out of the attacking force of 710 Lancasters and Halifaxes which dropped 1,069 tons of explosives and 1,391 tons of incendiaries, 94 bombers went down. German fighters were aided by clear weather and the improved technical skill of their night-fighter controllers, as well as their new airborne radar tracking device, the Liechtenstein.

But it was not enough to stem the tide. Despite heavy damage inflicted on the Allied air forces, the unprecedented aircraft production in America, Canada and Great Britain could easily absorb it. It was another story with the Luftwaffe. The ratio of losses to kills was disproportionately high and was all the more critical with German fighter output at a new low due to Anglo-American bombing. In spite of the Nuremberg successes, the German night-fighter defences were helpless against British electronic countermeasures, confusing German radar by "raining" metal pieces out of bombers. Inadequate situation reporting was another problem, because during the month all single-engine night-fighter units were disbanded and reassigned to daylight defence duty.

There was one bright spot — the scheme to revamp the German aircraft industry. In the face of the aerial crisis, Hitler had come to realise at last that, despite his earlier conviction that offence was the only answer, air supremacy over Germany could only be achieved through strong fighter defences. He now gave top priority to fighter aircraft production. Having come to that decision, he firmly believed that he could still win the war.

"The prerequisite for that," he pronounced, "is the 100 per cent fulfilment of the air force programme to clear the skies of Germany this year. I need tanks and guns in deadly earnest. But first of all we've got to have a fighter umbrella over the Reich. That's the alpha and omega of it all."[11]

Under the able direction of Albert Speer, Germany's armament minister, and his energetic deputy responsible for aircraft manufacture, Karl-Otto Sauer, the revitalisation plan took off in fine pitch, at full throttle. Factories were dispersed around the country and reinforced against air assault. Slave labour from the occupied countries, along with German convicts, were pressed into service by the thousands in the plants. A 72-hour work week was instituted and strict production quotas established. Construction of bombers was curtailed and production of Messerschmidt 109 and Focke Wulf 190 fighters was given precedence, rapidly expanded and accelerated. Critical manufacturing projects like that of the new jet airplanes were moved underground. The results were immediate and the programme surged ahead.

However, it was too late. In April the Americans succeeded in gaining air superiority over German airspace.

April-May 1944
KARINHALL, Germany

Hermann Goering was steadily losing favour with his Führer. April and May were not happy months for the Reichsmarschall. The Anglo-American air forces' bombing campaign continued to gain momentum, relentlessly hammering at German targets from one end of Continental Europe to the other. Concentrating mainly on petroleum targets, though not entirely at the expense of the aircraft plants, during April alone Doolittle's 8th USAF dropped 43,500 on Steyr, Augsburg, Poznan, Duba and Oschersleben. In south-east Europe, bombers from General Ira Eaker's Mediterranean Allied Air Forces (UASF 12th, 15th and RAF units) attacked the Romanian and Bulgarian oil fields at Ploesti, Sofia and Belgrade as well as rail networks to support the Russian army advance on the Carpathian mountains.

Over his strongest protestations — he was adamant that strategic forces should not be used for tactical purposes — Bomber Harris's RAF heavy-bombers, in support of the coming Normandy landings, were switched from German industrial targets to transportation centres in France and Belgium, among them railheads at Laon, Tours, Rouen, Juvisy and Lille. (As a compromise they also attacked Cologne and Essen.) This

effort was augmented by the 9th US Tactical Air Force medium-bomber Marauders dropping 8,800 tons of bombs on the
rail targets. In addition 2nd TAF fighters also struck at transportation — trains, trucks, bridges, railway junctions as well as
the V-1 launching sites.

Then, in May, practically the entire effort of the air forces
based in Britain was directed at targets in Belgium and France.
RAF Bomber Command made 28,500 sorties in attacks on
storage dumps, rail and training centres. Mailly, Bourg Leopold
and Boulogne were among those hit. Medium- and fighter-
bombers of the 2nd TAF and the 9th USAF dropped an additional 20,000 tons on France — road, rail and canal targets —
destroying 13 bridges over the Seine in the process.

But strategic targets were far from neglected. Harris's heavies raided Aachen and Duisburg on which they dumped 8,500
tons of explosives. Doolittle's bombers directed their efforts at
three types of objectives — the rail centres at Metz, Belfort,
Mulhouse and Hamm; oil refineries at Bohlen and Poolitz; and
manufacturing centres at Strasbourg, Poser, Berlin and Brunswick — dropping a total of 63,000 tons of bombs.

Planes from RAF Bomber and Coastal commands were ac-
tive laying mines in the English Channel and off the coast of
Norway to bottle up the German U-boats. Down south the
Mediterranean Air Forces continued their attacks on the oil
fields and communications systems. Bucharest, Brasov and
Ploesti were among those struck.

The sight of so many attacks in broad daylight over the Fa-
therland was driving Goering to despair. "I would have thought
it impossible that so many four-engine bombers could fly
around over German territory," he bemoaned. Ever since the
long-range Mustangs began escorting the bombers, he estimated the ratio of his pilots lost to enemy planes shot down
had increased from parity to five to one. In fact, the true figure

during the month of May was 530 American planes shot down versus 384 German fighters. Under the circumstances, that was not wholly unacceptable, considering the overpowering weight of American air power thrown against the Luftwaffe.

Nevertheless, now, more than ever before, Goering needed a *coup de main,* some sort of spectacular feat that would redeem him, and his Luftwaffe, in the eyes of the Führer. The spectre of the inevitable Allied invasion of the Continent loomed and Goering dreamed of creating a 1,000-fighter reserve with which to thwart the operation. But that was all it was — a dream, and a lousy one at that. With the Americans roaming all over the German skies, not a single fighter could be spared from protecting the homeland for far-flung gambles. In any case, it was far too late for such wild shenanigans.

June 6, 1944
NORMANDY, France

When the Americans, British and Canadians hit the beaches on the Calvados coast in the Baie de la Seine at dawn on D-Day, Hitler was sound asleep with strict orders — as usual — not to be awakened no matter what. Goering was getting in some early morning game hunting in the Schorfheide forest not far from his 100,000-acre Karinhall estate. But as it turned out it wouldn't have made a whole lot of difference if both of them had been on the flight deck when the Allies landed.

By the time they both learned of the invasion, Hitler couldn't make up his mind whether it was a sham or the real thing and refused to commit his Panzer divisions waiting in the Pas-de-Calais where his generals were convinced the true assault would take place. For Goering it was far too late to interfere with the Normandy landings; there was already an umbrella of 4,000 Allied planes over and about the beachhead. By afternoon he grudgingly gave orders for limited reconnaissance assaults that night and the following morning.

June 7, 1944: 1000 Hours
One Thousand Feet Over SWORD AND JUNO
BEACHES, France

Flying protective cover for British and Canadian troops fighting their way inland from the beaches around Bernieres-sur-mer, I suddenly spotted a German Junkers 88 diving through the 8/10ths cloud under which we were navigating. In an instant the enemy bomber hit the balloon cable of one of the landing craft and dissolved in a puff of smoke.

Directly ahead of us a dozen more 88s appeared, placing the 12 Spitfires of our squadron in the ideal attacking position. Flight Lieutenant Scotty Murray, to whom I was flying wingman, picked out the nearest one and opened fire. A perfect deflection shot set the enemy's port engine on fire as the pilot broke to the left. We then played hide-and-seek darting in and out of the clouds. I weaved steadily from side to side to throw the rear gunner off his aim. It was tricky trying to keep the Ju in sight, avoid getting hit and preventing a collision with my leader all at the same time.

Then as the German bomber gradually lost height, we were in the clear. When I gauged that I was about 400 yards behind it, I took aim and let go with my two cannons and four machine-guns. The volley knocked the bomber's tail off. We were now right down on the deck. The Junkers hit a fence and exploded in a ball of flame.

It was quite a morning for 401 RCAF Squadron. Besides Scotty's and my score, we counted seven other victories (two of them accounted for by the CO, Lorne Cameron), for a total of eight Huns destroyed. So much for at least one of Goering's "limited reconnaissance assaults." We celebrated in high style at lunchtime in the bar of the Tangmere officers' mess. But when our combat reports reached headquarters they are rejected by the ever-sceptical 83 Group AOC, Harry Broadhurst, who had a penchant for questioning claims, demanding absolute proof before he'd OK them. As one disgruntled flight commander complained: "That bastard Broady wouldn't acknowledge that the sun really does rise in the east and sets in the west unless he had a signed declaration from the Pope." Well bloody proof we gave the son of a bitch — in the form of cine-gun camera films and affidavits, forcing him to give credit where it bloody well was due.

This was one of the reasons that Broadhurst was generally disliked, not only by the pilots but by the ground personnel as well, in particular the air controllers, radio and radar operators, meteorologists and other technicians whose judgement he so often questioned. Well, they didn't trust him either.

June and July 1944
OVER THE NORMANDY BEACHHEAD AND BEYOND

By the middle of June, the 2nd TAF squadrons and those of the 9th USAF were operating from landing strips and fields on the beachhead. With scant opposition from enemy aircraft, they concentrated on paralysing road and rail movement from dawn to dusk leaving the Germans just the few hours of darkness to move up troops, supplies, guns and munitions. In addition, bridges were bombed and tank concentrations rocketed. This was dangerous work, not helped by inclement weather. It was tactical air support brought to the state of the art.

During this period, the strategic air forces continued to pound at the heart of Germany with particular emphasis on the oil industry. In July the 8th and 15th US Air Forces dropped 73,000 tons of bombs, while RAF Bomber Command added an additional 57,000 tons. Among the American targets were Munich, Friedrichshafen, Metz and Belfort. The British raided Stuttgart and Hamburg. Both air forces struck at petroleum plants in Wesseling, Bohlen, Merseburg, Vienna and Ploesti.

For Germany, the war in the air was reaching crisis proportions. Then an event took place that compounded the situation even further.

July 20, 1944
DER WOLFSCHANZE, OKW HEADQUARTERS,
EAST PRUSSIA, Germany

At 12.32 p.m. in the washroom of the Lagebaracke, the prefabricated building block Hitler had chosen to hold his morning conference before the scheduled arrival of Mussolini at the Wolfschanze that afternoon, Klaus Philip Schenk, Count von Stauffenberg, carefully broke a glass capsule with a pair of rubber-handled pliers, releasing acid which would eat through the wire to the explosive mechanism in approximately ten minutes. That would activate the two-pound plastic bomb he had brought with him.

This would be the third attempt that the aristocratic Stauffenberg — the very antithesis of Hitler, a trained cavalry officer with the organisational department of the army — was to make on the Führer's life. On two other occasions he had planned to assassinate him with a time bomb in his briefcase, but Hitler proved to be a tough target to tackle. He was well protected at all times by a bullet-proof vest and by three and a half pounds of laminated steel plate in his military cap. In addition to his bodyguard of sharpshooters, he always carried a revolver and was a crack shot. Only a few people close to him knew his timetable and he rarely showed up when and where he was expected. On both Stauffenberg's earlier assassination attempts, Hitler eluded him by simply failing to appear on schedule. But Stauffenberg remained dedicated to destroying Hitler whom he regarded as the "enemy of the people," even if it cost him his life. On this occasion, Hitler was exactly where he was expected to be.

After returning the bomb to his briefcase, Stauffenberg proceeded down the hall and entered the conference room where the meeting was in progress. He placed the briefcase on the floor just inside the oak slab, one of two supports, at the right end of the table, three places away from where Hitler was sitting. With the excuse that he was awaiting an urgent call from Berlin, Stauffenberg departed. Moments later, Colonel Heinz Brandt, first General Staff Officer to Chief of Operations General Adolf Huesinger, moved the briefcase to the outer side of the oak support. That simple gesture saved Hitler's life.

Suddenly the conference room dissolved in a blinding sheet of flame, accompanied by a loud roar. The walls and ceiling were torn to shreds. Chunks of concrete rained down from the roof. The oak table was hurled into the air and landed in a corner. Of the 24 men in the room, four were dead or close to it. Three of them were badly wounded while others suffered shock and superficial injuries.

Hitler escaped with flash burns to both legs and his right arm. His hair caught fire, his right hand was bleeding from superficial wounds and his eardrums were cracked. Though somewhat dazed and shaken, he was led away, with his uniform — particularly the trousers — in tatters. He resolutely refused to alter his schedule and greeted Mussolini as planned later in the day. The Italian Fascist leader, having lost power, looked far worse than the badly battered Führer. Ironically, Heinz Brandt, who had saved Hitler's life by moving the briefcase in which the bomb had been planted, was so severely injured that he died some days later.

This incident had far-reaching consequences for the Luftwaffe. Two of the bombing casualties were key air force figures. General Gunther Korten, who had taken over the reins of Chief of the Luftwaffe General Staff from Hans Jeschonnek, died of his wounds, while General Karl Bodenschatz, General Chief of Staff to the Air Force C-in-C, was badly crippled in the legs. Hitler appointed General Werner Kreipe to replace Korten, a hasty, ill-conceived decision made on the spur of the moment. But right then Hitler had more important and pressing matters on his mind, and he felt he could deal with the Luftwaffe and its problems later.

The main focus of his attention was in rounding up and punishing the conspirators responsible for the failed assassination attempt. Von Stauffenberg was, eventually, executed for his deeds. Soon the prisons and torture chambers were overcrowded with suspects. Over 7,000 arrests were made, of whom some 2,000 were found guilty and sentenced to death. "I want them hung up like carcasses of meat," Hitler pronounced and his bloodthirsty SS was only too willing to comply. At the Plotzensee barracks in Berlin the victims were strung up by piano wire and suspended from meat hooks while movie cameras recorded the grisly scene so that Hitler had the satisfaction of viewing his enemies in their final agonies.

The entire affair had a salutary effect on Hitler who believed that his survival was the result of an act of divine providence. He was thoroughly convinced that he had been spared to succeed, no matter what obstacles lay before him. At the same time this also stirred within him a fury and thirst for vengeance on anyone or anything that stood in the way of that goal. High on his list was that "damned Luftwaffe." And the situation in Normandy was doing nothing to improve his humour.

July 25, 1944
ST LO, NORMANDY, France

The Allied breakout of the Normandy beachhead was designated Operation Cobra. More than 3,000 aircraft were involved with 1,500 heavy bombers from Doolittle's 8th USAF employed in a tactical role, carpet bombing ahead of Lieutenant General "Lightenin' Joe" Lawton Collins' US VII Corps, flanked by the VIII Corps on the left and the XIII Corps on the right. Some of the bombs fell short inflicting casualties on the advancing troops. But the bombing crushed German resistance ending a week-long deadlock, and allowing American infantry and armour to pour south toward Avranches.

In the Caen area, which a week earlier had been softened up by 1,000 RAF heavy bombers dropping 7,000 tons of bombs on the suburbs of the city, with another 1,200 planes from 2nd TAF attacking tactical targets, British and Canadian troops drew off German tank forces and reserves in an advance south toward Falaise.

July 31, 1944
DER WOLFSCHANZE, EAST PRUSSIA, Germany

With reports coming in of the Allies advances in Normandy, Hitler was distressed over the Luftwaffe's shortcomings there and, at the same time, also concerned over home defence. After signing a decree two days earlier that henceforth only fighters would be produced, Hitler issued an order for Goering to examine ways of achieving local air superiority over the battlefield. "The Allies," he observed, "only like advancing when air power is on their side. That is why everything now depends on our fighter production. We must keep it top secret and start stockpiling in a big way. Then just watch the enemy gape when we turn the table on him four months from now."

On the last day of the month, Hitler had his right-hand man, General Alfred Jodl, Chief of Staff to Oberkommando de Wehrmacht (OKW) — German High Command — up on the carpet.[12]

> ... One must be clear [he berates him] that there can be no turn for the better in France until we regain air superiority, even temporarily. So it is my opinion that, however hard it may be at the moment, we must do everything to ensure that in the last resort we can hold the Luftwaffe formations at home as a last reserve in readiness to be employed at some point where we can turn the tables once more. I cannot say now where and when that point will be ... there is no doubt that if we could suddenly pump an additional 800 fighters and at once bring our fighter strength up to 2,000 — as we probably could — the whole crisis now would be overcome at once ....

At this, Fighter Command Chief Adolf Galland and Armaments Minister Albert Speer took instant and indignant umbrage. Pump an additional 800 fighters? Overcome at once? Turn the tables? C'mon! Confronting the Führer two weeks later they argued that the Luftwaffe should be withdrawn from the Western Front back to the Reich to protect the troubled armament industry. This sent Hitler into a rage. Although he had urged Jodl that "in the last resort we can hold the Luftwaffe formations at home as a last reserve in readiness," he furiously denounced Galland's and Speer's arguments, taking particular aim on the latter:[13]

I want no more planes produced at all. The fighter arm is to be dissolved. Stop aircraft production! Stop it at once, understand? You're always complaining about the shortage of skilled workers aren't you? Put them into flak production at once. Let all the workers produce anti-aircraft guns. Use all the material for that too. Now that's an order .... Every day I read in the foreign press reports how dangerous flak is. They still have some respect for that, but not for our fighters.

August 1944
IN THE SKIES OVER EUROPE

That Hitler's frantic, nonsensical instruction to Galland and Speer was never implemented was not surprising for two reasons. The first reason was that Hitler's growing megalomania was producing delusions of grandeur, erratic behaviour and unpredictable mood swings, in which he changed his mind from one day to the next. In those desperate days none of his impulsive edicts were taken too seriously by the OKW. Ride out the storm until it blows over. The second reason was the increasing pressure on the Reich from Allied air power during the month of August. Strategically, petroleum targets topped the list and the German oil reserves were hurting. Targets attacked by the Americans and British included Zeitz, Bohlen, Freital, Kolin, Poolitz and Hamburg-Meerbeck. Rail centres were also heavily hit, among them Saarbrucken, Mulhouse and Strasbourg. Aircraft factories at Anklam, Neustadt and Rakmel were pounded. In ground support operations the British tactical forces flew 33,000 sorties and the American fighter-bombers and medium-bombers a total of 32,500 missions in which they dropped 10,500 tons of bombs. Altogether this tactical effort destroyed 12,000 vehicles, 850 tanks and caused countless other damage.

The 8th USAF made a series of shuttle raids to Russia, then Italy, attacking on each trip. In all, the 8th and the 15th US Air Forces dropped 75,000 tons of bombs on German targets. In addition, RAF Bomber Command, flying over Germany in daylight for the first time since the early months of the war, dropped 65,000 tons of bombs, area bombing such targets as Kiel, Bremen and Brunswick. The British also dropped 2,000 tons of explosives on the V-1 and V-2 weapon sites, the most notable being the depot at Trossy-St Maxim. You don't halt fighter production with that sort of thing going on.

September 16, 1944
DER WOLFSCHANZE, OKW HEADQUARTERS, EAST PRUSSIA, Germany

At the regular OKW morning briefing, the news was even grimmer than usual. For Germany the war in the air had reached perilous proportions. The country was being savaged by Anglo-American bombers day and night. Before the month was out they would have dropped a massive 112,000 tons of bombs. Oil refineries at Sterkrade, Merseburg, Bratislava and Luktzkendorf, among others, were destroyed. The shortage of petroleum was now critical. Aviation fuel production was down to 10,000 tons a month compared to 150,000 tons in May. Moreover, the combined tactical air forces were devastating the German armies in the field. All of France was in Allied hands. In Belgium, the Wehrmacht still clung tenaciously to the Scheldt Estuary, preventing Allied shipping from reaching Antwerp. The Canadian Army was given the task of clearing it. The southern part of Holland was free and the British and American armies had reached the German border.

To inject a positive note into an otherwise glum aura pervading the gathered assembly, however, the Chief of Staff,

Albert Jodl, was able to toss out a small nugget. He reported that a handful of Panzer troops had driven back an American attack in the Ardennes. It was a minor soupçon considering the gravity of the situation, but at least it was better than nothing. And the word Ardennes electrified Hitler. He sprang to his feet. "The Ardennes," he announced excitedly, pointing to a map on the wall. "It is here I will attack!"[14]

His audience was dumbfounded. Attack? In the middle of a withdrawal? Jodl cautiously pointed out, "We don't have air superiority,"[15] recalling the German breakthrough of 1940 at Sedan under an unopposed Luftwaffe air umbrella of Stukas and Messerschmidts. But Hitler was so fired up over his spontaneous new brainchild that he pooh-poohed the caveat. "In bad weather, the enemy air force won't be flying either," he asserted bluntly.

Hitler's newly appointed Chief of the Air Staff, Werner Kreipe, noted dourly in his diary: "Führer's decision, counterattack out the Ardennes, objective Antwerp. Slice between the British and Americans — a new Dunkirk."[16] He made no comment on Jodl's misgivings about lack of air support. But this was not surprising. Kreipe was hardly an expert on air power. In fact, he was the wrong man in the wrong place at the wrong time, as Hitler soon realised.

September 16, 1944
ARNHEM, Holland

Operation Market Garden got underway. This was Field Marshal Bernard Montgomery's ill-fated scheme to shorten the war. It called for a series of airborne landings to seize bridges south of the north-south line of Arnhem-Nijmegen-Eindhoven while ground troops advanced south of Eindhoven to Nijmegen and then finally the last link, Arnhem. From there the Allies would turn eastward and take the Ruhr. However, things didn't quite go according to plan.

The southern bridges were captured without too much trouble, but at Arnhem the landings were hampered by poor weather and Luftwaffe fighters who clobbered the paratroop transports and airborne troop-carrying gliders. That was not enough to satisfy Hitler, however. He was furious that the landings had proceeded at all. Blind with rage, he took it out on his new Chief of the Air Staff.

September 18, 1944
DER WOLFSCHANZE, OKW HEADQUARTERS,
EAST PRUSSIA, Germany

Werner Kreipe, who had been on the job for less than three months, bore the full brunt of the Führer's wrath. He was blamed not only for what Hitler considered to be the Luftwaffe's latest blunder, Arnhem, but its incompetence in general. He ended his hour-long tirade by telling Kreipe, "I refuse to talk to you further. I need to talk to the Reichsmarschall tomorrow." He added sarcastically, "No doubt you are at least capable of arranging *that?*" [17]

September 19, 1944
DER WOLFSCHANZE, EAST PRUSSIA, Germany

On Goering's arrival at the Wolf's Lair, Kreipe warned him that Hitler was out for blood. When they met with Hitler, the German leader curtly dismissed Kreipe, to talk to Goering alone. The Chancellor rebuked his Reichsmarschall for what he considered the failure of the Luftwaffe, not only at Arnhem, but in general everywhere. Goering promptly blamed Galland for all its woes but that didn't satisfy Hitler. He ordered Goering to get rid of Kreipe, whom he labelled "defeatist and unreliable." He was so fed up with the Luftwaffe, in fact, that he didn't even bother to appoint another Chief of Air Staff. To fill the gap, he appointed as his Luftwaffe "representative" Generalmajor Eckhard Christian, an assistant to Jodl, who held no post in the air force and had no knowledge of its operations.

September 25, 1944
ARNHEM, Holland

After a week of bitter fighting, the airborne troops were finally withdrawn. Market Garden had been a costly failure. And there were two other bright spots on the horizon for the Germans. Poor weather had given them some respite from Allied bombing attacks on their oil refineries. And, thanks to the energetic efforts of Speer and his aircraft manufacturing deputy, Karl-Otto Sauer, fighter aircraft output reached its highest output of the entire war. On September 2, 876 Messerschmidt 109s and Focke Wulf 190s rolled off the assembly lines. Also the Me 262 and Arado 234 jet aircraft were then in production, though in extremely limited quantities. And, Hitler had finally given in on his insistence that the Me 262 carry bombs and allowed it to be employed as a fighter.

Given this set of circumstances, over the next month and a half, Adolf Galland busied himself shoring up his home defence squadrons to deliver what he called "Der Grosse Schlag " (The Big Punch). This was a highly ambitious undertaking designed to cripple the 8th USAF in a single concentrated one-day massive retaliation against the day-bomber force which Galland predicted would be "the largest and most decisive air battle of the war" and would re-establish Luftwaffe air supremacy or, at the very least, parity over Germany.[18] To do so he planned to assemble an astounding 3,700 fighters and pilots for the venture. In the initial action 2,000 fighters in 11 combat formations would be hurled at the invading armada. Then, in a second attack, another 500 fighters were to be thrown in. Finally 100 night-fighters would prowl the neutral borders of Sweden and Switzerland to pick off stragglers and damaged bombers. At that moment this plan had Goering's hearty approval but that was bound to be short-lived with the pressure the Reichsmarschall was under from OKW headquarters, as the Allied air offensive increased in intensity.

October, 1944
OVER THE WESTERN FRONT and GERMANY

The Allied strategic air forces divided their attention between strategic and tactical operations. RAF Bomber Command dropped 10,000 tons of bombs in the Walcheren area in support of the Canadian Army in its struggle to free the Scheldt Estuary. In addition it also dropped 50,000 tons of bombs on German targets including Duisburg, Essen and Cologne. The 8th USAF concentrated on oil targets at Buer, Sterkrade, Bohlen, Homberg and Regensberg and also raided Kassel, Cologne, Hamm and Munster, unleashing a total of 57,000 tons of bombs. German fighter losses continued to mount. It was bad news all round. Hitler exhorted Goering to smarten up his fighter pilots — or else.

October 26, 1944
BERLIN, Germany

Goering called his Gruppen Kommodores together for a high-level confrontation. "Mustangs are practically doing training flights over Bavaria," he raged, taking particular aim at Adolf Galland. He accused the fighter pilots of cowardice, of turning back from missions on the slightest pretext, of refusing to close with the enemy. From now on Jagdstaffeln (squadron) leaders would be held accountable for penetrating the fighter screens and zeroing in on the bombers. And group leaders themselves would fly, as well. Convulsed with anger, he tore Galland's medals from his chest and hurled them down on a table in front of him. "I'll put them back on when your damned fighter pilots start shooting planes down again," he growled. Goering had a special message for the General der Jagdflieger. "Unless you bring down 500 Flying Fortresses with your Grosse Schlag (Big Punch) you'll find yourself in the trenches," he warned Galland. Galland replied that he had set the date for late November, weather permitting, and assured him that Der Grosse Schlag would achieve Luftwaffe air superiority Germany. Goering merely glared at him, turned and stormed out of the room.[19]

November 2, 1944
GESENKIRCHEN, CASTROPAUXEL and LUENA OIL INSTALLATIONS, Germany

On that Thursday morning, two formations of 8th USAF, consisting of 325 and 650 Flying Fortresses, escorted by 600 Mustangs and 200 Lightnings of the 9th USAF crossed the Dutch coast on their way inland to Germany. Before they even reached the targets, Mustangs dived through a break in the clouds over Borkheide Airfield destroying 25 Me 109s and damaging 18 others. That was an inauspicious start for the Luftwaffe which scrambled 500 of its home defence fighters to stop the intruders. There was much worse to come. For a loss of 50 aircraft, the Americans destroyed 98 fighters and damaged countless others; 70 German pilots were killed or missing and another 28 wounded, among them three Staffeln leaders killed and three others wounded. For the first time the entire structure of the German fighter force was threatened — all in a single day. The situation had become so acute that Hitler ordered a complete review at his headquarters.

November 6, 1944
DER WOLFSCHANZE, EAST PRUSSIA, Germany

Hitler huddled with his Luftwaffe representative Eckhard Christian and the latter's aide, Major Herbert Buchs. Hitler's conclusions did not bode well for Galland's "Big Punch." After a heated discussion in which Hitler complained he was not being fed proper information or statistics the following exchange occurred:[20]

> Hitler: There must be someone to go through all these things properly and set out the deductions and conclusions. It must be somehow possible to get proper conclusions. We just can't say, 'Well, that's the way it is.'
>
> Christian: Führer, we're drawing up planning figures and forecasts all the time — Generaloberst Stumpff as Luftwaffe Commander is responsible for this. Galland as Inspector can talk to the units. The Reichsmarschall always has at his side ...
>
> Hitler: Well, all I can say is no one has ever shown me any figures of this kind.
>
> Christian: Führer, I've got these tables all drawn up.
>
> Hitler: But I've never really taken them apart. One's got to do that kind of thing for oneself.
>
> Christian: These figures are just preliminary ones. The assault Gruppe got 30 heavy bombers.
>
> Hitler: Thirty. And the AA shot down 30. That leaves 20 and those come from the 260 engagements. That's a rotten result. I put in 260 fighters and get 20 kills. So if I put in 2,000, I'd get 200 kills. This means I just can't count on these machines producing any ... and they're pouring out of the factories at the devil's own pace. They're just eating up materials.
>
> Christian: The real reason, Führer, is that the boys hadn't flown for ten days.

Hitler: Reasons, reasons. We're always hearing about "reasons."

Christian: Well that's the way things are. By contrast the Jagdgeschwader that took off in bad weather in the West landed back without loss, because it's flying every day, even in bad weather. You just can't get away from it.

Hitler: I don't want to say anything against the pilots. Let's stick to the kill figures for the moment: nothing can change those. It means that with 2,600 aircraft I can expect 200 kills. In other words any hope of achieving decimation by mass tactics is out of court. So it's nonsensical to keep on making machines just for the Luftwaffe to play numbers-games with.

For Der Grosse Schlag the writing was on the wall. The same was true for the General der Jagdflieger.

November 8, 1944
DER WOLFSCHANZE, EAST PRUSSIA, Germany

By this date Hitler's plans for his offensive had crystallised after careful review and study of the records of the 1940 Blitzkrieg attack at Sedan. "A single breakthrough on the Western Front!" he enthused. "You'll see! It will lead to collapse and panic among the Americans. We'll drive right through their middle and take Antwerp. Then they will have lost their supply port. And a tremendous pocket will encircle the entire English army, with hundreds of thousands of prisoners as we used to do in Russia."[21] His plan called for an advance by two Panzer and one regular army division through the Ardennes between Monschau and Echternach, sweeping across the Meuse River on the second or fourth day, bypassing Brussels and seizing the prize of Antwerp within a week.

The timing of the attack was slated for later in the month. By that time the Wehrmacht would have accumulated the

17,500 cubic metres of fuel needed to implement it. Code-named Wacht Am Rhein (Watch on the Rhine), the opening would not take place until at least five days of poor flying weather were forecast. Hitler's chief meteorologist, Dr Werber Schwerdfeger cautioned; "The only thing which is not in our favour is the air situation. That is why we are now forced to take advantage of the bad winter weather. The air situation forces us to do so." Dr Percy Schramm, the official record keeper, echoed the same assessment, "The attack can only be carried out at a time when the prevailing weather conditions will be a considerable handicap for enemy air forces."[22]

Luftwaffe air support for Wacht Am Rhein was another matter.

November 13, 1944
GATOW AIRFIELD, Germany

Adolf Galland would later recall:[23]

> In the middle of November I received an alarming order, the whole impact of which I could not foresee. The fighter reserves were to be prepared for action on the front where a great land battle was expected in the West. This was incredible. At this moment I lost all spirit for the further conduct of hostilities.

It was goodbye to the Big Punch! Logistics for such a readjustment were overwhelming — tactics, equipment, armament and experience had been geared to the aerial defence of the Reich. The pilots, and this included the leaders, needed new, special training, but that was out of the question; shortage of fuel due to the Allied raids on the German oil refineries prevented it. The move to smaller airfields in the west near the front line required the total reorganisation of the squadrons whose strength of 70 aircraft was much too large for the size of those advanced bases.

But all this was completely out of Galland's hands. Though he had recently been promoted to Generaleutnent (Lieutenant General) — "Bad sign, that means it won't be long before they sling me out" — and was still technically the General of Fighters, he was being divested of all responsibility except for two Jagdgeschwaderen under his command, all that was left of the Home Defence Force.[24]

Hitler had entrusted the General of Bombers, Dietrich Peltz, to command fighter support for his offensive. A most unlikely choice, and a poor one, Peltz had not the slightest conception of what fighters or fighter operations were all about. But unlike the blunt, outspoken Galland, he was willing to follow orders without question and had always been a supporter of the Führer and his wishes.

November 14, 1944
DER WOLFSCHANZE, EAST PRUSSIA, Germany

In an operational order detailing the conduct of the Luftwaffe for Wacht Am Rhein Goering, under the heading Conduct of Battle, stated: "A single concentrated strike against all airfields near the front to knock out close support forces." He also ordered that all fighter aircraft be capable of arming for fighter-bomber missions within 24-hours' notice.

November 21, 1944
MERSEBURG OIL YARDS, Germany

Hitler's reservations over mass fighter attacks against American daylight raids and preparations for aerial support for his offensive notwithstanding, OKW sanctioned a dress rehearsal for Der Grosse Schlag, at the first opportunity. It presented itself on the moderately inclement morning of the 21st of the month and the stage setting couldn't have been more choice. The target for the 1,149 Flying Fortress bombers of the 8th USAF escorted by 858 Mustang fighters was right in the heart of Germany providing the German home defence fighter force at least four hours of fighting time over the Reich in which to hassle the invaders.

But as the American hordes pressed across the border into Germany the weather began to sour. It started to rain and the entire sky became overcast. Reluctant to commit the fighters under such conditions, headquarters grounded them, temporarily. Over the Hanover area, the invaders broke through the clouds and at this point the order went out for the Luftwaffe fighters to take off. But it was too late to do any damage. The Flying Fortresses were already over the target dropping their bombs without the slightest interference. The day ended in disaster for the Luftwaffe which lost 62 planes, 20 of them from one Gruppe alone. That was the last anyone was going to hear about the "Big Punch."

November 24, 1944
LORRAINE, France

It was slow going, but General George Patton's United States Third Army occupied Strasbourg having captured the ancient fortress of Metz three days earlier. However this plodding style of warfare did not suit the pistol-packing general. He hankered for a breakthrough and knew that this depended on tactical air support. That night he huddled with General Otto "Opie" Weyland in charge of the 19th US Tactical Air Command of the 9th USAF.

November 26, 1944
MISBURG, Germany

When between 50 and 80 Focke Wulf 190s pounced on the force of 1,000 Flying Fortresses and Liberators as it crossed into Germany, five of the fighters were shot down in as many minutes. But that was only the start. Closer to the target near Hanover, the fighter formation from 301 Jagdgeschwader lost 26 pilots killed and 30 wounded. Altogether Luftwaffe casualties for the day were 57 pilots killed and 30 wounded. On two succeeding days casualties totalled another 150, bringing the total Luftwaffe losses for the month of November to 404 aircraft destroyed and 244 pilots killed against American losses of 155. Oberstleutnant Walther Dahl, commander of 300 Jagdgeschwader best summed up the situation:[25]

> November 1944's flying was the toughest I had been through in the whole war. The odds were 20 to 1 and often as much as 30 to 1 against us. We were taking casualties every day. Our aircrew reinforcements were short on quality and they didn't get enough training. And shortage of fuel was making itself more and more felt.

November 28, 1944
SCHONWALDE AIRFIELD, Germany

As Goering pulled up in a luxurious Mercedes to visit Johannes "Macky" Steinhoff's Jagdgeschwader 77 "Red Hearts," it began to rain. Goering singled out one of the pilots lined up for inspection and asked: "Could you today, in this weather, fly deep into enemy territory — say France or Belgium — attack aircraft with your cannon, and fly back here again?"[26] Puzzled, the young flyer replied that the only catch that he could see would be navigation. That seemed to satisfy the Reichsmarschall that the success of Operation Bodenplatte — the code name (alluding to low level) he had given to the raid on Allied tactical airfields — would not be a problem.

November 30, 1944
JAGDKORPS 11 HEADQUARTERS, ALTENKIRCHEN,
Germany

Redeployment of all Jagdgeschwaderen to take part in Bodenplatte was almost complete. Dietrich Peltz had settled his headquarters in a comfortable inn on the outskirts of the village of Altenkirchen. As he perceived it, there were two objectives to the low-level air raid. The first was to concentrate the attack at dawn when it was least expected and neutralise all the Allied tactical air bases in Belgium, France and Holland. That was a tall order; altogether there were more than 30 of them and it would require perfect weather conditions — clear skies with perfect visibility. That accomplished, and with the 9th US Tactical Air Force and the British 2nd Tactical Air Force no longer a threat, Luftwaffe fighters would be left free to establish an umbrella over the German armies in the field. Meanwhile German bombers could strike at American columns to the rear while night-fighters could also attack targets and shield the advancing armies. Heady, hopeful stuff, but it had Hitler's tacit blessing and Goering indicated he would be 100 per cent involved in the operation.

December 2, 1944
SAAR, Germany

Opie Weyland's 19th US Tactical Air Command (TAC) flew 281 sorties to pave the way for George Patton's troops to occupy Saarlouis. Two days later, thanks to the pummelling by medium-bombers, the town was in American hands and a bridgehead was firmly established across the Saar River. Patton was now anxious to exploit his advantage. With proper air support, he was optimistic he could break through the rigid German defences and punch his way right to Berlin. To launch such an enterprise he believed that carpet bombing in the St Lo style would catapult the Third Army across the Rhine. Weyland was just as keen as Patton over the prospect. He agreed to present the proposal at a meeting of the Allied air commanders scheduled for December 5 at General Carl Spaatz's headquarters just outside Paris.

December 2-5, 1944
THE SKIES OVER GERMANY

Despite the transfer of fighter Jagdgeschwaderen to the west to support the coming offensive, they were still sorely needed to defend against Allied air raids which continued without let-up during the first week of December. On the 2nd, the 8th USAF launched two major attacks at Cologne and Bingen, while the 15th, based in Italy, bombed oil plants and refineries at Blechhamer in Lower Silesia and Floridsdorf near Vienna. The following day the Americans committed mainly fighters over the Aachen-Duren area. Then, on December 4, the rail network of Kassel-Behra-Giessen-Mainz was attacked. These operations cost the Germans 65 pilots, 47 of them killed.

On December 5, Doolittle was instructed to bomb Berlin. The weather was anything but favourable for the venture; the skies over the German capital were completely overcast. But that did not stop the 427 Flying Fortresses and their Mustang escorts from reaching the target by 1045 hours and bombing it without hindrance. So far not a single Luftwaffe fighter had been seen. They were in the air but the heavy cloud prevented them from finding their quarry. And when the defenders finally did make contact with the 8th USAF bombers, the Mustang fighter screen was so formidable they were unable to penetrate it. It was midday before they were able to engage the American fighters — with disastrous results. German casualties totalled 75, with 53 pilots killed, 22 wounded, including a Gruppe and two Staffeln leaders lost. Only five American planes were shot down.[27]

December 5, 1944
GENERAL SPAATZ'S HEADQUARTERS, PARIS, France

Among those attending the air commanders' conference were such heavies as Bomber Harris, Jimmy Doolittle and Arthur Coningham, along with the supreme commander Dwight Eisenhower. Also present were 9th USAF commander General Hoyt Vandenberg's representatives, Brigadier General Elwood Quesada, commander 9th TAC, Brigadier General Dick Nugent, 29th TAC commander and Opie Weyland.

Spaatz and Doolittle wanted Eisenhower's permission to use the heavy bombers in a tactical role to break the Western Front stalemate. That got things rolling for Weyland who proposed bombing an advance line ahead of the Third Army which would allow it to cross the Rhine then advance down behind the German armies. This won unanimous approval. The next day, Spaatz, Doolittle and Vandenberg arrived at Patton's headquarters at Nancy to draw up plans for a massive bombardment by 3,000 bombers escorted by 1,000 fighter-bombers. Weyland pronounced that Operation Tink would be the "biggest operation of its kind in history. The ground forces must realise that this provides the surest way to a quick and decisive breakthrough."[28] It was now a question of waiting for clear weather to implement it.

December 10, 1944
BAD NAUHEIM, Germany

Hitler moved his headquarters from the Wolf's Lair in East Prussia, west to the Eagle's Aerie at Bad Nauheim, ten miles north of Frankfurt, to be closer to the action when Wacht Am Rhein got underway. "This will be the great blow that must succeed," he proclaimed. "If it does not succeed, I no longer see any possibility of winning the war."

December 12, 1944
DER ADLERHORST, Germany

All the army generals about to take part in the forthcoming offensive gathered together in the command bunker of Der Adlerhorst (the Eagle's Aerie) for last-minute instructions from the Führer himself. Numbered among them were: Generalfeldmarschall Karl-Gerd von Rundstedt who had been reinstated as Commander-in-Chief in the West and who wanted no part in the plan — on the grounds that the Wehrmacht lacked sufficient strength for it to succeed; Generalfeldmarschall Wilhelm Keitel, chief of the Oberkommando der Wehrmacht (OKW) — German High Command; his chief of staff General Alfred Jodl, and General Hasso von Manteuffel, chief of the 5th Panzer Army, who had worked out the tactical details for the attack. It was a grave collection of yes-men.

Security was tight as a drum. Ever since the failed attempt on his life on July 20, Hitler had been paranoid. Behind each general's seat stood an armed, black-uniformed SS guard. Indeed on arrival, each officer had been stripped of his briefcase and weapons and forced to sign a declaration that what he was about to hear would be kept secret on penalty of being shot!

Hitler made his entrance at six o'clock that evening. To those who had not seen him recently, his appearance came as a distinct shock. He looked stooped and lurched when he walked. His face was puffy and pale and his eyes had a glazed look. His right hand shook so uncontrollably that he had to steady it with his left. But a lot of the old fire was still there; his ability to incite and inspire and his powers of persuasion had not deserted him.

To make his point he evoked the legend of his idol, Frederick the Great, who had turned certain defeat into victory at the climax of the Seven Years' War. Hitler was now convinced, or so he told his generals, that he could do the same. Strategically the plan was his and his alone and was based on his belief that the Allies were divided, each with their own interests at heart. "The aim of the United States," he proclaimed, "is to be the heir of England. Russia aims to secure the Balkans, the Dardanelles, Persia, Persian oil, the Persian Gulf. England aims to maintain her position, to strengthen her position in the Mediterranean." Therefore, he concluded, one thunderclap was all that is now needed to tear the Russo-Anglo-American alliance apart.

The recapture of Antwerp would achieve that objective. With the Allied armies split in two, the British would have to evacuate the Continent, just as they did four years earlier at the time of Dunkirk, or face capture. Then, with his new V-2 rockets, Hitler would paralyse England and force her out of the war. This would enable Germany to halt the Russian advance and create a stalemate which he was sure would bring the United States onside to join in stemming the Communist tide.

The generals obediently accepted this assessment without argument. What else could they do? After all, *befehl ist befehl* (orders are orders)! What was left hanging was the question of air support. Again Hitler painted a rosy picture. Interference by the Allied air forces would not be a problem, he assured his captive audience. His meteorologists had forecast that beginning Saturday, December 16, four days hence, the kick-off date for the Ardennes offensive, poor flying conditions would prevail for at least a week. He then made the stunning announcement that, despite losses sustained from daylight bombing raids, thanks to the sterling manufacturing efforts of Albert Speer, Luftwaffe fighter strength now stood at 3,600 aircraft. And, without revealing the nature of Bodenplatte, he alleged that everyone, but the Allies in particular, was in for one giant surprise when the weather did clear.

December 15, 1944
JAGDKORPS 11 HEADQUARTERS, ALTENKIRCHEN
east of BONN, Germany

In the strictest secrecy, Dietrich Peltz summoned all his air commanders to a briefing on Bodenplatte. The plan called for Jagdgeschwadern 12, a total of 33 Gruppen (wings), to simultaneously attack the Allied tactical airfields at low-level to avoid radar detection. As a further precautionary measure, all radio frequencies were to be changed to prevent interception by the Allied "Y" direction-finding listening device. Also the FUG25 (IFF — identification friend from foe) equipment was to be removed from all aircraft. The raid had been plotted with meticulous attention to detail. The emphasis was on surprise, thus the need for the tightest security. No date could be set until forecasts showed perfect weather — clear, cloudless conditions. Then, and only then, would the nearly 1,300 pilots spread over 37 airfields and airstrips be briefed — at the very last minute.

Instructions were explicit: complete radio silence was to be observed up until the very moment of the attack. All Jagderschwerden were to fly low across the front lines simultaneously at daybreak or as near to it as possible.

Each JG would receive aerial photographs of the individual targets assigned to them with which they could brief their pilots. To ensure maximum surprise, the operation called for target airfields to be attacked simultaneously, or as close to it as possible.[29]

Outward and return flight paths would be charted on the pilots' operational maps but, to maintain security, only the far side of the German lines would be marked. Then, if a map fell into enemy hands, the location of the German bases could not be identified.

Endnotes

1 Willi Frischauer, *The Rise and Fall of Hermann Goering,* pp. 138-139.

2 Werner Gerbig, *Six Months to Oblivion,* p. 25.

3 Danny S. Parker, *To Win the Winter Sky,* p. 22.

4 Parker, p. 22.

5 Parker, p. 23.

6 Edward Jablonski, *Flying Fortress,* p. 133.

7 Jablonski, p. 137.

8 Comment to author October 14, 1943.

9 Parker, p. 51.

10 Jablonski, p. 148.

11 Parker, p. 28.

12 Parker, p. 34.

13 Parker, p. 31.

14 Parker, p. 35.

15 Parker, p. 35.

16 Parker, p. 35.

17 Parker, p. 36.

18 Parker, p. 90.

19 Parker, pp. 92-93.

20 Gerbig, pp. 25-27.

21 Gerbig, pp. 28.

22 Parker, p. 14.

23 Parker, p. 132.

24 Parker, p. 92.

25 Parker, p. 132.

26 Parker, p. 132.

27 Hugh A. Halliday, *Typhoon and Tempest: The Canadian Story.*

28 Parker, p. 122.

29 Gerbig, p. 74.

Flying Officer Hugh Fraser of 439 Squadron at
Eindhoven was on a reconnaissance flight when
the battle broke out. He managed two kills.
(Department of Defence)

Left to Right: Flight Lieutenant Lyle Shaver, Squadron Leader
Jim Beatty and Flying Officer Hugh Fraser. Shaver is showing-
off a souvenir from the battle. (Department of Defence)

CHAPTER 3

THE BEST-LAID PLANS

O n Saturday, December 16, 1944, General Omar Bradley, commander of the US 12th Army Group, considering the possibility of a German attack through the Ardennes, scoffed that, "No damn fool would even try it." Early that morning, Field Marshal Bernard Montgomery commanding the 21st Army Group noted that, "The enemy is at present fighting a defensive campaign on all fronts; his situation is such that he cannot stage a major offensive operation." Nevertheless Wacht Am Rhein should not have come entirely as a surprise. The ULTRA code-intercepting operation provided indications of a German build-up. But these signs were either misinterpreted or dismissed out of hand, or both.[1]

Following a short but sharp artillery barrage, before first light that misty morning, the Germans began their advance through the Ardennes with 24 army divisions, ten of them armoured, on an 80-mile-wide front between Monschau and Trier. The terrain was rugged and heavily wooded with countless gorges so that movement was necessarily restricted to the few roads available. This made it vital to seize the various junctions.

December 16, 1944
JAGDKORPS 11 HEADQUARTERS, ALTENKIRCHEN, Germany

Dense, soupy ground fog and light rain grounded Dietrich Peltz's fighters leaving him no choice but to advise his superior Generalleutnant Josef "Beppo" Schmidt in command of Luftwaffen Kommando West that Bodenplatte would have to be postponed indefinitely, until the weather improved and, according to the meteorological reports, that appeared to be at least a week away. Schmidt instructed him to do what he could in the meantime to support the advance. Peltz ordered his commanders to do so the following morning. His job was not made any easier by the fact that his Jagdgeschwadern were based on airfields much too far apart from each other over a breadth of some 250 miles between Oldenburg and the Rhine-Maine area. It made co-ordinated operations between his Jagdgeschwadern difficult, and in duff weather, well nigh impossible.

9th US TACTICAL AIR COMMAND HEADQUARTERS, VERVIERS, Belgium

Totally unaware that the Germans were on the march less than 30 miles away, Pete Quesada and Hoyt Vandenberg were focusing their undivided attention on air support for George Patton's Third Army offensive as well as cover for two other proposed offensives for the First and Ninth American armies.

Later in the day, aircraft from Quesada's 67th Tactical Reconnaissance Group on a scouting mission reported 75 German trucks and some tanks in the vicinity of the US 28th Division, while Nugent's 29th TAC reported heavy enemy traffic on the Koblenz and Trier railroads and highways.

SUPREME HEADQUARTERS ALLIED EXPEDITIONARY FORCE, The TRIANON PALACE, VERSAILLES, France

When this news reached the Supreme Commander Dwight Eisenhower who was in conference with Omar Bradley discussing the 12th Army Group's proposed offensive, the latter shrugged it off as merely a "spoiling action" to upset his own plans. Eisenhower was not so sure but made no move to release two reserve divisions held back for just such an emergency. His suspicions that this was probably a major operation were confirmed, however, when, just before midnight, an ULTRA decrypt was received stating that Jagdkorps 11 headquarters had issued an order to its Jagdgeshwadern to support the German 5th and 6th armies the following morning. Another decrypt, this one from Generalfeldmarschall von Rundstedt, the C-in-C in the West, clinched it. It read:[2]

> The hour of destiny has struck. Mighty offensive armies face the Allies. Everything is at stake. More than mortal deeds are required as a holy duty to the Fatherland.

December 17
THE EIFEL COUNTRY, Germany

The weather was still murky and wet, a chilly 45 degrees and drizzling. But visibility was just enough for both sides to put their planes in the air. By concentrating on logistical targets, like supply depots and communications centres in the rear area, the American Lightnings and Thunderbolts managed to lure the German fighters away from the Ardennes front over the Eifel mountains where most of the air fighting took place.

This left the German ground forces without air cover or support, but it didn't make any difference. Coming as a complete surprise, the slender, fragile front, defended by a mere four divisions of the US 8th Corps commanded by Major General Troy Middleton, crumbled under the brute force of 1,000 enemy tanks and assault guns. Jolted into action and reality at last, Supreme Allied Headquarters Expeditionary Force (SHAEF) rushed the weary American 82nd and 101st Airborne Divisions, recuperating from the failed Arnhem operation, into the breach as reinforcements.

In the air, it was quite a different story, and not a good one for the Germans. At day's end Dietrich Peltz ruefully counted up his Jagdkorps' losses of 79 planes destroyed, with 55 pilots killed and 24 wounded, among them a Gruppe and a Staffel leader killed and two Staffeln leaders wounded. At this rate of attrition, his force of 1,500 serviceable Messerschmidt 109s and Focke Wulf 190s (contrary to Hitler's boast to his generals of a strength of 3,600), even fighting in inclement weather — or because of it — could be whittled down so badly in just a single day that Bodenplatte might quickly become an impossibility.

December 18, 1944
THE WESTERN FRONT

Allied strategic bombers shifted their weight from strategic targets in Germany to communications centres behind the battle zone to stop supplies from getting through and to bombing airfields on either side of the Rhine. Meanwhile the US 9th Tactical Air Force concentrated on targets within the combat area. Though the weather was still poor Peltz's fighters did manage to interfere with these operations but in the process lost 33 planes with 21 pilots killed and another 12 injured.

December 19, 1944
THE WESTERN FRONT

The Germans had reached Stavelot and Houffalize, the latter being defended by the US 82 Airborne Division. Ten miles to the south, the US 101st Airborne Division, completely surrounded, determinedly held onto the key road junction of Bastogne. Patton's Third Army was given orders to relieve it in 48 hours. In the mist, fog and cloud above the battlefield, Coningham's 2nd Tactical Air Force joined Vandenberg's fighters in attacks on tactical targets while the 8th USAF continued its raids on supply lines and centres behind the combat zone.

December 20, 1944
THE WESTERN FRONT

Patton began his move to relieve the 101 Airborne at Bastogne. This holdout and another at St Vith upset the German timetable and they were desperately trying to capture both road junctions before the weather improved and they would come under incessant air attack. Mosquito bombers from the 2nd TAC attacked targets at night to add to the destruction wrought by day-fighter-bombers. Again Peltz's fighters offered resistance, at times successfully, but he was beginning to have serious doubts that he would ever be able to launch Bodenplatte due to the continuing poor weather and increasing losses.

December 21-22, 1944
THE WESTERN FRONT

By this time all railways between the Luxembourg front and the Rhine had been paralysed by Allied tactical bombing. But the weather deteriorated to the extent that airfields on both sides were fog bound. The entire Allied tactical effort amounted to an abysmal 191 sorties. However, at night RAF Bomber Command was able to put up 234 of its heavies in attacks on Bonn and Cologne. Next day in Bastogne, Brigadier General Anthony McAuliffe rejected a German demand to surrender the 101st Airborne with a contemptuous "Nuts!"

December 23, 1944
THE WESTERN FRONT

As the sun finally made its way through the mist and clouds after a week of frustrating murky weather, George Patton remarked, "What a glorious day — for killing Germans!"[3] And as it turned out, in the air at least, it was just that. That morning, with a fighter escort of 400 Mustangs, 419 Flying Fortresses struck at rail junctions west of the Rhine. American, British and Canadian fighters and fighter-bombers hit at tactical targets in the battle zone. Peltz's fighters offered stiff resistance but it was terribly costly — 98 German fighters lost, 63 pilots killed and 35 wounded. And although the weather had improved it was still not clear enough to undertake the low-level Bodenplatte operation which called for absolutely unlimited visibility.

Christmas Eve, 1944
THE GERMAN AIRFIELDS

After the current losses it was remarkable that Peltz's Jagdkorps 11 was able to get between 700 and 800 fighters airborne in what was described as the "greatest German effort since D-Day."[4] Early in the day, they were first scrambled against 2,034 bombers from Doolittle's 8th USAF, the largest mission — No. 706 — in its history, escorted by 700 fighters. The targets were the German airfields; the objective was to put them right out of business. Once the Focke Wulf and Messerschmidts had tackled that assignment they were then faced with defending against more than 1,200 Spitfires, Tempests and rocket-firing Typhoons striking at tactical ground targets. It was a black day for the Jagdkorps — 106 aircraft shot down, 85 pilots killed, among them two Gruppe commanders and five Staffeln leaders, and another 21 pilots injured.

There was other bad news. The German offensive had been brought to a halt. Hitler knew he was beaten on the Ardennes front but he was still determined to capture Antwerp, his last and only hope of still winning the war. He now cast his eyes on the Eifel country to the north as a new venue from which to launch a fresh attack.

JAGDKORPS 11 HEADQUARTERS, ALTENKIRCHEN, Germany

Dietrich Peltz knew now that he could not postpone Bodenplatte much longer. Luckily, with a great deal of sweat, most of the airfields could be repaired reasonably quickly as could many aircraft damaged on the ground. But by far his biggest headache was the mounting daily losses which, at this stage, could only be replaced with pilots lacking combat experience and who, in many cases, were inadequately trained.

Christmas Day, 1944
THE ARDENNES, France

The Americans began their counter-attack as the Battle of the Bulge reached its climax. Peltz marshalled all his fighters to try and stem the tide turned against the Wehrmacht. But the overwhelming force of Allied Mustangs, Thunderbolts, Lightnings, Spitfires, Typhoons and Tempests made the task impossible. During the day's fighting, Jagdkorps 11 lost another 62 planes with 49 pilots killed. *Fröhliche Weihnachten, Luftwaffe!* Merry Christmas, Luftwaffe!

Boxing Day, 1944
THE ARDENNES, France

On this date the American 4th Armoured Brigade finally broke through to relieve the "Battered Bastards of Bastogne," the 101st Airborne Division. The Ardennes offensive was lost for the Germans as the Allies seized the initiative. But the weather had worsened in Britain and over parts of the continent. Freezing fog over the British Isles limited the 8th USAF to flying only 150 bomber sorties. During the morning in north-west Europe fog grounded the fighters on both sides, but later in the day Allied fighters created havoc on German supply lines and transportation. By day's end they had accounted for 60 more German planes destroyed with 49 of their pilots dead.

DER ADLERHORST, GERMANY

For the Germans, the situation had so deteriorated that OKW-head Keitel's chief of staff Alfred Jodl forbade any further traffic movements in daylight. He recorded that:[5]

> On the entire front, there was the heaviest enemy low-flying attacks ... which made movement and supply nearly impossible for the entire day ... considerable destruction of vehicles as a result of low-flying attacks .... The Luftwaffe could only offer localised and temporary relief in the face of massive employment of enemy aircraft over the battle zone.

In fact, Peltz's commitment of 400 fighters was simply overpowered by the 3,500 Allied fighters and fighter-bombers.

That evening in the Eagle's Aerie, Jodl confronted Hitler, "We must face facts. We cannot force the Meuse." The Führer answered, "Yes, we have had unexpected setbacks because my plan was not followed to the letter, but all is not lost." Goering did not agree and told Hitler so. "The war *is* lost," he maintained and suggested he seek a truce. He recommended that Hitler contact Count Folke Bernadotte, whose father, brother of King Gustavus V of Sweden, could probably help with armistice negotiations. This so enraged Hitler that he flew into a screaming frenzy. "I forbid you to take any step in this matter," he ranted. "If you go against my orders I will have you shot." The Reichsmarschall, realising he had gone too far, retired to his Karinhall estate where he told his wife Emmy, "This is the final break. He does not believe me anymore." His salvation would be Bodenplatte he decided. It was the only chance left to him.[6]

December 27, 1944
THE WESTERN FRONT

It was another bad day for the Luftwaffe. Although weather conditions in England limited Doolittle's 8th USAF to 575 bombing sorties against German rail targets at Gerolstein, Euskirchen and Hilleshen east of the Ardennes, the tactical air forces wrought havoc with transport, troop movements, tanks and gun emplacements on the battlefield. Jagdkorps 11's casualties amounted to 50 planes lost, 36 pilots killed, 14 injured with one Gruppe commander and four Staffeln leaders killed.

DER ADLERHORST, Germany

After meticulously studying the day's reports, Hitler decided to create a diversion by attacking through the Eifel country to the north, the objective still being the port of Antwerp. He instructed Jodl to issue an order to von Rundstedt to begin the new offensive — Operation Northland — immediately. At the same time he called Goering telling him to guarantee air support. The Reichsmarschall was beside himself with joy. Here was the opportunity he had been waiting for to get back in the

Führer's good graces. He wasted no time conferring with Beppo Schmidt and Dietrich Peltz. If there ever was a time for Bodenplatte, given a break in the weather, this was it.

December 28, 1944
JAGDKORPS 11 HEADQUARTERS, ALTENKIRCHEN, Germany

Dietrich Peltz's Bodenplatte plans coincided geographically with Operation Northland. All 21 of the Allied tactical airfields in Europe targeted for the low-level attack were in the north-west: 13 in Belgium, six in Holland and one in France. He estimated that by committing his fighters parsimoniously against Anglo-American air activity, at the current loss rate he would still have 800 available among his front-line Jagdgerschwadern 11 and 50 more among his supporting JGs along with some 30 Me 262 jet aircraft.

Schwartz Tag (Black Day) December 29, 1944
THE WESTERN FRONT

While the tactical air forces continued to hammer at targets from over the battlefield — some 2,300 machines were aloft that day — Peltz, carefully shepherding his Jagdgerschwadern for Bodenplatte, sent up only 130 fighters, but still lost a third, five of them to a Canadian Spitfire pilot in a spectacular dogfight between Osnabruck and Rhine, making him an instant ace. For Flight Lieutenant Dick Audet of 411 Squadron RCAF, flying from Heesch Airfield in Belgium, it was the first time he had seen, let alone engaged, an enemy aircraft. He was a quick study indeed.

Meanwhile, with clear weather now prevailing over England, Doolittle sent 1,315 of his bombers escorted by 572 Mustangs to drop 3,500 tons of bombs on German rail communication centres at Bullay, Kaiserslautern, Mainz and Bischoffsheim as well as bridges at Altenahr, Auskirchen, Irlich, Remegen and Merchnich. Not a single German fighter tried to stop them.

The accumulated effect of Allied air activity on the Wehrmacht over the previous six days was becoming catastrophic. Ammunition, fuel and supplies were not reaching the front. Vehicles and tanks were stalled, artillery stilled. Headquarters OBWest reported that "the severity of the efforts of the enemy air force could definitely be compared to that of Normandy."

December 30, 1944
THE WESTERN FRONT

Heavy fog, cloud and sleet limits operations for both Allied tactical and strategic air activity and Luftwaffe fighter operations. Operation Northland was about to get under way, however, and German meteorologists forecasted fine, clear weather in the next day or so.

Morning of December 31, 1944
NORTHERN GERMANY

With much improved weather, an American bomber force of 1,300 Flying Fortresses, heavily escorted by Mustang fighters, raided the Hamburg-Haarburg refinery and the hydrogenation plant at Milsburg. On the way to and from the targets, the armada was intercepted by Adolf Galland's home defence Jagdgeschwadern 300 and 301, with between 150 and 190 Messerschmidt fighters, 50 of which were lost.

Late Afternoon
JAGDKORPS 11 HEADQUARTERS, ALTENKIRCHEN

Dietrich Peltz finally received the weather report he had been praying for. For New Year's Day there would be clear skies with unlimited visibility. Although at one time or another 137 of his fighters had been in the air over the Ardennes since morning, the signal "Varus 1.1.45 Teutonicus" brought them in. It was a code issued to all Jagdkorp 11 JG commanders to end all flying for that day and to alert them that Bodenplatte was on. Later another signal, "Hermann Time 0920," gave the hour of attack.

The two signals displayed a typically Germanic bent for the historic. Hermann did not have anything to do with Goering but was the German name for their leader Amernius who, in AD 21, destroyed the Roman legions under Varus. Teutonicus was the name of the German military religious order. Though typically militant in nature, they served their purpose. When picked up by ULTRA, they kept the Allies guessing, just as the Germans intended.

That Evening
DER ADLERHORST

Der Führer had the last word. With the full knowledge that Bodenplatte was mere hours from getting underway, Hitler, brimming with confidence, addressed his people in a radio broadcast:[7]

> Only the turn of the year causes me to speak to you today, my German men and women .... Although our enemies have predicted our collapse during every one of the past years, they set special hopes on 1944 .... But once again we have turned fate away .... That this fight is an incredibly hard one is due to the enemy's aims ... to exterminate our people. When destroying our towns, they do not only hope to kill women and children, but also to eliminate our 1,000-year-old civilisation .... Our people are resolved to fight the war to victory under any and all circumstances ... the world must know that this State

will, therefore, never capitulate .... Germany will rise like a phoenix from its ruined cities and go down in history as the miracle of the 20th Century ...! We shall fulfil our duty faithfully and unshakeably in the new year too, in the firm belief that the hour will strike when victory ultimately will come to him most worthy of it, the Greater German Reich.

Endnotes

1 Lidell B.H. Hart, *History of World War II,* p. 639.

2 Danny S. Parker, *To Win the Winter Sky,* p. 146.

3 Parker, p. 221.

4 Parker, p. 266.

5 Parker, p. 317.

6 Parker, p. 319.

7 Parker, p. 363.

Flight Lieutenant Dick Audet of 411 Squadron
at Heesch shot down two Folcke Wulf 190s.
He had become an ace on December 29,
1944, when he shot down five enemy planes
in one day. (Department of Defence)

Looking over the damage done to his Spitfire on December 24.
The Germans did not let up in the days leading up to Operation
Bodenplatte. (Department of Defence)

CHAPTER 4

TAKE-OFF

Bombs dropped on the railway stations at Brussels and Liege shortly after midnight proved to be the herald of the low-level attack on Allied tactical airfields to come nine hours later. That was not part of the plan. They were simply unloaded by the four Arado 234 jets led by Einsatzstaffel III KG 51 Kommodore Diether Lukesch to get rid of them. Historically this marked the first-ever jet night-bombing attack. The aircraft were on a weather reconnaissance mission preceding the launch of Bodenplatte. Though in some areas there was some light rain and snow, their report was favourable.

By Sunday morning, some British airfields had to be sanded because ice had formed on the runways and taxi strips from the overnight rain. On other fields snow had to be cleared. While this slowed things up a bit these were minor inconveniences that were soon rectified. On German fighter strips in the low-lying areas, early morning fog had settled in, delaying take-off. But this was no major problem either. Shortly after sunrise it had dispersed.

New Year's Day, 1945

BETWEEN 0600 and 0940 HOURS
Weather: Extremely cold, but clear and bright.
DELMENHORST, QUAKENBRUCK, VECHTA and
BISSEL AIRFIELDS, Germany

Brimming with confidence, at 0730 hours, Oberstleutnant Johann Kogler's Jagdgeschwader 6 — 70 machines strong — took to the air for their meticulously prepared attack on Volkel Airfield in Belgium. It seemed a lead-pipe cinch — all in a morning's work. The Messerschmidts of Gruppe III, commanded by Major Helmut Kuhle, flew top cover to Hauptmann Ewald Trost's Gruppe I Focke Wulfs which would lead the attack. Following close behind would be Gruppe II led by Hauptmann Johannes Naumann in a second sweep. Then to complete the assault, Gruppe III Messerschmidts would make a third run at the field from above.

Gruppe II from Quakenbruck and Vechta led off followed by Gruppe III from Bissel, with Gruppe I from Delmenhorst bringing up the rear. No sooner was Gruppe III airborne than Oberleutnant Hans Pfliederer's Messerschmidt suddenly lost speed and crashed into the trees around Delmenhorst Airfield, killing the pilot. Shortly afterwards the Geschwader suffered its second casualty. Feldwebel Karly Schubert, a veteran air fighter with Gruppe I, described it:[1]

> I was leading a vic .... After we got airborne ... we headed for the Zuider Zee. Right over its southern tip, [Oberfeldwebel] Walter Jung went down. We assumed he must have collided with another machine. We never found out what happened to him — his machine probably caught fire when it crashed in a meadow beside the lake.

The three Gruppen assembled over Quakenbruck, followed the Ju 88 trail-blazer on a south-westerly course to Veghel, then turned south-east. However, the navigation of Hauptmann Karl Bibsiem, the Ju 88 trailblazer pilot, proved faulty. He flew straight on past the turning point, with the result that the fighters found themselves too far to the west. The field that lay ahead of them was not Volkel at all but the newly constructed Heesch Airfield ten miles north-east. Only nine of the German fighters managed to find Volkel, while the others simply got lost.

HEESCH AIRFIELD, Holland

Flight Lieutenant John Edison was in his control tower early. At 0850 hours he directed the take-off of 411 Squadron on an armed reconnaissance foray in the Osnabruck-Munster area. Thirteen minutes later he gave 442 Squadron the OK to leave the ground and sweep the Lingen-Munster district. In the group was a section led by Flight Lieutenant Norm Keene and made up of Flying Officer Len Wilson and Flight Lieutenant Dave "Tex" Pieri. Wilson had not originally been slated to fly the sweep, but he had filled in for one of his comrades who's hangover was so bad that he wanted to go back to bed. Wilson agreed to take his place.

By 0914 the 12 Spitfire IXs of 401 Squadron, under the temporary command of Flying Officer Doug Cameron, who was leading Yellow Section, were on the runway ready to take off. Cameron was fuming. Although Edison had given the squadron clearance for take-off, for some inexplicable reason, the pilots of Red Section in the vanguard, led by Flight Lieutenant Johnny MacKay, were still sitting on their butts.

In the officers' billets, Al Bathurst was dead to the world, sleeping off the effects of the night before.

VOLKEL AIRFIELD, Belgium

Two of the 122 Wing squadrons, 56 and 486, led by Squadron Leaders David Cotes-Preedy and A.E. "Spike" Umbers, respectively, with wing leader John Wray in the vanguard, had been in the air for over half an hour on an armed reconnaissance of the Paderborn region.

Like his counterpart, J.C. Meyer, Commanding Officer of the US 32nd Fighter Group over at Asch Airfield, Wray had an inkling that one day the Germans might attempt a low-level raid. Near the Vokel air strip there was a railway loading station the Germans had used for storage and the railway line led directly into Germany. Wray had considerable experience in low-level attacks. For these reasons he said later, "I always tried to ensure that three of my five squadrons were off the ground at first light ..."[2]

A third unit, Jimmy Thiele's No. 3 New Zealand Squadron, had yet to take-off. Pilot Officer Ron Pottinger, who had over-celebrated the end of his ops tour the night before woke up with a king-size hangover. But his room-mate was in even worse shape and persuaded Pottinger, much against the latter's better judgement, to fill in for him as the squadron "spare" — a standby role to take the place of any of the pilots who were unable to get off, for one reason or other. Thankfully for Pottinger, who was still nursing a throbbing head, this did not happen and, once 3 Squadron was airborne, he began taxiing back to the dispersal. Two others on the field, Pilot Officers Robert Adcock and Bill Bailey were also strapped in their aircraft with the engines running.

PADERBORN, LIPPSPSINGE and GUTERSLOH AIRFIELDS, Germany

The most successful fighter pilot in the sky that New Year's Day morning was destined to lead the most successful raid of the entire Bodenplatte operation. The tall, dashing Oberstleutnant Heinz Bar, Kommando of Jagdgeschwader (Udet) 3, with more than 200 victories to his credit — 21 of them four-engine bombers — ranked among the top ten German aces. Composed of Gruppe I under Oberleutnant Fritz Seidel, Gruppe III commanded by Hauptmann Karl-Heinze Langer, and Gruppe IV under the temporary leadership of Leutnant Erich Mueller, JG 3 had been singled out to attack Eindhoven Airfield, where the rich prize of two Typhoon fighter-bomber wings and a Spitfire reconnaissance wing awaited them.

At all three airfields, the pilots were awakened before first light when reveille sounded. Then after breakfast, they were briefed at 0700 hours, given maps with the warning that Eindhoven "is swarming with Spitfires," and told to keep a sharp lookout for any that might already be airborne.

Take-off took place simultaneously from all three airfields at 0830 and the Jagdgeschwader formed up over Lippstadt and headed west where a Ju 88 led the formation across the Rhine. They flew over the Ruhr, passed the first checkpoint at Dorsten and crossed the Dutch border some 15 miles north of Venlo. Twenty minutes from the target, the snow-covered plain of Brahast stretched before them, the town of Helmond on the left. At this point several Staffeln had broken away from the rest of the formation. They had, in fact, gotten lost and found themselves headed toward Gilze-Reijen Airfield where a parachute landing was expected, not an air attack. Meanwhile over Sonse Heath, Bar led his men south making a wide sweep around Eindhoven, crossing over the town and roaring in toward the field from the south-west.

EINDHOVEN AIRFIELD, Holland

B-78 was buzzing like a beehive. All three wings were gearing up for one kind of operation or another. Even the airfield Auster artillery spotting light aircraft was airborne. First off the deck was a flight of 439 RCAF Squadron Typhoons from 143 Wing. Led by Flying Officer Bob Laurence, it was made up of Flying Officers Hugh Fraser, Bill Anderson and Sam Angelini, and took off at 0830 hours for a weather check over St Vith in the Ardennes.

At that very moment, Flying Officer Gordon Hill of 416 Squadron from Brussels-Evere, who had limped in with his shot-up Spitfire the day before, arrived at the airfield control truck. He had been told that the air cooler had been replaced and his aircraft was now fully serviceable. It looked great. Hill went inside the truck to ask the controller to phone for a battery cart, the auxiliary power needed to get the engine started.[3]

Half an hour later, Squadron Leader Harold Lambert, commanding officer of 168 Squadron from the same wing, also led a flight of six Typhoons toward St Vith. His mission was to assist in the advance of the "Battered Bastards of Bastogne," the US 101st Airborne Division.

At 0901, three flights of Spitfire IXs from 414 RCAF Squadron took off. The first led by the commanding officer, Squadron Leader Gordie Wonnacott, headed for Cologne on a tactical reconnaissance sweep. Another pair, made up of Flight Lieutenants Jim Donovan and Paul Grier, set course for Munich on a similar mission. A third flight, with Flying Officers Ian Woloschuk and Bill Sawyer, had as its target, Nees-Cologne.

By this time Bob Laurence's weather recce flight reported that cloud had begun to clear around most of the immediate area, although there was still some mist over the Ardennes.

A Typhoon of 168 Squadron flown by Flight Lieutenant Harold "Gibby" Gibbons had just taken off on an air test and now, flights from the RCAF squadrons, 430's new Spitfire XIVs and Typhoons from 438 and 440 Squadrons, began taxiing out to the take-off point. Aircrewmen perched on both wingtips of the aircraft to guide the pilots through the eight-inch frozen ridges on either side of the taxi strip as well as around bomb craters.

The Spitfires were led by flight commander Jim Prendergast, of 430 Squadron. Pete Wilson, the new CO of 438 Squadron, led seven other Flying Officers including his Number Two Ron Keller, Andy Lord, Bill Beatty, Don Campbell, Allan Harle and two others. One of the squadron's pilots was nowhere near the runway. Phil Macklem was standing in front of the dispersal watching and waiting for an Anson transport to fly him back to England. He'd been taken off ops the day before, having finished his combat tour. 440 Squadron RCAF was split into two sections. Flight Lieutenant Ernie Savard acted as Red Section leader while Pilot Officer Dick Watson headed up Blue Section. Among those making up the two flights were Flying Officers Ted Smith, Iva Gunnarson, Currie Garner, and bridegroom-to-be, Ed Flanagan.[4]

439 Squadron RCAF's Typhoons had been fitted with rockets and were neatly lined up in front of a hangar. The CO, Squadron Leader Robert Crosby, inevitably nicknamed "Bing" after the famous crooner, was driving his jeep from the convent billet to the dispersal, Flight Lieutenant Johnny Carr in the passenger seat. Leading Aircraftman Len Weir was at the wheel of a truck taking Flying Officers Johnny Johnson and Jack Roberts to the maintenance hangar.

At exactly 0910 hours, Father Michael, the Catholic padre with 143 Wing, began saying Mass.

DARMSTADT-GREISHEIM, BABENHAUSEN and RHINE-MAIN AIRFIELDS, Germany

At 0810 hours the three Gruppen of a badly under-equipped Jagdgeschwader 4 got airborne, led by its commander Major Gerhard Michalski. Though they had suffered severe losses over the last week — Hauptmann Wilhelm Steinmann's Gruppe I could only muster ten Me 109s, for example — the pilots looked forward with anticipation to attacking Le Culot near Brussels where, from reconnaissance photos, they knew 100 American P-47 Thunderbolts, along with medium- and heavy-bombers, were all neatly arrayed, just waiting to be pounced on. Once airborne, the three units rendezvoused over Bingen then headed west toward Belgium in the wake of Feldwebel Gunther Kotschote's twin-engine Ju 88 trailblazer. The formation flew on to Hunsruck then, ten minutes later, reached the first fix marked on the pilots' maps distributed at the briefing just before take off, Bullay on the Moselle River. They then proceeded west to Prum in the Eifel country, arriving at approximately 0840 hours, just as the sun began penetrating the morning mists. So far so good, they were now within a half hour's flying time to the target. Then disaster struck.

A few minutes later, en route to Le Culot, JG 4 sustained the first of the casualties that were about to reduce it to less than half of its fighter strength. Over Palenburg, Unteroffizier Gunther Schwarzenau from Major Max Schroder's Gruppe II, bailed out after his FW 190 was hit by ground fire. Near Hannut, Unteroffizier Horst Thanaan crash-landed his Focke Wulf after running into heavy ack-ack. Both pilots survived to be taken prisoner.

The most critical loss at this stage, however, was that of the Jagdgeschwader's pathfinder, Gunther Kotschote, who was forced to pancake his Ju 88 trailblazer in a field after it had been riddled by light flak. In a stroke the Geschwader had lost its seeing-eye dog. Gerhard Michalski did his best to steer his 55 FW 190s and Me 109s to the target but in the confusion resulting from the loss of Kotschote as their guide, the JG Kommodore had lost his bearings and his attempt proved hopeless. Drifting aimlessly in circles some ten miles south of Brussels searching for

Le Culot fighter base without success, the formation soon became lost and thoroughly disoriented. The three Gruppen separated from one another, each one deciding to fend for itself. The inevitable result was that, in the absence of any cohesion or leadership, many Staffeln, as well as lesser Vic formations (V-shaped, similar to flying formations of geese), broke away preferring to seek out targets on their own.

Some latched onto Schwarm formations of double pairs as stragglers from the various Geschwarden spread out over the countryside, while others attacked Allied ground targets in the Ardennes in the vicinity of Bastogne. Although they were missing about half their Staffeln which had gone their separate ways, Max Schroder's Gruppe II FW 190 pilots found themselves over St Trond-Brustem, convinced they had at last found their designated target. This mistake was understandable. Le Culot and St Trond were less than ten miles apart, and from the air, the frozen, snow-covered ground surrounding made it difficult to differentiate one airfield from the other. That similarity was reinforced by the fact that both fighter fields were packed solid with American P-47 Thunderbolts. The FW 190 pilots got ready to attack, only to find, to their complete surprise, that another Jagdeschwader, the famed Richthofen JG 2, had beaten them to the punch. But that didn't bother anyone — except perhaps the field defenders — the more the merrier!

FURSTENAU, NORDHORN and PLANTLUNNE AIRFIELDS, Germany

At Furstenau Airfield, Pips Priller, utterly frustrated over having to split up his JG 26 for the double-pronged attack on the twin Brussels airfields of Evere, west of the city, and Grimbergen to its north, close to the town of Vilvoride, waited impatiently for the signal to take off. Finally, at 0814 hours the flares went up and, once in the air, Gruppe I under Major Karl Borris was joined by Gruppe III from Jagdgeschwader 54 from Varrelbusch, led by Oberstleutnant Hans Dortenmann, which boosted Borris's spirits no end — he needed all the reinforcements he could get. Over the past month he had lost 16 of his pilots which left him with a fighter strength of just 67. Like his own Gruppe and that of Major Anton Hackl's (Gruppe II), Dortenmann's pilots were also equipped with "Long Noses," the Focke Wulf 190 D-9s (known as "Doras"). But his outfit too had suffered heavily — as recently as the day before. The most it could muster was 17 Doras.

Simultaneously, a much stronger force of over 100 planes, comprising the other two JG 26 Gruppen II (Doras), and III (Me 109s), took off from Nordhorn, where a three-piece band gave the pilots a martial send-off, and from Platlunne, led by Anton Hackl and Hauptmann Walter "Count" Krupinski, respectively. Fortunately they were destined for a much more fruitful mission than their companions in Gruppe I and the JG 54 contingent.

Flying at various altitudes of between 150 and 500 feet, well spread out to avoid collision, the two combined formations of FW 190s and Me 109s followed the first leg of their mission leading directly to Spakenburg at the tip of the Zuider Zee where they altered course for Rotterdam.

Between Utrecht and the Dutch port, trigger-happy German ack-ack gunners from the 16th Flak Battery guarding the V-2 rocket sites, opened fire on their own aircraft. Although they had been alerted earlier to expect large low-flying formations of Luftwaffe fighters over their area, either they never received the signal or else suffered from a bad case of the twitch — perhaps both. Their first victim was Oberleutnant Franz Kunz of Gruppe I, who was severely injured when his Focke Wulf crashed near Polsbroek. Next to fall was one of JG 54's pilots, Unteroffizier Gerhard Kroll and two of his 26

Geschwader confrères, Obergfriete Manfred Neissen and Oberfahnrich Helmet Heuser. After absorbing their share of "friendly" ack-ack, all three managed to belly land their FW 190s safely on land near Borken east of the island of Tolen.

The remainder of the two formations swept west away from Rotterdam and their trigger-happy countrymen in the vicinity, and vectored south in the direction of their allocated targets. Crossing over the Scheldt Estuary and Walcheren Island, they were fired upon again, but this time at least, the flak was "un-friendly" — most unfriendly and very accurate. That precision of the Canadian anti-aircraft gunners sounded the death knell for four of Hackl and Krupinski's fighters. Me 109 pilots Oberleutnant Harald Lenz and Gefreite Horst Sengspiel from the Count's Gruppe III, along with Unteroffizier Leo Speer from Hackl's Gruppe II, met their fate after their fighters sustained solid strikes from the bursting flak shells. Both pilots crashed to their deaths into the icy North Atlantic waters off the Dutch coast. Speer's wingman Obergefreite Hubert Lott managed to jump clear of his FW 190 but just as his parachute sprung open the harness came loose. With nothing to brake his fall, Dutch civilians on the ground and his comrades in the air alike, watched in horror as his helpless figure tumbled earthward to its death.

Over the River Scheldt just north of Antwerp, flying as he said "into the barrel of a 3.7 cm AA gun," Stabfeldwebel Hans-Joachim Steinkamp's FW 190 was riddled with shellfire from British anti-aircraft batteries. Steinkamp turned north. He had every intention of trying to make it back to the German lines until he looked at his port wing. Most of it was missing. It was a wonder he was still flying. Without a second thought, the JG 54 veteran of the Russian Front and the summer battles over France, bailed out of his stricken machine and parachuted down into the middle of the tiny hamlet of Hults where he was taken prisoner. In captivity he remained as unflappable as he had been through his combat career, his confidence in a final German victory unshaken. Spouting the party line, he told his interrogators, "The faith of the whole German nation is now in the hands of the Führer, who will find a way to save Europe from Bolshevism. How and when, only the Führer knows." (Heil Hitler!)

As the formations crossed the border in Belgium to make their final approach to their objectives they encountered Spitfires from the St Denis-Westram-based 308 Polish Squadron. In the brief but bloody skirmish that ensued the Poles knocked five of the Luftwaffe fighters out of the sky without a loss themselves. Flight Lieutenant Zbigniew Zimgrodski quickly put Gruppe I's Obergefreite Dieter Kraegerloh out of action. The hapless FW 190 pilot later recalled his plight:[5]

> I was only 21 years old …. My plane was hit several times. While I was flying further, my engine stopped and I attempted a crash-landing. I was too low to bail out. The flaps did not respond, so I could not reduce my speed. It hit the ground very hard. My safety belts were torn and I smashed into the dashboard. I broke my back and my legs were pinned in the cockpit. I could only wait until a doctor gave me first aid before I could be moved from the wreckage.

Further west, Pilot Officer Andrezj Dromlewicz splintered Feldwebel Paul Dreutschmann's FW Dora with a burst of cannon fire. The JG 54 pilot managed to jump free from his aircraft and hit the silk, only to land in the freezing River Durme where a Belgian policeman arrested him. Shivering and despondent, he still had enough spirit left in him to throw his revolver into the icy river when his captor demanded he hand it over to him.

Three other Focke Wulf Long Noses from Hans Dortenmann's Geschwader were shot down in the same fight, all of them plunging into the streets of the village of Sinai and killing the pilots. Flight Sergeant Zymunt Sisynski ended Unteroffizier Heinz Schulz's career as a fighter pilot. Sergeant Stanislaw Breyner accounted for the other two Doras destroyed.

At around 0920 what was left of the JG 26 Gruppe I and JG 54 Gruppe III formation, reached their target, which they had been instructed to attack in three waves. But as Grimbergen loomed before them, to their chagrin, they saw that the field was virtually deserted except for four Flying Fortresses and a lone Mustang parked between the hangars. Pips Priller was completely pissed off. Due to improper communications, his JG had been fired on by their own troops and now it was clear that the reconnaissance people hadn't done their job either. All this effort, all these casualties, just to end up finding a goddam empty airfield. That was Bodenplatte for you. A total waste of time. A complete balls up. After signalling Karl Borris to take over and try and make the best he could out of a downright, thorough shambles, Priller turned away in absolute disgust and started back to Furstenau.

By comparison, Hackl and Krupinski's Gruppen II and III struck it rich, as if they'd been hung with horseshoes. Not only had their casualties been minimal, but as Evere Airfield hove into view at precisely the same time that Priller came upon the near-empty Grimbergen — 0920 hours — they spied Spitfires all neatly parked in rows on one side and a line of planes of multi-engine design on the other, as well as other fighters with their engines running, waiting to take off. At this exciting and critical point, to his dismay, Krupinski was forced to radio Hackl to take over both Gruppen. His engine was missing after being hit by flak and he was unable to go on. Hackl ordered all pilots to jettison their drop tanks and get ready to wade in.

BRUSSELS-EVERE AIRFIELD, Belgium

On the way from the 421 Squadron billet by truck, Flying Officer Ken Langmuir was suffering from a monumental hangover from the New Year's Eve celebration the night before. When they arrived at their dispersal, those on readiness went to their lockers to get their flying gear — parachutes, Mae West life preservers, helmets and so on. Langmuir considered himself lucky he wasn't one of them. He stepped outside to breathe in the nice brisk fresh air and clear his head watching aircraft from the other squadrons taxi out. He threw a baseball around with several others and, as he would later say, they were simply "shooting the shit."

B-56 was covered in ice as a result of freezing rain overnight. Before the first patrols could take off, the runway and taxi strips had to be sanded. So, even though those on call from 403 and 416 Squadrons had been up for hours, it was not until 0900 that the first flight of Flight Lieutenant Dick Reeves and his Number Two, Flying Officer Mackenzie "Mac" Reeves, got airborne after the controller had warned them to take it easy on the brakes to avoid skidding. Twenty minutes later a second patrol left the ground — Pilot Officer Steve Butte and his wingman Sergeant Pilot Doug Lindsay.

Meanwhile 416 Squadron had been brought to readiness and the pilots' 12 Spitfire XVIs, headed by Flight Lieutenant Dave Harling, got ready to begin taxiing out. Directly behind him was his Number Two, Warrant Officer Lou Jean. Next in line in the Number Three slot was Flying Officer Len Commerford, and Eric Downer, who had joined the squadron on Christmas Day, filled the Number Four position.

After a pleasant night with the Belgian lovely he had met at the dance hall in Brussels, Flying Officer Bill Roddie, who had had "his ass shot off" the day before in the Rhine-Munster sector, enjoyed a breakfast of croissants and coffee with her and her family that morning. He then set out for the airfield, a half an hour's walk away, where he arrived at 0905 hours. Precisely 15 minutes later, Harling taxiied onto the Evere runway.[6]

BRUSSELS-GRIMBERGEN, Belgium

Group Captain Alexander Gabszewicz and his adjutant who had arrived at the field (which at this stage was non-operational, a fact that had escaped German Intelligence), the day before to make arrangements for moving Gabszewicz's 131 Polish Spitfire Wing from St Denis-Westram Airfield, were in the best of spirits. All details for the transfer had been completed and approved. The accommodations and facilities they considered highly satisfactory by tactical air force standards. At 0900 hours they had just emerged from their billets and were getting ready to drive over to the mess for breakfast after which they planned to make a last-minute check of all their arrangements.

GROSS-OSTHEIM, DARMSTADT-GREISHEIM and ZEILLHAUSEN AIRFIELDS, Germany

VROOM! VROOM! A collective guttural roar of some 30 BMW 18-cylinder engines rent the early morning silence as mechanics revved up the Focke Wulf 190 fighter motors in readiness for take-off. Around 0630 Hauptmann Horst von Fassong, an ace with 100 victories to his credit, had begun briefing his Gruppe III at Gross-Ostheim. A Junkers 188 nightfighter stood by waiting to lead the entire Jagdgeschwader (JG 11), headed by Oberstleutnant Gunther Specht, flying with Gruppe I in an FW 190 from Darmstadt-Greisheim to the target. Each pilot was given a clearly marked map showing the route from the front lines near Limburg to the objective and the return direction.

They would fly at an altitude of 150 feet to avoid detection by Allied radar. Strict radio silence was to be maintained, no matter what. The Jagdgeschwader formed up over Aschaffenburg where it was to be joined by Gruppe I and the Messerschmidt 109s of Gruppe II from Zeillhausen. From there, following the Ju 188 pathfinders, they flew west toward Aachen then followed the Meuse River north, passing over Emael, Kanne, Vroehoven and Veldvezel, places made famous during the 1940 blitzkrieg.

A hitch in the operation had occurred just after 0800 hours when a slight mist drifted over most of the German fighter fields, delaying take-off for half an hour. This upset the timetable as far as the ack-ack batteries were concerned, and when the trailblazing Junkers dropped their flares, they were mistaken for hostile signals. As the fighters of JG 11 neared the lines, they were greeted by flak from their own anti-aircraft gunners. Fortunately no damage was done. But several minutes afterwards, Oberleutnant Adolf Fiedler's Focke Wulf 190 was hit by British anti-aircraft fire near Aachen. Wounded in the head, he lapsed into unconsciousness, yet recovered, and was still able to make a forced landing in a field where he was rescued by his captors.

By 0935 the German force was in sight of its target, Asch Airfield. A slight ground haze covered the snow-swept countryside. This, and the fact that the FW 190s and Me 109s, some 70 fighters in all, were hugging the ground at treetop level, allowed them to race in to attack the field from the north-east completely undetected. The surprise was complete!

ASCH AIRFIELD, Belgium

Around 0700 hours, fog moved in, threatening to ground all activity. Gradually, however, it began to clear enough for take off at any rate. Undaunted by 9th Tactical Air Force Command chief General Pete Quesada's refusal to grant him permission to mount an early morning patrol over the airfield, acting CO of the 352nd Fighter Group J.C. Meyer wolfed down a quick, typical wartime breakfast of powdered eggs and coffee, lit his pipe, and determined to take another stab at it. Meanwhile, at 0842 hours the 391st Fighter Squadron, armed with 500 pound bombs and led by Captain Eber Simpson, took to the air to bomb German tanks near St Vith in the Ardennes. Their sortie was successful. For the loss of one P-47 which was hit by light flak, though the pilot managed to belly land it safely in a field south of Liege, the squadron had accounted for several enemy tanks. Then, unbeknownst to the others back at Y-29, on the way home they had run across two Me 109s south of Malmedy which Lieutenants John Bathurst and Donald Holt promptly shot down.

By this time, headquarters had had a change of heart. Yes, Quesada told Meyer, he could fly a preventive patrol — but with only 12 Mustangs — provided he could assure that 36 fighters from his 352nd Group would be available as escort for the US 8th Air Force bombing mission to targets in the Kassel and Koblenz-Trier regions. Roger! No problem at all!

Meyer assigned the 487th Fighter Squadron with himself as leader and the other two sections led by Major William "Bill" Halton and Captain William "Whiz" Whisner. But first, control radioed the "Thunderbirds" of the 390th Fighter Squadron to take off first. As soon as they began orbiting the field on their way to the front, Meyer signalled his team to get ready for their own take-off. Meyer and his wingman, Lieutenant Alex Sears, reached the runway first. Slamming their throttles forward, they tore down the runway heading due east. The time was exactly 0940 hours as they lifted their wheels.

OPHOVEN AIRFIELD, Belgium

Shortly after take-off, three of 41 Squadron's Spitfire pilots were forced to abort their mission and turn back due to engine failure. They landed back at Y-32 at approximately 0855 hours, just a few minutes before the four 610 Squadron pilots got airborne to patrol the Maeseych region.

Meanwhile, Squadron Leader Don Benman led the remainder of his unit down the Rhine north of Koblenz. One section tackled a convoy of 17 railway cars, inflicting severe damage with their machine-gun and cannon fire. At the same time Flight Lieutenant Robert Harding and Flying Officer Ned Gibbs shot up a three-ton barge plying its way up the river. Mission completed, the squadron reassembled to return to base.

MERZHAUZEN, NIDDA, ETTINGHAUSEN, ALDERNSTADT and COLOGNE-WAHN AIRFIELDS, Germany

Bodenplatte instructions to Gruppe I of the famed Richthofen Jagdgeschwader (JG 2) as read by their commander, Hauptmann Karl Hrdlicka, to his pilots at 0600 hours were simple and straightforward: "Take off 0800. Form up over map square 'Papa-Oscar 4 and 5' and wait for Gruppen II and III to join. Attack to be carried out in conjunction with SG 4. Close Support Geschwader."[7]

Gruppen I and III of the JG 2 Geschwader — commanded by Oberstleutnant Kurt Buhlingen, an ace with 100 victories — had only recently been equipped with the new long-nosed Focke Wulf 190 D-9s (Doras) housing the powerful 1,770 horsepower BMW engines. In fact some were so new, so fresh off the line, there hadn't been time to paint their markings on them. The other wing, Gruppe II, flew Me 109s. Some of the FW 190s with the support Geschwader had rockets, usually used against the American bombers, affixed for the raid.

It was still dark when the pilots began arriving at the airfield by truck from their billets in town. In addition to the directional briefing they were given aerial reconnaissance photos of the target, St Trond-Brustem, showing some 130 tightly packed American fighters and a half a dozen four-engine bombers parked on the airfield, almost wing-tip to wing-tip — a turkey shoot!

The plan called for all Gruppen to rendezvous over Koblenz, then fly south over the Schnee Eifel in the Ardennes before turning north-west to head for St Trond. Gruppe III had just reached Westerwald when suddenly Unteroffizier Fritz Altpeter's FW 190 Dora began to belch black smoke then caught fire. At just over 100 feet Altpeter was unable to bail out and crashed to his death near Diersdorf.

Then Feldwebel Karl Tschelesnig had trouble retracting his undercarriage, so he landed for hasty repairs. He took off again and raced to catch up with the rest of his Staffel. Just east of Verviers his FW 190 was hit by enemy flak. Tschelesnig dived into some trees to evade the gunners. Miraculously, his aircraft emerged from the foliage but it was so badly damaged that, after coaxing it up to 600 feet, Tschelesnig took to his parachute.

Meanwhile, Oberstleutnant Alfred Druschel's SG 4 Schlackgerschwader (Support Wing) Gruppe III had taken off from Cologne-Wahn Airfield to rendezvous with Buhlingen's JG 2 two miles south of Aachen, the only German city then in Allied hands. As the formation approached the ancient Holy Roman Empire centre, it came under accurate and severe American anti-aircraft fire which claimed, as one of its four victims, Albert Druschel, a veteran of 800 missions, who had only taken over the leadership of SG 4 that morning. A shattered second-in-command, Major Gunther Dornbrack, had no choice but to take over on the spot.

JG 2 advanced further to the battlefield area, but even before reaching the target, the Geschwader lost 13 more aircraft to American flak. Unterfoffizern Otto Dost, Friederich Opteenhostert and Oberfeldwebel Fritz Schuler were all shot down and killed. Near Eupen, Unteroffizern Hans Wyssola,

Georg Wilkens and Wilhelm Scherwadt had to bail out of their riddled machines to be taken prisoner. Unteroffizier Helmut Breitweg crash-landed and was captured, while Unteroffizier Ernst Klein plunged to his death in the same vicinity. Unteroffiziern Siegfried Binger and Michael Speiss, and Obergefreiter Hubert Schyma all bailed out and were captured after being hit near Malmedy-Verviers, while, closer to the target, Leutnant Christfried Clemens was shot down and killed near Sittard.

The vaunted Richthofen Jagdgeschwader had already lost 15 pilots before firing a shot, added to the four pilots lost to the close support Sturmgeschwader, two of the Luftwaffe's most experienced leaders among the victims.

ST TROND-BRUSTEM AIRFIELD, Belgium

While some of the pilots of the 9th USAF's 48th and 404th Fighter Groups were making their way down to the dispersal areas, the others, particularly those from the former group, were still in bed sleeping it off. As the 48th's diarist noted:[8]

> At 0845 when some of the Group had taken their hangovers to work and most had kept them in bed, an amazing thing happened. An unfamiliar drone of engines was heard ...

RHINE, TWENTHE and DROPE AIRFIELDS, Germany

At 0630 hours when Hauptmann Hans-Georg Hackbarth briefed his Gruppe I pilots of Oberstleutnant Herbert Ihlefeld's Jagdgeschwader 1 "Oesau" at Twenthe, on the "Big Show" planned for that morning, they felt a sense of relief. For most of the outgoing flight, the FW 190 pilots would be flying over territory occupied by their own troops. Guided by two Ju 88 trailblazers and joined by Gruppe III of the Geschwader, led by their new commander, Hauptmann Harald Moldenhauer, from Rhine Airfield, equipped with Me 109s, the gaggle of 55 aircraft were to fly to Spakenburg at the southern tip of the Zuider Zee then proceed westward to the Dutch coast. From there they were to fly down over the North Sea hugging the shoreline, then crossing in over Belgium between Blankenberge and Knocke and heading south in the direction of Bruges. Their target was Maldegem Airfield (B-65) which faulty German intelligence had mistakenly advised was the home of 485 Royal New Zealand Air Force Squadron. In fact the unit had moved south several days earlier, leaving only 17 Spitfires being modified for operational service. The pilots had also been told to expect to find Tempests and Mustangs as well as Spitfires parked on the field, another juicy bit of misinformation. Both Gruppen were to make five passes over the target. Gruppe II of JG 1, after taking off at 0730 from their airfield at Drope north of the Rhine, followed a similar route as the rest of the Geschwader. At 0900 hours the 30 FW 190s roared in from the south-west to attack their target, St Denis-Westrem Airfield near Ghent.

Due to a mix-up in communications, German naval anti-aircraft gunners opened up on Gruppe I's Focke Wulf 190s on the Dutch coast south of Rotterdam. They had mistaken them for low-level RAF fighters which they were accustomed to seeing daily. Hackbarth lost two of his pilots right off the bat, Unteroffiziern Egon Comtesse and Heinz Jurgan, an artist by trade and a veteran of 80 combat flights in North Africa, Italy and Romania. A third pilot, Unteroffizier Heinz Bohmer, managed to keep his battered FW 190 aloft above the Old Meuse River, but it was a losing battle. He finally lost his plane and his life as well, when he crashed into the ground south-east of Dordrecht. A further casualty was the Geschwader leader, Herbert Ihlefeld, whose aircraft was hit by flak as the formation flew past The Hague. However, he successfully managed a belly land in a farm field. Although he escaped without injury it was still, all in all, hardly an auspicious beginning for the attack on the unsuspecting B-61 and B-65 Allied fighter fields.

On arrival near Bruges, the raiders began organising the attack on Maldegem Airfield. Number 4 Staffel from Gruppe I, led by Oberleutnant Hans-Gottfried Meinhof, immediately lost one of its five pilots, when Unteroffizier Alfred Fritzsche was hit by flak and crash-landed, severely burnt. Meinhof's Gruppe detached itself to seek out the secondary target of Ursel Airfield. Once again, German intelligence proved faulty. Its information showed a squadron of 12 Spitfires located on the field, but these had returned to England the day before, leaving only a few bombers being repaired. The time was approximately 0900 hours.

URSEL AIRFIELD, Belgium

After breakfasting in the abandoned leather factory that served as a mess hall, Leading Aircraftsman Edward Green and the seven other airmen who were billeted in an old bakery a mile from the field, proceeded by truck to the Motor Transport Section of which Green was a member. Green was told to get a small van to pick up a work party on the opposite side of the field and take them to the control tower where a badly damaged Mosquito that needed repair work was parked. Nearby was the shot-up Flying Fortress from the 486th Bomber Group of the 8th USAF that American mechanics had been repairing for some weeks, as well as two RAF Lancaster bombers that had pranged on landing after being clobbered by anti-aircraft fire. They stood by the airfield oil dump and the Spitfire bomb dump. Here the Spitfires that daily flew over from Manston on the British south-east coast would load up before going on to dive-bomb the German V-2 rocket sites.

Green was on his way with his party when he remembered that he had forgotten to check another truck for fuel and mileage.

He stopped his van and ran back to where the truck was parked. In the far distance he could hear the sound of aircraft. That must be the Manston Spitfire squadron, he thought.

By this time it was 0900 hours and Sergeant Peter Crowest with the other members of the air controller's crew were positioned in the tower at the down-wing end of the runway against which there were low concrete walls as a shelter in case the field came under fire. This was fortuitous because the field had absolutely no ground defenses.

BRUGES, Belgium

In the Cornet d'Or Hotel, the two Anson crews — Flight Lieutenants Bob Fowler and Bruce White and Flying Officers Russ Hunter and Norm Powell — were still sound asleep after their night on the town.

ST DENIS-WESTRAM AIRFIELD, Belgium

All three squadrons of Group Captain Alexander Gabszewicz's 131 Polish Spitfire Wing were in the air flying Mark IXs. First off the ground at 0815 hours was 308 Squadron led by Flight Lieutenant Ignacy Olszewski, its targets, a ferry and enemy installations near Wounstreecht. At 0835 Squadron Leader Marian Chelmecki's 317 took to the air. Its objectives: German military targets at Werkindan on the Wahl River. Finally, 302 Squadron, commanded by Squadron Leader Maria Duryusz, took off at 0840 on an armed reconnaissance in the Lyons-Amersfoort-Zwell-Appledoorn region.

There were still at least 30 Spitfires left on the ground. One of the most tempting targets was an American Flying Fortress that had been forced to land on the field two days earlier after being badly shot up. A maintenance crew had been flown in to repair it. It was in such sorry shape that they did not envy the chore.

Back at St Denis-Westram, the church was crowded with those attending New Year's Mass. It was a cause for celebration — the first free New Year in the last four years. That service was about to be rudely interrupted.

DORTMUND, BONNINGHARDT and DUSSELDORF-LOHAUSEN AIRFIELDS, Germany

Gruppe II of Jagdgeschwader 77, the Herzas, (Red Hearts) JG was a storied outfit. It had participated in nearly every major operation since the occupation of Denmark and Norway in 1940, including the abortive Allied airborne Arnhem assault, in which the unit had been crippled badly, losing some 19 pilots. Like all home defence Jagdgeschwadern, JG 77 suffered from the malaise of heavy losses, and by inexperienced, untrained replacements.

On December 29, after JG 77's Kommodore, Major Johannes Wiese, was shot down and wounded, Major Erich Leie, with over 100 kills to his credit, took over command — just in time for Bodenplatte. His Jagdgeschwader's target was the Belgian airfield of Antwerp-Deurne.

The direct route was 100 miles, but to ensure surprise, the prescribed course marked on the pilots' maps called for the Jagdgeschwader to fly north, then sweep around Rotterdam and head south, which doubled the distance. Conditions were ideal as the 100 Messerschmidt 109 fighters took off from the three airfields shortly after 0800 hours and climbed to 150 feet. They headed north across the Lippe River and, 15 minutes later, were over Borken where they turned south toward Rotterdam. There, infuriatingly, near the front lines, the German naval ack-ack guns let fly at them. Leutnant Heinz Abendroth was the first to take a hit but managed to bail out, only to be taken prisoner. Unteroffizier Johann Twietmeyer suffered a similar fate when he parachuted to earth near Rosendaal. Over Antwerp, running into flak again, this time from the enemy, Leutnant Heinrich Hackler, commander of Gruppe II and a veteran with 56 victories to his credit, became entangled in balloon cables protecting the Belgian port. One of them tore off the port wing and his Messerschmidt plunged into the ground, killing him.

A mile or two east of the bank of the Scheldt River, Woensdrecht Airfield (B-79) came into view. Mistaking it for the target, Vic formations of three Me 109s from Gruppe I swooped down to rake it with fire. But as far as they could see, there was nobody home. In the process, the Gruppe got separated from the rest of the formation which pressed on. Ahead, the other Gruppen could see the docks and cathedrals of Antwerp. Directly in front of them was Antwerp-Duerne Airfield, yet, incredibly, they didn't even see it. They began circling about in search of the target.

WOENSDRECHT AIRFIELD, Holland

Only two of the five Spitfire squadrons were on the field. The two RAF squadrons, 66 and 127, were in the air escorting Mitchell medium-bombers to Dasburg. There were neither aircraft nor pilots from the Dutch squadron, 322; only the ground crew had arrived from England. On their approach, Gruppe I failed to see the aircraft of the other two squadrons, 331 and 332 Norwegian, because of a slight haze at ground level that sharply reduced visibility, as well as the Germans' inexperience with low-level strafing.

ANTWERP-DEURNE AIRFIELD, Belgium

There were two wings at B-70 — 145 composed of four Spitfire squadrons, and 149 comprising five Typhoon squadrons. As well, there was a Dakota unit from Transport Command stationed there. It had snowed overnight and ice covered the runway preventing those units assigned to various missions from taking off. All personnel were relegated to digging snow and clearing the ice.

RHINE, HESEPE, ACHMER and VORDEN AIRFIELDS, Germany

The plum target of Brussels-Melsbroek was the field picked for Major Ludwig Franzisket's Jagdgeschwader 27, and it was in good shape to tackle it. Its four Gruppen of Me 109s had been replaced by FW 190s of Gruppe IV from JG 54 at Vorden. Taking off from all four airfields, shortly after 0800 hours were Gruppe I, led by Hauptmann Eberhard Schade; Gruppe II, commanded by Hauptmann Gerhard Hoyer; Gruppe III, under Hauptmann Emile Clade; and Gruppe IV, led by Hauptmann Hans-Heinz Dudeck. A total of 70 FW 190s and Me 109s formed up over Spakenburg to begin the 200-mile flight to the target led by two Ju 88 trailblazers. They also suffered the dangerous indignity of being fired upon by their own ack-ack batteries. Just before they reached Utrecht German flak shot down two of their own aircraft and another was lost the same way as they flew over the front lines.

As they neared the target, part of Emile Clade's Gruppe III decided to attack Gilze-Reijen field outside of Bruges, while the rest of the formation proceeded on to the primary target of Melsbroek.

BRUSSELS-MELSBROEK AIRFIELD, Belgium

All three squadrons of 139 Bomber Wing were in the air. The 35 medium-bomber Mitchells of 98, 180 and 320 Squadrons, escorted by Spitfires from Woensdrecht, were on their way to bomb the road centre at Dasburg, leaving only a few of the spares behind.

Flight Lieutenant Edward Dutt and the pilots of 16 Photographic Reconnaissance Unit (PRU) had been briefed for a flight around the Ruhr to reconnoitre the German airfields in the area. They were due off at dawn but after inspecting the taxiway and runways, the airfield staff ruled them temporarily unfit due to icing. So the pilots waited in the Operations Room for further instructions.

After breakfast, Flight Lieutenant Hugh Tudor and Flying Officer Ian Ewing of 140 Squadron were just getting into a jeep to drive over to the field which was across the road from the officers' mess. They were ready to fly a Mosquito back to England to pick up Tudor's father. Ewing suddenly remembered he'd forgotten his pipe and went back to the billets to get it while Tudor waited in the vehicle enjoying the early sunshine. "It was a lovely clear morning," he recalled.[9] Their CO, Squadron Leader Richard Walton, who had been flying the night before, was still in bed, fast asleep.

Squadron Leader Mike Shaw had one hell of a hangover, after celebrating the New Year and his DSO the night before. Now the commander of 69 Squadron was reminded by his carousing companions of the night before that he had agreed to test fly the repaired four-engine Sterling bomber. It was a maiden trip in the type for him, and bleary-eyed though he was, he was reasonably confident he could handle it without too much trouble.

By 0920, the PRU Spitfires of 16 Squadron were still on the ground, alongside Mosquitoes from 140 Squadron, low-level night reconnaissance twin-engine Wellingtons ("Wimpies") from 69 Squadron, a covey of lumbering Handley-Page Harrows from 217 Transport Squadron, several P-47 Thunderbolts, the Flying Fortress that had landed with its hydraulics all shot-up the day before, and, of course, the repaired Short Stirling bomber waiting to be air tested.

MALMSHEIM, KIRRLACH, and ST ECHTERDINGEN AIRFIELDS, Germany

Metz-Frescaty was the only airfield targeted for Operation Bodenplatte in all of France. Jagdgeschwader 53, commanded by Oberstleutnant Helmut Bennemann, a veteran ace with over 100 victories under his belt, had been selected to lead the attack. Thanks to excellent photographic reconnaissance of Y-34, intelligence was able to accurately pinpoint actual targets on the field.

Hauptmann Karl Luckenbach's Gruppe III had been assigned to take out the anti-aircraft defenses in and around the field, while the other two Gruppen, II and IV, led by Hauptmannen Julius Meimberg and Heinz Muer, were to hit the parked P-47 Thunderbolts of the three squadrons of the American 386th Fighter Group, in a series of at least three low-level passes. The planes were to come in on the deck, strafe the field, then, pulling up in stall turns, whip around and come back again from the opposite direction in a very professional, perfectly coordinated attack. Even the unbloodied novices were gung-ho.

All three Gruppen of some 70 Me 109s took off at dawn, formed up at 150 feet, and headed due east across the Franco-German border. However, through no fault of their own, Gruppe III never made the rendezvous. They were bounced by a patrol of American P-47 "Thunderbuggies," and two German pilots were wounded. Forced to jettison their tanks when the mélée began, low on fuel, the Gruppe had to return to Kirrlach as soon as it ended. That left JG 53 short-handed by 20 planes. Bennemann decided to continue on anyway, and by 0930 hours Metz-Frescaty Airfield was in sight.

METZ-FRESCATY AIRFIELD, France

At 0828 hours, 11 Thunderbolts of the 387th Fighter Squadron, led by Major Arlo Henry Jr., left the ground for an armed reconnaissance in the St Ingbert-Neunkirchen-Nohfelden-Dilberg area. Carrying 500-pound bombs under each wing, they reached St Ingbert 22 minutes later where they attacked a rolling train, destroying five freight cars and severing the rail line. By 0913 the P-47s began landing back at Y-34.

Once they were safely down, the 388th Fighter Squadron, led by Captain Jerry Mast, took off for Homberg. Because no one in the formation had dropped out, the spare, First Lieutenant Lavern Alcorn, headed back to Metz-Frescaty. By 0930, the third fighter squadron in the Group, the 386th, prepared to get airborne. The 12 Thunderbolts assembled at the southwest corner of the field.

Normally there were two "alert" Thunderbolts positioned at the end of the runway, just in case. But this morning, of all mornings, only one pilot stood guard, Captain Tom Stanton from the 386th Fighter Squadron. His wingman, Flight Lieutenant Samuel Lutz had yet to join him. That was not really out of the ordinary. The "alert" precaution was never taken very seriously, since nobody really expected anything to happen. Lutz was still warming himself over a gasoline fire before climbing into his P-47 and joining his section leader on readiness.

GILZE-REIJEN, Holland

At 0829 hours Flight Lieutenant Jim Young of 2 Squadron took off with his wingman, Fllight Lieutenant Ed Packwood, on a tactical reconnaissance mission in the Leewen-Hilversum-Arnhem area. Three minutes later Flight Lieutenants Dave Mercer and John Lyke from 268 Squadron were airborne on a similar sortie in the direction of Utrecht.

After breakfast at 0850, Flight Lieutenant Bill Baggs who was still in his uniform — he hadn't bothered to change into battle dress — and the other members of 164 Squadron were being transported from the mess to the airfield.

Fifteen minutes later, at 5,000 feet over Amersfoort, Ed Packwood spotted two twin-engine Ju 88s with what he took to be their escort, more than 30 Me 109s and FW 190s headed west on the deck. He and Jim Young pulled up into the sun, then wheeled around and dived down onto the rear of the German formation.

From 150 yards astern, Packwood let go a five-second volley of machine-gun bullets and cannon shells at an Me 109, striking the cockpit and fuselage, and pulverising the machine. The port wing broke off and the aircraft flicked over onto its back and hit the ground aflame. Jim Young, his leader, meanwhile had radioed base to expect an attack at any moment. His timing was right on.

BOORTMEERBEEK, Belgium

At 0815 hours, radar operator Leading Aircraftsman Ron Staughton had been on tube duty for over two hours when he picked up an echo on his screen indicating five plus aircraft within the radar's maximum range of 160 miles. From the goniometer direction finder, it appeared they were coming from the vicinity of Stuttgart. Five plus turned rapidly to ten plus, then 20 plus, then 40 plus. Staughton called into the headset directly linked to the plotting room at 83 Group headquarters at Eindhoven. "There are 150 plus bogies headed south west," he reported. "Correct that to 250 plus — range 80 miles," he amended quickly. "Nonsense," the controller replied. "You've probably got a spurious echo" (malfunction or, by today's standards, a computer glitch). "Anyway the Huns haven't got that many aircraft." (Shades of Pearl Harbor when the United States Army Information Center duty officer at Fort Shafter dismissed radar operator Private George Elliot's report from Kahuku Point that a large formation of 140 planes was approaching the island.)

"I've been at this job for a long time," he retorted angrily to the controller and sent for his commanding officer, Flight Lieutenant Owen Halfhid to confirm his sighting and speak to the disbelieving individual. Halfhid grabbed the headset and shouted to him, "Look, there's over 1,000 aircraft headed our way." Again the controller argued that it was probably nothing more than a "spurious echo." By this time Halfhid could hear the aircraft overhead. "If you don't believe me, you stupid prick, go outside and see for yourself!" he yelled.

Though a complaint from Halfhid was filed for attention at the highest level — Air Vice-Marshal Broadhurst, the Air Officer commanding 83 Group — no inquiry resulted. The only report was an innocuous statement issued from Supreme Headquarters Allied Expeditionary Force (SHAEF) that: "All formations approached low enough to avoid radar detection." Clearly a white-wash.

Had Staughton's warning been heeded, there would have been time to put some Allied patrols in the air to meet the German invaders head-on, since there were planes standing on readiness or getting ready to take off on most of the fields. As Staughton summed up the affair: "Someone should have been strung up by the balls."

Endnotes

1 Werner Gerbig, *Six Months to Oblivion,* p. 97.

2 Norman Franks, *The Battle of the Airfields,* p. 40.

3 Gordon Hill, correspondence, July 20, 1996.

4 Jim Prendergast, interviews and correspondence, May 1996 to September 1997.

5 Danny S. Parker, *To Win the Winter Sky,* p. 24.

6 Ken Langmuir and Eric Downer, interviews, June 15 and August 22, 1997.

7 Gerbig, p. 86.

8 Parker, p. 416.

9 Franks, p. 116.

Leading Aircraftsman Ron Staughton
whose radar warning of approaching
German planes was ignored.
(Ron Staughton)

CHAPTER 5

STRIKE

Poised to pounce on their unsuspecting victims, Generalmajor Dietrich Peltz's Jagdgerschwaden had at least achieved one of their aims — that of complete surprise. But as the Prussian military strategist, Karl von Clausewitz, once said, "war is full of surprises." And what happened during the next 40 minutes certainly proved that and then some!

MOMENT OF IMPACT

Between 0900 and 0940 hours
HEESCH AIRFIELD, Holland

The Ju 88 trailblazer that led the three Gruppen of Johann Kogler's Jagdgeschwader 6 got lost and led them away from their intended target, Volkel. They ended up heading towards Heesch, ten miles away instead, and the Canadians on the field and the Germans in the air were both caught by surprise.

In the control tower, mistaking Gruppe's III Messerschmidts for American Mustang P-51s, Flight Lieutenant John Edison thought, "Shit, the Yanks are off course!"[1] The sight of flak bursts fired by the RAF Regiment guarding the field soon clued him in. They weren't allies! In the living billets, the sound of the 44-mm cannons going off startled Flying Officer Al Bathurst out of his slumber. He jumped out of bed and promptly slipped in the vomit the pilot in the next bed had deposited before passing out the night before. He then dashed outside and slipped on the snow. It just wasn't his morning. He should have stayed in bed.

When the Germans appeared over the field heading due south, Flying Officer Doug Cameron of 401 Squadron, still pissed off at Flight Lieutenant Johnny MacKay because he hadn't got his Red Section off the ground, and as a result was left waiting to take his Yellow Section off, pondered: "Am I better to duck behind my bullet-proof windshield or to try and swing the aircraft around and duck behind the bullet-proof shield behind the pilot's seat?"[2] He did neither. Instead, he called on the blower to tell MacKay (the acting CO) to get the hell off the deck — now! Both sections took off pronto. Airborne, Cameron, a real pro, automatically adjusted his rudder control so that his Spitfire was skidding left and right somewhat, enough to upset the line of fire of any aircraft trying to shoot at him. In no time at all he had climbed to 1,000 feet over the field. Looking down, he saw two Me 109s flying in echelon between 100 and 200 yards behind the main group, which by this time had crossed over the field. They had peppered it without result because they had been so startled at finding themselves over it, they could not line up their sights well enough to take proper aim. By then practically all the Spitfires at Heesch were in the air.

EINDHOVEN AIRFIELD, Holland

Wing Commander Kit North-Lewis of 124 Typhoon Wing happened to be looking out the window of his headquarters when, suddenly he saw a string of aircraft in line astern which he immediately recognized as Me 109s. There were at least a dozen of them. He wondered "what the hell they were doing in Eindoven."[3]

It came as a distinct surprise because not since the days in Normandy during June, July and August had enemy aircraft ventured over allied fighter fields — and then only singly or in pairs. When he rushed outside he was even more astounded at the sight of a flock of FW 190s as well — that made 25 enemy fighters in all circling the field at low level. They immediately began straffing runs on the parked aircraft on the field.

Leading Aircraftsman Desmond Shepherd, an armourer with 137 Squadron, had just finished breakfast and was sauntering across the runway. But he also kept a sharp eye out for aircraft taking off and landing. He knew that several patrols had been scheduled for the morning, some of which were already in the air. Then suddenly he was startled by the sound of gunfire and an Me 262 twin-engine jet roared right over his head, followed by several FW 190s. Then, coming from the opposite direction, he saw some Me 109s.

As the enemy fighters opened fire from both ends of the field, in desperation Shepherd threw himself on the grass. As he watched the scenario unfold, two of the leading planes of each group collided with each other head-on, falling to the ground in flames not far from where he lay. The pilot of one of them struggled to try and get out but the 190 exploded, spewing pieces of burning debris in all directions.[4]

Flight Lieutenant Ed MacKay and the other pilots of 438 Squadron, who had the morning off, were still in their pyjamas asleep in the convent where they were billeted in town, when the noise of flak guns, cannon fire and aircraft engines jolted them awake. They rushed to the windows to see Messerschmidt 109s and Focke Wulf 190s whizzing over the rooftops. They dressed hurriedly and dashed outside to commandeer one of the ever-ready transports standing by to take them to the air-field. As they scrambled into the trucks they shouted to the Dutch sentries posted at the gates to fire at the enemy planes. Then they had to order a ceasefire when the gunners started shooting at a pilot in his parachute.

Flying Officer Pat Pattinson of 182 Squadron, who had been on readiness since first light, was waiting impatiently to be relieved so that he could go and get some breakfast when, as he later recalled, "all hell broke loose."[5] Gunfire seemed to erupt from everywhere and aircraft seemed to be diving from all directions. The squadron's wooden dispersal hut escaped unscathed, however, because it was hidden between the marquee and the woods behind it.

Flight Lieutenant "Gibby" Gibbons of 168 Squadron was lifting his Typhoon off the runway when the FW 190s and Me 109s from the Udet Jagdgeschwader (JG 3) began their attack. When he saw one of the grey-green 190s — flown by Feldwebel Gerhard Leipholz — closing in behind him, Gibbons had just enough flying speed to be able to whip around in a steep turn that put him on his assailant's tail. He managed to shoot him down, but another 190 riddled his Typhoon with its fire. Gibbons was dead by the time his aircraft skidded onto the field on its belly.

BRUSSELS-EVERE AIRFIELD, Belgium

Flying Officer Ken Langmuir of 421 Squadron, who was playing catch and just "shooting the shit"[6] outside dispersal, looked up to see what he judged to be a disorganised group of American Mustangs flying over the field. It was not an unusual sight, not worth a second thought. The occupants of the Belgian airfield had grown quite accustomed to such things. In this case, however, the "disorganised Mustangs" were, in fact, a group of long-nose Focke Wulf 190D-8s and Messerschmidt 109s from JG 26's Gruppen II and III, led by Major Anton Hackl. (Hauptmann Walter "Count" Kruprinski had been forced to cop out after the engine of his 109 was hit by flak.) Suddenly machine-gun, cannon fire and bomb bursts erupted all round. Langmuir ran inside the dispersal and dived under a table. "For all the good it would do, but I was frightened out of my flying boots — I'd never been bombed before." As one missile after another exploded, he could hear the crash of broken glass. "It sounded like the whole world was blowing up out there." He wasn't far wrong.

Of the four Spitfires from 416 Squadron turning off the taxi strip to take off, only the leader and commander of the flight, Flight Lieutenant Dave Harling, made it into the air. Hackl's 109s targetted the Spitfires on the runway and taxi strip as well as those lined up at the edge of the field, while another bunch concentrated on taking out the anti-aircraft guns. One of the first Spitfires to be hit was that of Harling's Number Two, Warrant Officer Lou Jean. He quickly jumped out of his aircraft, as did Len Commerford directly behind him. Commerford forgot to unplug his radio cord before jumping down off the wing which jolted him momentarily until he yanked it loose and completed his leap. Both pilots took cover behind some metal drums. Jean complained of a pain in the leg. He had taken a splinter of shrapnel from a cannon shell, but that was the least of his worries. Right now, the premium was on staying put. The fourth member of the flight, Flying Officer Eric Downer, also abandoned his aircraft and dived into a ditch between two hangars from where he claimed he, "had the best seat in the house."[7]

In addition to Hackl himself, Unteroffizier Lutz-Wilhelm Burkhardt, Oberleutnant Adolf Glunz and Leutnant Siegfried Sy were responsible for this carnage.

BRUSSELS-GRIMBERGEN AIRFIELD, Belgium

Group Captain Alexander Gabszewicz and his adjutant casually drove over from their billet to the officers' mess for breakfast and took their sweet time about it. There was no point in rushing; Gabszewicz' 131 Polish Spitfire Wing — 302, 308 and 317 Squadrons — wouldn't be moving in from St Denis-Westram until well after lunch. While quaffing their morning coffee, they heard aircraft approaching, assuming them to be one of the early patrols from nearby Evere Airfield. But, glancing up they saw the long snouts of the FW 190 Doras from Gruppe I, of JG 26. It was led by Major Karl Borris, after the Geschwader Kommodore Pips Priller had left the scene in downright disgust. Gabszewicz's adjutant immediately identified them. "They're bloody Focke Wulfs," he shouted and pulled the vehicle to a halt so that they could bail out and take cover in the nearest ditch.[8]

The six planes on the field, four Flying Fortresses, one of which was being serviced by the ground crew, a Mustang and a twin-engine Mosquito, were quickly destroyed by the attackers from JG 26 and JG 54. Having run out of aircraft targets, according to Unteroffizier Hans Kukla, they made "three attacks on the hangars, without great effect." But Gabszewicz quickly marshalled the ground troops on the field, and their small-arms fire joined with the ack-gunners from the RAF Regiment in the defense of the base.

A cheer went up as a 190, piloted by Feldwebel Gunther Egli from the 54th Geschwader, crashed on its belly right in the middle of the field after being hit by the gunners. Egli was taken prisoner. On his second strafing pass, Freiheurer Hans-Joachim Werner's Focke Wulf (Gruppe I, JG 26) took several hits and he was forced to bail out over the field. But the gunners could not take credit for the demise of a third victim, Leutnant Theo Nibel, from JG 54, even though that was decidedly more credible than the Belgian farmer who claimed he'd shot him down with a blast from his shotgun. In fact, Nibel's FW 190 D hit a partridge head on, knocking a hole in his radiator. Though he immediately lost all power in his engine, he was, nevertheless, able to make a perfectly normal wheels-down landing on a RAF airstrip at Wemmel. In captivity, Nibel described it:[9]

> I had the mission of silencing the flak at Grimbergen. We flew a total of three attacks on the flak, which returned fire strongly. When I pulled up after the third attack, my engine quit. I suspected flak had hit the engine. I had reached an altitude of 100 metres and had to decide quickly between a parachute jump and a crash landing. I lost height quickly, and

> was forced to make a belly landing. I found a freshly turned
> field beside a farmhouse and made a perfect landing.

The raid on the worthless, non-operational (so designated at
this stage by a white cross displayed on the field) station had
cost the marauders dearly. Twelve of the JG 26s Gruppe I never
made it back to Furstenau, and those who did manage to get
home were badly shot up. For Gruppe III JG 54 it was an abat-
toir. Of the 17 FW 190s that took off that morning only seven
returned.

ASCH AIRFIELD, Belgium

The first to spot the attackers from Oberstleutnant Gunther
Specht's Jagdgeschwader 11 were the flak gunners protecting
the airfield. As the 352 US Fighter Squadron leader, J.C.
Meyer, lifted off the runway in his Mustang, "Petie II," he saw
ack-ack bursts at the far end of the field. He immediately called
up the control tower on the radio transmitter but nothing was
showing on their screens. Almost simultaneously, however,
the Thunderbolts from the 390th Fighter Squadron, led by
Captain Lowell B. Smith, which were orbiting the field in
preparation for an offensive patrol, spotted German fighters
diving on Ophoven Airfield to the north, the home of 41, 130,
350 and 610 Spitfire Squadrons. Then, Smith reported 50-plus
FW 190s and Me 109s approaching Asch on the deck from the
north-east.

Meyer had no sooner got airborne when to the "astonishment and disbelief" of the squadron's ground support officer,
Major Dick DeBruin, "I saw an enemy fighter plane 'on the
deck' flying directly across the path of J.C's take-off ... [It] was
a German FW 190."[10] But Meyer's Mustang was not Gefreite
Gerhardt Bohm's target. The JG 11 Staffel 9 pilot had his

sights on one of five C-47 Dakota transports parked on the north-west side of the field. But then he was in Meyer's sights. J.C pressed the firing button on his control column to let off a quick burst of fire. As usual his aim was dead on. The FW 190 crashed beside one of the transports, exploding on impact. That was number 23 for J.C. Meyer — his very first on a take-off. His combat report detailed that victory:[11]

> Immediately upon getting my wheels up, I spotted 15-plus 190s headed towards the field from the east. I attacked one getting a two-second burst at 300 yards, 30 degree deflection, getting good hits on the fuselage and wing roots. The E/A (enemy aircraft) half-rolled, crashing into the ground.

ST TROND-BRUSTEM AIRFIELD, Belgium

As the badly depleted ranks of the FW 190s and Me 109s pilots of the famed Richthofen Jagdgeschwader 2, led by Oberstleutnant Kurt Buhlingen, came in low over the perimeter of another of the three American bases in Belgium, to attack the Thunderbolts of the 48th and 404th Fighter Groups, the anti-aircraft gunners let fly with everything they had.

The 48th Fighter Group diarist described the action:

> An unfamiliar drone of engines was heard — the first was immediately recognised as an Me 109. The plane was accompanied by five more of Goering's Groundhogs and they were busily preparing to clobber St Trond-Brustem Airfield. Upon the alarm that enemy planes were attacking the field, offices and boudoirs were evacuated for more substantial dugouts .... By this time the Mes had made their pass and were preparing to take another one from the opposite direction. For a while

they were all over hell and gone and half of Belgium. They strafed the runways, they strafed the planes, they strafed everything that got in front of them. Later a pilot who was captured said that all he did was press the trigger every time the field swung in front of him. The ack-ack boys on the field made a good showing for themselves .... Damage to our aircraft [however] was negligible in spite of the amount of Nazi ammunition expended. We had two of our planes slightly damaged. Most of these were back in flying condition within the next few days.

Having been alerted by other planes already in the air, the ack-ack batteries were ready and waiting. In the first few minutes — and that was about as long as the raid lasted — ten planes were shot down. Both Unteroffizieren Adolf Redlich and Helmet Bollwerk spun into the ground and were killed. Leutnant Werner Edelhoff was luckier: he was able to take to his parachute. As he floated down to earth, half the pilots from the 493rd Squadron rushed out onto the open field to form a welcoming committee. By the time Edelhoff hit the ground he faced at least nine carbines and machine-guns. When interrogated he remarked bitterly, "This is just as the Führer said it would be, Germany yesterday, Belgium today and the United States tomorrow."

The part played by the Gruppe II FW 190s from JG 4, led by Major Max Schroder, which had stumbled into the mêlée by accident, mistaking the field for their own appointed target of Le Culot, was minimal. They lost one plane to ground fire. When Gefreite Walter Wagner calmly lowered his flaps and wheels, the ack-ack gunners held their fire, allowing him to land his slightly damaged machine right in the middle of the airstrip. The Americans were overjoyed at having in their possession an FW 190A-8 almost intact.

WOENSDRECHT AIRFIELD, Holland

At 200 feet off the ground, the Messerschmidts of Gruppe I of the Jagdgeschwader 77 zoomed in across the field they had mistaken for Antwerp-Duerne, their intended target. It didn't make a whole lot of difference. The mist obscured the aircraft on the field, so that they never even got a chance to fire off a shot.

ANTWERP-DEURNE AIRFIELD, Belgium

Approximately 12 Me 109s from Gruppe III of the 77 Geschwader began the attack on B-70 sweeping in over the field at heights of between 150 and 200 feet from across the Scheldt River embankment to be met by fire from the airfield ground defences. That was the only resistance they encountered thanks to the snow and ice covering the runway, which kept all aircraft on B-70 grounded. But the assailants caused little damage.

On this clear, slightly hazy morning, Flight Lieutenant Stan Eaton and his fellow pilots with 257 Typhoon Squadron watched the giant fleet of German fighters crossing the airfield from the embankment side. They appeared to be in complete disarray, flying like a great gaggle from heights varying from 150 to 300 feet. There was some firing at a few of the attackers but the combination of the embankment and the disorder of the attackers saved the Typhoon wing from large-scale destruction.[12]

In fact the attack was amateurish, sloppy and totally uncoordinated. Flight Lieutenant Ronnie Sheward of 263 Squadron was flabbergasted. "Weave, you stupid bastards!" he shouted at the enemy. Later he noted, "They strafed a few aircraft but put up a very poor show." The 193 Squadron diary stated, "they stooged around like a Sunday picnic," while the 329 Free

French Squadron reported, "the Me's seemed to be playing possum with the gunners." Denys Gillam, commander of 146 Wing, was the most scathing of all when he said, "on the whole the enemy put on a very poor show. If any of my boys put on a show like that I'd tear them off a strip."[13]

This performance by the Red Hearts was particularly frustrating for the pilots at Deurne who were stuck on the ground; the 109 pilots' poor flying would have made them such sitting ducks from the air. But Gillam's men could only, in his own words, "sit on the deck and swear at the ack-ack gunners."[14] They may have underrated their effectiveness, however, because by expending 1,270 rounds of ammunition they had some success. Of the 30 Messerschmidts out of the 100 from JG 77 that actually did manage to find the field, six pilots were killed, four taken prisoner and another ten aircraft went missing. Damage to the aircraft at Deurne was slight. A Dakota transport, a B-17 Flying Fortress bomber and one Typhoon were hit and destroyed and ten others suffered some damage.

MALDEGEM AIRFIELD, Belgium

It was almost too good to be true. The 17 Spitfires at the RAF maintenance depot waiting to be put into operational service were all neatly lined up in a row, presenting a perfect target for the Messerschmidts of Gruppe III and Focke Wulf 190s from Gruppe I of Oberstleutnant Herbert Ihlefeld's Jagdgeschwader 1. When they moved out several days earlier, 135 Wing had taken their airfield defences, and all that stood in the raiders' way were a pair of stationary 20-mm cannon, two Vickers machine-guns, a few rifles and some handguns. It was no wonder that in a few minutes, 11 of the Spitfires were set on fire and two others were damaged.

URSEL AIRFIELD, Belgium

The aircraft noise that Leading Aircraftsman Edward Green with the 424 RAF Rearming and Refuelling Unit had taken to be a squadron of Spitfires arriving from Manston on the British east coast, actually came from three Focke Wolf 190s of Oberleutnant Hans-Gottfried Meinhof's depleted Staffel of Gruppe I (JG 1). In the control tower, the corporal in charge of the fire truck parked outside and asked Sergeant Peter Crowest for permission to use his Sten gun. Crowest barked, "Stay under cover you stupid bastard!"[15] The only defense against the attacking planes came from an RAF sergeant armourer who rushed out of his store hut, got down in a ditch and opened up with a machine-gun, following the bullets with curses.

With no Spitfires to shoot at, the German pilots took aim at the two damaged aircraft under repair. With a loud explosion the Mosquito near the control tower exploded in flames. Had Edward Green not stopped to check on the truck behind him, he and his repair crew, on their way to the Mosquito, would have been right in the line of fire.

Immediately after the Mosquito exploded in fire, the American B-17 Flying Fortress under repair also erupted in flames. Then the oil drums adjacent to it took direct hits and exploded in flames. Suddenly people were scurrying about in all directions, taking cover in nearby ditches as the FW 190s straffed the field from one end to the other, firing at will. Green later recalled that with the sun glinting on the enemy aircraft, it was as if they were on a weekend trip "with not a care in the world."[16]

The Flying Fortress was a total write-off. But The American repair crew were far from unhappy over its demise — weeks of frustrating, unrewarding work had at last come to an end.

In addition to the Mosquitos and the B-17, two Lancaster bombers, also under repair, were blown up.

THE CORNET D'OR HOTEL, BRUGES, Belgium

Flight Lieutenant Bob Fowler and his companions were awakened with a start by the sounds of gunfire as the Germans made their runs directly over the Cornet d'Or Hotel. They pulled on their uniforms and dashed outside where a crowd had gathered at the hotel entrance. One plane flew so low Fowler thought it "was going to take the roof off." What was happening still hadn't quite sunk in. But when one aircraft swept over the top of the hotel, made a couple of rolls, then dived to the right, Flying Officer Norm Powell turned to Fowler and said, "That damned thing had crosses on it!" [17]

Fowler later stated:

> It was a standard short-nosed Focke Wulf 190 and was the best close-up view of a German fighter flown by a German pilot that I had ever been treated to in my whole war. The paint was a bit dingy, but there was such a lot of detail I wished I could have had a better look at it. I didn't have to wait long. We moved out into the street to have a better view of the sky, and in the next few minutes we had more 190s and 109s to look at than we had ever seen before, and not very far away to the east they seemed to have plenty to shoot at.

It was clear to everyone that this was certainly no air show or even a drill. This was an air raid in progress. It did not go unnoticed either that the Messerschmidts and Focke Wulfs were diving in the direction of Maldegem where Powell and his friends had parked their Ansons for repairs. Without further ado, they commandeered the handiest military vehicle to take them to the airfield.

ST DENIS-WESTRAM AIRFIELD, Belgium

A cacophony of machine-gun, cannon fire and exploding bombs suddenly drowned out the organ music and choral singing in the church in celebration of mass. Everyone in the congregation rushed outside to see what was happening. Planes seemed to be everywhere diving and twisting and firing at everything in sight. Ugly pillars of smoke were rising in the direction of Ghent. The congregation ran inside to take refuge and prayed as they had never prayed before.

With their tanks nearly dry, the Spitfires of Squadron Leader Maria Duryusz's 302 Squadron, which had successfully attacked targets near Wounstreech, began landing at the very moment the FW 190s from Hauptmann Herman Staiger's Gruppe II of JG 1 swept in on the field from the south-west. One Spitfire was hit by friendly flak and nine others parked on the ground were destroyed or damaged by the attackers. Miraculously the others got down safely, despite the interference, without being hit. Flight Lieutenant Walclaw Chojnacki of 308 Squadron was also in the circuit. He had a hung-up bomb and after unsuccessfully trying to jettison it, was ordered to return to base. This was an unusual instruction since standard procedure under such circumstances was to bail out for fear that the bomb might detonate on landing. Nevertheless, Chojnacki arrived over the field just as Gruppe II began its first run. He had just lowered his wheels when three FW 190s appeared before him. Chojnacki immediately retracted his undercarriage, focused on the rear plane, pressed the gun button and, from 800 yards, blew its tail off. The German plane cut through a tree, bounced off the roof of a building and smashed into a parked Flying Fortress. But, just then, three other 190s dived down on Chojnacki's Spitfire, opening fire and sending it plunging into the ground where it exploded, killing him.

VOLKEL AIRFIELD, Holland

Despite the JG 6 snafu with casualties and faulty navigation, B-80 did not entirely escape notice from the Luftwaffe. After much scouting around, nine FW 190s and Me 109s, and a lone Me 262 jet did manage to find the target. But their attack was hardly worthy of a medal. They made a few hasty, half-hearted passes but with zero results except to scare the shit out of Pilot Officers Bob Adcock and Bill Bailey who, strapped into their Tempests, had the disconcerting experience of seeing bullets striking the ground all around them, though luckily missing their aircraft.

Pilot Officer Ron Pottinger, the 3 Squadron spare pilot, who hadn't been needed, had climbed out of his Tempest by this time and was chatting with the ground crew when the Germans opened fire. Everyone ran for cover. Pottinger dashed for his tent, pulled out a rifle and, in frustration, began firing at the marauders, not sure he was accomplishing anything but it felt better than doing nothing.

BRUSSELS-MELSBROEK AIRFIELD, Belgium

After retrieving his pipe from his room, Flying Officer Ian Ewing, along with Flight Lieutenant Hugh Tudor of 140 Squadron, was leaving the officers' mess for the second time that morning to take their Mosquito to England to pick up Ewing's father. Outside the billets a small crowd had gathered. Watching a trio of fighters swooping at low level across the airfield, someone shouted, "Christ! Look at those three Hurricanes." Having spotted the black crosses on the wings, "Hurricanes be buggered," someone else yelled, "They're 109s!"[18]

Seconds later the sound of cannon fire sent everyone scurrying for cover. Tudor and Ewing rushed inside to waken their CO Richard Walton and his navigator Flying Officer Bill Harper and tell them about the attack. At first they didn't believe it, but the sound of gunfire and the sight of the tail wheel of an aircraft right outside the window soon convinced them. All four put on tin helmets and went outside where, from the playing field next to the billets, they took pot-shots at the intruders with their Smith and Wesson .38 revolvers.

Coming in from the west from JG 27's point of view, the raid was a model of precision and efficiency. The only resistance was from ground fire and ack-ack guns, but it was heavy. Gruppen I and II attacked in straight runs along Melsbroek's north-south runway, while Hauptmann Hans-Heinz Dudeck's Gruppe IV came in from the south-east with the sun at their backs while Gruppe IV, JG 54 joined in the attack. On their first pass, Dudeck's pilots destroyed the Stirling four-engine bomber that Wing Commander Mike Shaw was going to flight test as well as a twin-engine 140 Squadron Mosquito and the private plane of the AOC of 2nd TAF, Air Marshal Sir Arthur Coningham. "In retrospect," Shaw said later, "I breathed a sigh of relief — I didn't have to fly the goddam thing."

GILZE-REIJEN AIRFIELD, Holland

Hauptmann Emile Clade's Gruppe III from JG 27, meanwhile, had zeroed in on the Typhoons packed into Gilze-Reijen Airfield. The truck carrying 164 Squadron's pilots had just arrived on the airfield when bullets and cannon shells started flying in all directions. Flight Lieutenant Bill Baggs, the Canadian member of the unit, leapt from the vehicle onto the muddy field with his companions. Baggs went splat into a puddle in his nice clean uniform. That riled him even more than the danger of being strafed or bombed. "Out there in the open field, hugging the ground, I felt naked and dirty," he said.[19]

HEESCH AIRFIELD, Holland

Flying Officer Doug Cameron of 401 Squadron, who had spotted two of Major Helmut Kuhle's Gruppe III Me 109s (JG 6) flying in echelon behind the main group, dived down, took aim at the Messerschmidt on the right. His cannon and machine-gun fire ripped into the 109 just behind the cockpit. A quick flash of flame told him he had burst open the oxygen tank. The aircraft nosed over, crashed into the field and exploded. Next, Cameron focused on the leader. A short burst exploded that 109s oxygen tank as well, and it too hit the ground and blew up. Two down and he was still not through.

He looked about to make sure no one was on his tail, and saw another Me 109 to his right some distance away. It was all alone and must have been lost. Cameron opened fire at the extreme range of 1,000 yards but managed to hit the Messerschmidt's engine. The German pilot then turned to port and began heading in Cameron's direction. He fully expected a dogfight, but to his amazement the Messerschmidt suddenly turned north-east and began hightailing it for home. Cameron followed, closing the gap, but the German took no evasive action. Cameron pulled up beside the Messerchmidt to find the pilot slumped over. Then the 109 started to lose height and finally skidded into a field on its belly.

Flight Lieutenant Johnny MacKay, who had led his section away from the field, was vectored by Flight Lieutenant John Edison to the Reichwald area where he repeated Cameron's hat-trick. First he spotted one of Gruppe III's Me 109s flying north-east, apparently another lost German pilot. MacKay snapped off a long burst without result. He then closed in directly behind his quarry and this time his fire sent it crashing in flames.

During the encounter, MacKay had become separated from the rest of his section and he now set course for Heesch — on the deck. Near Nijmegan he could see two aircraft headed in his direction. He watched and waited and as they neared him he identified them as a Tempest chasing an FW 190. Suddenly, with a skilful manoeuvre, the German pilot reversed the situation ending up on the Tempest's tail. MacKay pulled up behind the German fighter and opened fire with what was left of his ammunition. That spent, he closed to within 30 yards of the Focke Wulf. The pilot panicked, went into a series of wild flick turns, and struck his port wing on a frozen lake. The 190 did a cartwheel and exploded.

MacKay now headed for home but ahead he saw an Me 109 flying west, blocking his way. He had no choice but to bluff it out. He pulled in as close as he could, forcing the Messerschmidt down on the deck where it hit some trees and disintegrated. Meanwhile Flying Officer Bob Foster also damaged an FW 190.

EINDHOVEN AIRFIELD, Holland

Squadron Leader Pete Wilson, the newly appointed CO of 438 Squadron, and his Number Two Flying Officer Ron Keller started their take-off run as the German attackers from the Udet Jagdgeschwader surged down the runway on the deck from the opposite direction toward them, but when Wilson was hit in the stomach by a bullet, he throttled back, pulled his Typhoon off the end of the runway, climbed out of the cockpit and collapsed. Keller got airborne but did not stay that way for long. A 190 sneaked up from behind and underneath and shot him down in flames, killing him.

The others in the squadron never even came close to getting off the ground. They never had the chance. Pilot Officer Don Campbell was trapped in his cockpit by the strafing and decided to stay put. He hunkered down behind the instrument panel and although his aircraft was hit several times he escaped injury. But his Typhoon effectively blocked Flying Officer Bill Beatty from trying to take off, so Beatty hastily taxied off the runway to his left, jumped out of the plane and ran for a foxhole, dove in, and landed right on top of an air-control airman. In short order the pair were joined by two others who flopped on top of them. The noise around them was frightening: the roar of air-craft engines, the crackle of machine-gun and cannon fire, the blast of bombs bursting, the thunder of the ack-ack guns.

Both wings of Flying Officer Andy Lord's Typhoon were set on fire. Because the fuel tanks were in the wing roots, there was no time to lose. Lord yanked off his helmet, stood on the edge of the cockpit and jumped more than ten feet to the ground. "A wonder I didn't break a leg or something."[20] By this time his dander was up. He pulled out his .45 Colt and began firing at the "strafing suckers, so low I didn't need to raise my arm. They were all over the place, right on the deck shooting us up real good. It was a madhouse. Our ack-ack was firing away with some success, smoke from burning aircraft, ours and theirs, bombs exploding, enemy planes crashing on the field, parachutes coming down, ammo exploding from our burning kites." By the time Lord calmed down, he saw some other pilots waving to him to join them in a shell crater, an invitation he happily accepted.

Back at dispersal, because the flight room walls had only clay tile siding which offered little protection, Flying Officer Bob Spooner who had taken charge, ordered all pilots and ground crew to take cover in the underground shelter. But Spooner and the squadron's armourer, Flight Sergeant Ron Large remained in the dispersal room where, armed with an unwieldy Bren gun propped up on the door, Large fired back at the attackers while Spooner kept him supplied with fresh ammunition. One Focke Wulf 190 came in so close that they could see the pilot looking down at them from 50 feet. Just then pieces started to fall off the aircraft, the pilot lost control, and it crashed on the runway.

After extricating himself from his aircraft, Flying Officer Allan Harle made for the adjutant's office of the nearby 440 Squadron dispersal where those in the orderly room were hiding under chairs and tables. Outside a bomb went off and Harle was injured by flying glass.

Meanwhile the 440 Squadron pilots led by Flight Lieutenant Ernie Savard who were waiting in their Typhoons at the end of the runway became head-on targets for the attackers. Pilot Officer Dick Watson, who was leading Blue Section, opened fire on one of three FW 190s flying straight toward him. He damaged it but his own aircraft was set on fire forcing him to abandon it.

Flying Officers Iva Gunnarson, Currie Gardner and Ted Smith also abandoned their aircraft. Ed Flanagan was not so fortunate. As he began to extricate himself from the cockpit a 20-millimetre cannon shell pierced the bubble hood from behind and exploded against the instrument panel in front of him. Shrapnel splattered his face, severely pockmarking it. Fortunately he was wearing his goggles and his eyes were spared. But there was worse to come. As he climbed out of his Typhoon an FW-190 strafed it, wounding Flanagan in both thighs. Luckily he had no broken bones, and although the flesh wounds were bleeding profusely, he was still able to walk, even wearing his parachute. At least that gave him some protection.[21]

One of the ground crew nearby who had taken shelter under the control tower nearby crawled out and shepherded Flanagan towards it. But that was the last place he wanted to be; it was too good a target. Twice he crawled back out from underneath and twice the crewman, with the best of intentions, dragged him back.

As soon as the Germans attacked, for protection Ernie Savard turned his Typhoon in the opposite direction so that the armour plating behind the seat was between him and the enemy aircraft. But he knew he couldn't stay there for long. He unfastened the safety harness and started to jump out. But in the heat of the moment he'd forgotten to unplug his radio transmitter and oxygen mask which hung him up. Looking up, he saw that the FW 190s were turning around to resume their strafing run and, realising he would not have time to escape, he climbed back in the cockpit, turned on the gun button and started firing his cannon at the approaching Germans. At the same time he ducked as low as possible hoping the Typhoon's giant Napier Sabre engine would give him some protection. Savard could hear and feel the thud of enemy gunfire striking his aircraft. By the time the 190s flew past he decided to make his exit from the cockpit, this time without his flying helmet.

Vainly searching for a place to hide, he saw the Germans beginning another run, scrambled under the tail of his aircraft and lay down on the frozen ground. From there he saw a ribbon of strikes a mere four feet away, heard his aircraft being hit again and set on fire. Now he had to move and bolted to a shell hole only 50 yards away.

"More enemy aircraft were about to attack again," Savard recalled:[22]

But I felt I had enough time to reach the shell hole before they would be able to get lined up on us. I ran as fast as I could over the frozen ground, slipping and sliding and I am sure that I actually dove into the shell hole from several feet away. It was mostly filled with old jerrycans and wire netting but there was still enough space to give fairly good protection.

It was then that I noticed a small mound of sand at the end of the runway about 50 or 60 yards away. It would be about five or six feet in length and about four feet high. There were about seven or eight pilots using it to try to hide from the attacking fighters. If it hadn't been for the situation we were in, the scene around the sand pile might have been humorous. When an attack was about to start from the north and when the direction was from the south, they would all hurry to the opposite side. There wasn't nearly enough sand for all of them to hide and only the fastest were hidden. As for the slower ones, there were butts and other parts being well outside the edges of the mound. Before the next attack, I stood up and yelled at them to join me. Apparently they hadn't noticed the shell hole and now they all made a dash for it.

A young airman, hit in the gut by gunfire, had reached the shell hole before Savard dived into it. He was in bad shape, semi-conscious and moaning. The pilots took out their first-aid kits which held morphine syringes. But no one had ever shown them how they should be administered. In any case it was too late. By this time the airman was beyond help. He had stopped breathing. Frustrated by his death, when the Germans next attacked, the pilots fired their service revolvers at them. "This was dangerous," Savard admitted. "If we were seen, all a fighter had to do would be to make a steeper attack and fire right into our shelter and kill us all."

When Flying Officer Ted Smith climbed out of his aircraft, he saw another Typhoon on fire some 100 yards away. Realising it would no longer be a target, he made for the tail of it but could get no closer than 10 feet due to the heat from the blaze. Then the cannon shells from the aircraft began to explode all around him and he decided to make for a bomb crater 200 yards away. However, he found it almost impossible to reach it due to the weight of his flying boots on the ice and snow. He gave up and crawled, hugging the ground as best he could. The situation reminded him of the pet dog he'd had as a youngster. Every time the doorbell rang, Lucky would try to burrow into the linoleum on the kitchen floor to hide under the stove.

From where he lay he watched Flying Officer Currie Gardner hightailing it across the field toward a fence where tall grass surrounded a fence post. But his yellow Mae West life-preserver made him a conspicuous target. Smith shouted, "Take off your Mae West, Currie! Take off your Mae West!" But with the clamour of cannons, machine-guns and bombs exploding, he couldn't be heard. Fortunately, Smith reached the bomb crater.

He dived in head first, landing on top of Ernie Savard, who was packed in there along with Iva Gunnarson and a couple of others. Angrily, Savard barked at Smith "Why the hell don't you watch what you're doing?" Smith, who was known for his short fuse, uncharacteristically apologised.[23]

Flight Lieutenant Jim Prendergast of 430 Squadron and his Number Two, Flying Officer Ken Gilmour, had reached the take-off point, as ground crewmen on either Spitfire's wing-tip guiding them through the ice and snow. Two Typhoons were ahead of them preparing to take off. Before turning onto the runway to follow them, Prendergast glanced back over his shoulder to see if there were any aircraft landing or in the circuit. There weren't, but what he did see, to his absolute horror, nearly made him jump out of his skin. Fifteen to 20 yellow-nosed Messerschmidt 109s were streaking across the perimeter of the field and down the runway toward them, the leading edges of their wings flashing fire and flame from their machine-guns and cannons. Following in their wake was another group of 109s at least 30 strong. In two minutes, Prendergast estimated, well over 100 enemy aircraft had attacked the field.[24]

The two Typhoons were both hit blocking the Spitfires' way. One had stopped and the pilot was slumped over in the cockpit. The other was standing on its nose and was on fire, the pilot climbing out of it. Prendergast was trapped. Pondering what to do, he saw another group of German fighters taking a second strafing run. Prendergast turned his aircraft towards them and let go with everything he had, his machine guns and cannons and did manage to "hit some aircraft."

At this point he realised his two ground crewmen were still sitting on the wing-tips looking at him, wondering what he was going to do next, when "damned if the Huns didn't turn around and come back a third time — very unusual. I decided it would be better for myself and my ground crew to get out of there." He waved them off, bailed out himself, then the three of them, along with Gilmour and his two mechanics, tried to make themselves as scarce as possible in the frozen piles of snow.

Prendergast's Spitfire became a prize target for the Germans and sustained a fair amount of damage. Gilmour's aircraft was also hit but damage to it was minor. Gilmour and the four crewmen escaped unharmed but Prendergast himself was wounded in the head when a stray bullet ricocheted off the taxiing strip and creased the back of his flying helmet. It gave him one hell of a headache but at this moment his concern was that it might be reason enough to bring his tour to an end, the last thing he wanted with the end of the war so close.

Two other members of his squadron, Flight Lieutenant Robert Gill and Flying Officer Bill Golden, did not escape injury either. Gill suffered a slight head wound while still in the cockpit of his Spitfire. But that wasn't all. He climbed out, slipped on the ice and broke his arm. While still strapped in his aircraft, Golden received body wounds from an exploding cannon shell.

The airfield controller had no sooner put the phone down after requesting a battery cart to start up Flying Officer Gordon Hill's repaired Spitfire, which had been shot up the day before, than the raid began. "Twenty minutes later," the 416 Squadron pilot from Brussels-Evere recalled, "I no longer had an airplane. I did, however, have a good case of the 'shakes' as more than one aircraft had had a go at the control truck."[25]

The raid took its toll of innocent bystanders as well. Watching the action from outside the 438 Squadron dispersal, which was set back in the woods and got off scot-free that morning, Flying Officer Phil Macklem, who had finished his ops tour and had been waiting for a transport to fly him to England, was hit in the shoulder by a piece of flying shrapnel from a bomb dropped by an Me 262 jet. The wound wasn't serious but it delayed his return to the UK for another two days.

As soon as the firing and bombing started, Father Michael, who had just begun Mass, ordered everyone to "hit the deck and stay there and you'll be OK." However, one of the airmen panicked, ran outside the dispersal and tumbled into a slit trench. He should have listened to the padre. A bullet struck him in the knee.

When he heard the firing and explosions, Squadron Leader Hart Massey, the 439 Squadron Intelligence Officer and son of Vincent Massey, Canada's High Commissioner to Britain, left his trailer to go outside and see what was going on. He hit the deck but it was not enough to save him being wounded in the head, the chest and rump.

The 439 Squadron's CO, "Bing" Crosby, with Flight Lieutenant Johnny Carr beside him, got as far as the Salvation Army building before cannon shells began exploding about their jeep. They jumped out of the vehicle and sought the safety of a ditch. In another truck nearby, driver leading Aircraftsman Len Weir, and his passengers, Flying Officers Johnny Johnson and Jack Roberts, also decided to abandon their transport and took cover behind the wheel of the three-ton truck. To their consternation, one of the tires took a direct hit from a cannon shell.

The remainder of 440 Squadron not being shot at on the field, stayed inside their dispersal. But they weren't spared either. Although it was protected by a blast-proof wall, it took the full force of an exploding bomb that knocked over tables, desks and chairs and smashed every window in the building. Many of the occupants suffered cuts to their face and hands from the flying glass.

Situated near the centre of the field, the Motor Transport section building made a tempting target for the raiders. Inside, two tracer bullets pierced Corporal Jerry Porter's greatcoat which was hanging on a hook, burning two holes in it. Since there were no suitable replacements in stores at Eindhoven, Porter continued to wear it. Later, on leave in England, a little old lady in a pub asked him: "Were you wearing it at the time?"[26]

Nearby, the brand-new portable wooden cookhouse parallel to the perimeter didn't escape attention either. This angered Chef "Taffy" to no end. Grabbing a Bren gun he shouted, "Who the hell do these bastards think they are?"[27] and began blazing away through the window. It was a brave attempt but Taffy was badly wounded as a result.

Everywhere there was chaos. Trucks, huts, buildings were all taking a fearful pounding. In one truck, the "Breakfast Special," Leading Aircraftsman Ron Norris was struck by cannon fire. He died of his wounds the next day. Another casualty was Flight Sergeant Reginald Bazley, crew chief of 137 Squadron, who was wounded in the hand. One of the other NCOs rushed outside to get the first aid box. But it was to no avail; he was too late. By the time he returned to administer first aid to the flight sergeant, Bazley was dead.

Leading Aircraftsman Desmond Shepherd, still sprawled on the grass, did not dare move as bullets and cannon shells whistled all around. He could see pilots jumping from their aircraft parked along the taxi strips and at the end of the runway waiting to take-off. One of the attacking FW 190s was shot down on the other side of the field and crashed into a parked Spitfire. Shepherd tried in vain to burrow into the ground but it was impossible, the ground was frozen solid. An empty cannon shell casing fell on his forage cap which, although he wasn't wearing a tin helmet, nevertheless saved him from a head injury. When the casing cooled off, he slipped it inside his battledress blouse to keep as a souvenir.[28]

BRUSSELS-EVERE, Belgium

The three abandoned 416 Squadron Spitfires effectively blocked the eight others in the squadron following them, their pilots were forced to evacuate their own aircraft quickly. This left five pilots, two of whom were, as yet, totally unaware of the attack in the air, to defend the airfield against some 100 enemy planes. The anti-aircraft defences had been temporarily taken out on the Germans' first pass.

Almost as soon as he got airborne, Flight Lieutenant Dave Harling had an Me 109 in his sights. He pressed the gun button and sent the enemy plane crashing into the ground. But simultaneously Gruppe III Unteroffizier Heinz Gehrke sneaked up behind him so close he couldn't miss. His cannon fire sent Harling's Spitfire crashing into a Brussels house, killing him but, miraculously, sparing the occupants.

At that precise moment, Flight Lieutenant Frank Minton, the 127 Wing IO (Intelligence Officer) received a phone call in the operations trailer at the far end of the runway. The message was cryptic. "Large gaggles of Huns near your airfield," the voice barked. "Get your Spits off!"[29]

"You're too late," Minton replied. "If I stick this phone outside you'll hear their bloody cannons!"

ASCH AIRFIELD, Belgium

After his take-off victory, 352nd Group Commander J.C. Meyer immediately tacked on to another FW 190 which he chased to the vicinity of Liege.[30]

> On my first attack I got good hits at 10 degrees 250 yards [an excellent position]. The E/A [enemy aircraft] half rolled and recovered just on top of the trees. I attacked but periodically had to break off because of intense friendly ground fire. At least on three occasions, I got good hits on the 190, and on the last attack the E/A started smoking profusely and then crashed into the ground. Out of ammunition, I returned to the field, but could not land as the field was under attack. I

proceeded west and was bounced twice by 109s and was able
to evade by diving and speed ....

In his report J.C. omitted to record that this second victory for
the morning brought his score of aircraft destroyed in the air
to 24.

Like Meyer's first victim, Gefreite Gerhardt Bohm, Leutnant
Georg Fureder from Gruppe II had also lined up his sights on
one of the Dakotas but not by choice. His original intention
had been to attack one of the Thunderbolts parked on the eastern part of the airfield. However, his approach angle had been
too steep to take proper aim, so he pulled back and picked a secondary target. Suddenly tracer bullets whizzed by the wing-tips
of his Messerschmidt as two Thunderbolts, flown by Captain
Lowell B. Smith and his wingman Lieutenant Bob Brulle,
latched onto his tail. Luckily for Fureder, their aim was off, allowing him to take evasive action by climbing steeply to port
as his attackers slid underneath him and broke away. But the
two Thunderbuggie pilots quickly found two other targets
which they soon dispatched, sending both of them crashing
into the airfield. This is Brulle's report of the action:[31]

> I jettisoned my bombs and did a steep wing-over, getting into
> position on the tail of an FW 190. I started firing and closed
> to 100 yards, observing many strikes. He exploded when he hit
> the ground. I then got on the tail of another FW 190 and used
> up the rest of my ammo while firing at him. When I broke off I
> saw him trailing smoke, but never saw him hit the ground.

At almost the very same moment, Second Lieutenant Melvin
Paisley, Lieutenants Currie Davis, Joe Lackey and John Feeney
brought down several FW 190s. Paisley explained his own
unique form of attack:[32]

... on the way in, I jumped an Me 109. Instead of using my guns, I chose to initiate my attack with the rockets I was carrying. I missed him with the first two but got him with the third.

Among the victims in one-eyed Oberstleutnant Gunther Specht's Jagdgeschwader 11 in this initial, sharp exchange were: Oberfeldwebel Karl-Heinz Sistenich, Feldwebelen Harald Schwarz and Herbert Kraschinski, Oberleutnant August Engel, all killed; Feldwebelen Karl Hiller, who was severely burned when his FW 190 which had been set on fire crashed near Maastricht where he was taken prisoner.

ST DENIS-WESTRAM AIRFIELD, Belgium

As soon as the Germans attacked, 308 and 317 Squadrons were immediately recalled. East of Ghent, Sergeant Stanislaw Breyner of 308 spotted two FW 190s flying on the deck in the direction of St Denis-Westram and dived to attack. But, before he could open fire, the German pilots panicked, pulled up too sharply and stalled. One crashed into a building, the other spun into the ground.

At the same time, the squadron's leader, Flight Lieutenant Ignacy Olszewski, attacked several other 190s causing them to separate and allowing other members of the squadron, led by Flight Lieutenant Bronislaw Mach, to give chase. Meanwhile, Flight Sergeant Zygmunt Socyzinski polished off another of the attackers, opening fire from 100 yards, sending it diving into the ground.

Pursuing the other gaggle, to the north-east near Termonde, Mach closed in behind one of the German fighters opening fire from 200 yards and closing to 100. The 190 rolled over and crashed but the pilot managed to bale out, landing in the Scheldt River. Mach then became embroiled in a tussle with two FW 190s, one of which he damaged. He then followed the other one down from 2,000 feet to the deck. His fire blew the cockpit canopy off the enemy aircraft which crashed into a field near Terneuzen.

By this time Olszewski and the rest of the squadron were nearing base from which they could see smoke rising. At this point Flight Sergeant Josef Stanowski was forced to break away from the squadron formation and make a beeline for the airfield because he was almost out of fuel. By the time he reached it, FW 190s were everywhere beating it up. Stanowski sighted on the nearest one, flown by Unteroffizier Karl Hahn, and let go a well-aimed squirt with his machine-guns and cannons that set it on fire and sent it crashing into the ground. He then turned into another 190, this one flown by the Gruppe II commander, Hauptmann Hans-Georg Hackbarth, and opened fire from 100 yards. The Focke Wulf's wheels dropped down. Stanowski fired again sending it into a dive right into the centre of Ghent where it plowed into the back of a flower shop and smashed through the front window throwing Hackbarth's lifeless body out onto the street. Completely out of fuel by this time, Stanowski had to make a forced landing north-east of the town.

Over the airfield now, Olszewski and the rest of the squadron had the height advantage as they waded into the low-flying enemy fighters. Olszewski singled out one of them and fired. Hit by his cannon shells the 190 flicked onto its back and crashed east of Ghent. At 3,000 feet Flying Officer Tadeusz Szlenkier went to the rescue of another Spitfire which had a 190 on its tail. From 250 yards he opened fire just as the German aircraft started to level out. His bullets and cannon shells smashed into the enemy's right wing, then it turned over on its back and hit the deck near the small hamlet of Rosdam. But in the process Szlenkier's Spitfire had been hit by flak, forcing him to crash-land.

By the time he arrived over the airfield, Warrant Officer Zeonbieuz Wdowczynski, despite a rough running engine, managed to down one of the raiders just east of Ghent when he was immediately set up by another 190. He managed to out-manoeuvre his adversary but stalled in the process. Then his engine packed up altogether and he had to crash-land.

Meanwhile, Pilot Officer Andrezj Dromlewicz chased a 190 which was attacking a Spitfire. Closing to within 30 yards he used up all his cannon shells before his quarry pulled up sharply in a climbing turn. Dromlewicz opened up with his machine-guns blasting pieces off the Focke Wulf's starboard wing and the pilot took to his parachute.

Bronislaw Mach's Number Three in his section, Warrant Officer Stanislaw Bednarcyzk, went to his leader's rescue when he saw a 190 firing at him. A short, sharp burst from Bednarcyzk's Spitfire sent the enemy fighter crashing into the ground just north of the airfield.

At this point Squadron Leader Marian Chelmecki's 317 Squadron arrived on the scene. Clouds of black smoke were rising from the field. As the pilots waded into the midst of the German fighters, Flight Lieutenant Czeslaw Mroczyk took a shot at the 190 nearest to him. It went completely out of control, forcing the pilot to bail out. Taking to his parachute was nothing new to Unteroffizier Fritz Hoffmann, who had been shot down twice before. This time he ended up in a British POW camp but not before being roughed up by Dutch civilians and police. As Mroczyk pulled up Chelmecki, the squadron commander, saw another 190 slide in behind the tail of the Spitfire. Chelmecki deftly — and bravely — edged in between the Focke-Wulf and the Spitfire forcing the German pilot to make a steep turn to port. Chelmicki climbed into the sun, levelled out then, seeing an FW 190 about to start a strafing run across the field, dived down, clobbering it with his machine-guns and cannons from 400 yards. But he lost sight of it in the smoke from a burning Flying Fortress that had been set on fire at the beginning of the German attack. However, the 190 had been badly damaged by Chelmecki's fire and went completely out of control. It struck a small building, caught fire and crashed into a nearby railway line.

A little to the east, Flight Lieutenant Zbigniew Zimgrodski scored hits on an FW 190 that belched black smoke, but he had to break off his attack when another German fighter latched onto his own tail. Breaking around, he saw another 190 chasing a Spitfire. Though he scared off the enemy it was too late to save the life of Flight Lieutenant Tadeusz Powierza, whose aircraft plunged into the ground, killing him.

Sergeant Kelnis Hubert reached the base at 2,000 feet and with a well-aimed burst, shot down an FW 190 300 feet below him. Like Stanowski's earlier victim it too crashed into the centre of Ghent. Climbing away, Hubert tackled the rearmost aircraft of a formation of three 190s. He saw flames streaming from his target but had to pull aside to force another 190 to break away from an attack on a Spitfire.

Warrant Officer Stanislaw Piesik targeted two FW 190s just finishing their strafing run. He set one of them on fire just as tracer shells zipped by his cockpit. Piesik broke around to take a 190 head-on noticing hits on the enemy's engine cowling.

Flight Lieutenant Roman Hrycak took aim on an FW 190 which was diving down to attack the base's fuel dump. In the miasma over the field, he was unable to see the results of his shooting but observers on the ground confirmed that the enemy plane had crashed behind some nearby buildings.

Flight Lieutenant Czeslaw Mroczyk's Spitfire had been damaged during the fighting and he asked his squadron commander Chelmecki for permission to land. But as soon as he touched down, his engine died — he had run out of fuel. With that aircraft blocking the runway, Chelmecki had to divert the other Spitfires in the air to Ursel and Courtrai airfields.

VOLKEL AIRFIELD, Belgium

The minute the raid by Jagdgeschwader 6 began, the control tower advised the squadrons in the air that the field was under attack. Leading 486 Squadron near Deurne, its CO, Spike Umbers, spotted three FW 190s, one on the deck, two at 6,000 feet. Umbers dispatched a section to attack the higher pair and went after the one below himself. With a short, sharp burst of fire he sent the German aircraft crashing into the ground in flames.

Steering his section toward Volkel, they encountered a lone Me 109 at 1,500 feet. But when the pilot saw the Tempests, he instantly dived to the deck to join a group of other 20 Me 109s. Disregarding the odds, Umbers closed in from behind and the 109 went into a series of violent gyrations, weaving from one side to the other. Umbers stayed on its tail and got off a burst. The port wheel of the Messerschmidt dropped down and the fighter hit the ground and exploded.

By this time Umbers was out of ammunition and as the section arrived over Volkel, an FW 190 was racing across the field firing into the middle of it. Umbers ordered Flying Officer Bill Trott to take care of it. It took only three quick bursts to send the 190 flopping over onto its back and diving straight into the ground.

Some moments later, Trott and his wingman Pilot Officer C.J. "Butch" Steadman chased after a lone Me 109 flying close to the ground. Trott emptied his ammunition, seeing strikes on the enemy aircraft which, though damaged, continued to fly. Steadman was unable to finish the Messerschmidt off. He too had run out of ammunition. Earlier, he had spent half of it in a futile attempt to attack three Me 262s and later an FW 190. The two Tempest pilots could only watch as their quarry, the wounded Me 109, blissfully flew on.

The section Umbers had earlier assigned to tackle the pair of FW 190s was led by Pilot Officer Gus Hooper who zeroed in on one of them sending it crashing into a field. He was then attacked by an Me 109 which he scared off with a sharp burst before his ammunition ran out. His Number Three, Pilot Officer Jim Shedden, also shot down an FW 190 which hit the ground violently and exploded into small pieces.

While all this was taking place, Tempests from 3 and 56 Squadrons who had completed their armed reconnaissance were also on their way back to Vokel. Flying Officer Don Butcher, who had dived down to investigate two columns of black smoke rising from the field, spotted four Me 109s on the deck. Butcher singled out one of them while Flight Sergeant Maurice Rose took aim on another. Butcher opened fire from 20 yards at a speed of 440 miles an hour. As white smoke streamed from the Messerschmidt, it lost speed, allowing Butcher to get in close and finish it off. Firing again at point-blank range, he broke hard to starboard just as the Me 109 hit the ground and caught fire.

Rose had opened fire on his target from 200 yards out and although he had used up most of his ammunition, he failed to see any strikes. He let go a final burst at 100 yards then radioed for anyone with ammunition left to come and "finish the bloody Hun off!" Suddenly the Me 109 pulled up vertically to 1,500 feet, then rolled over on its back and the pilot, Unteroffizier Rudolf Schlossborn, bailed out. His aircraft crashed into a field near Lieshart and caught fire.

After his 56 Squadron had successfully completed their attacks on German locomotives near Paderborn, Flight Lieutenant Jock Ross also led his Tempests back to Vokel when he heard it was under fire. Pilot Officer Dave Ness, a Canadian, spotted two Tempests on the deck chasing an Me 109 south. As the enemy plane broke away, Ness, accompanied by Pilot Officer Harold "Artie" (after the noted band leader) Shaw, went after it. Ness got in several bursts and black smoke belched from the Messerschmidt's engine. Ness continued to fire but had to break off when oil covered his windshield, blotting out his forward vision. Shaw now closed in to complete the job. Flames burst from the Me 109s engine as Shaw riddled it with his fire. The pilot pulled back his cockpit canopy as the propeller began to windmill. Too low to bail out, he tried to force land, but as the 109 struck the ground wheels-up, it tore through a row of trees, turned over onto its back and broke apart.

The RAF Regiment gunners also scored a hit against an Me 109 which began to trail smoke as it flew over the field. It finally crashed less than a mile away. In all, three Me 109s were destroyed right over Volkel. Besides Unteroffizier Rudolf Schlossborn, who managed to bail out, Unteroffizier Hans-Joachim Rose was so badly shot up, he had to make a forced landing and Hauptmann Willi Kindler was shot down and killed.

GILZE-REIJEN AIRFIELD, Holland

When Flight Lieutenant Dave Mercer of 268 Squadron, flying with Flight Lieutenant John Lyke, spotted three Ju 188s escorted by five FW 190s at zero feet over Utrecht, he came to the same conclusion that Flight Lieutenant Jim Young of 2 Squadron had. It was an airfield raid by a small bombing force escorted by fighters.

They were cruising at between 5,000 and 6,500 feet when they spotted the enemy formation flying very low beneath them. Mercer radioed Gilze-Reijen — "Longbow" — that the German aircraft were probably about to attack the field. He then dived down to attack.

Singling out one of the Junkers, he opened fire sending it crashing into a clump of trees where it burst into flames. Then he and Young beat a hasty retreat back to base, staying close to the ground, not wanting to stick around and tangle with the FW 190s which began to chase them.[33]

The attack was a unique spectacle. For the first time, and perhaps the last, in WW II at any rate, here was the spectacle of jet bombers and piston-engine driven fighters executing a co-ordinated air raid. Six Aredo 234 jet bombers from Staffel 9/KG 76 led by Oberleutnant Alfred Stark combined with a dozen or so FW 190s and Me 109s from JG 3. While the bombers dropped light fragmentation bombs on the field, the fighters went after the parked aircraft.

Flight Lieutenant Bill Baggs recalled:[34]

> I can't remember seeing the 190s, but the Messeschmidts were milling around at reduced speed circling about making them easy targets to the anti-aircraft gunners. There didn't seem to be any teamwork. Each fighter seemed to go in individually. It was as if they'd got lost and didn't quite know what to do next.

In fact the gunners did have a field day. The 18 guns which fired off 803 rounds, destroyed three Me 109s, damaged five others and brought down one of the Ar 234s. One of the German pilots managed to bail out right onto the field and was promptly locked up in the guardroom.

In the middle of the fracas John Lyke, who had lost touch with Dave Mercer in the mêlée over Utrecht, returned to Gilze and landed. As he touched down, his Mustang was shot up by a 109. One of the ack-ack gunners managed to wing the 109 in turn, but it flew off, its fate unknown.

HEESCH AIRFIELD, Holland

The remaining 401 Squadron aircraft that had not left the ground when the attack began were sitting neatly arrayed armed with 500-pound bombs. The pilots scrambled to get into their planes and take off. But first, for the sake of manoeuvrability, the bombs had to come off — unofficially. The RAF manual stated that a bomb "already armed" could not be removed from the aircraft or it would explode. Armourer Cecil "Smokey" Mann knew better. After all he'd been around explosives for four years and knew them inside out.

These particular bombs were fused in the nose. To detonate them, the firing pin had to be driven into the detonator causing it to explode which, in turn, ignited the powder in the main chamber exploding the bomb. To achieve this, the bomb had to drop perpendicularly so that the nose, which was heavier than the rest of the bomb, hit the target first. But with a parked Spitfire, the belly of the bomb was only 20 inches from the ground, which meant that if it was released, the nose would not tilt down sufficiently to detonate.

With enemy machine-gun and cannon fire spraying all over the place, there was no time to lose. While the rigger strapped the pilot into the cockpit and the fitter waited to start the engine, Mann climbed up on the wing of the Spitfire, reached over the pilot's shoulder and calmly pressed the electronic bomb-release button. The pilot blanched but there was only a dull thud as the bomb hit the ground. While the fitter started the engine, Mann and the rigger swung the tail sideways past the fallen bomb. Other crews hastily followed Mann's example.

Meanwhile the Canadians in the air at the time were enjoying great success. Flight Lieutenant Dick Audet of 411 Squadron who, three days earlier, had become an instant ace by shooting down five planes in a single encounter, became separated from the rest of his flight and was attempting to reform with them south-west of Enschede when he was bounced by four Typhoons mistaking his Spitfire for an Me 109. Audet deftly broke through them and they missed him altogether. But in the process he lost complete sight of his own formation. He decided to call it quits and turned back toward base. At 9,000 feet he spotted an FW 190 4,000 feet below him heading towards

Enschede. As soon as he saw Audet, the enemy pilot went into a shallow right-hand turn. Audet latched on to him easily opening fire and scoring hits on the enemy aircraft which rolled over and spun down spitting flame, finally crashing into the ground.

Regaining height, Audet saw another 190 heading in the same direction. The enemy pilot tried to flee but was unable to jettison his drop tank. Audet's fire shot away pieces of fuselage and rudder, then the 190's engine stopped, causing his adversary to overshoot. As Audet wheeled around for a second attack, the enemy pilot tried to find a place to land. Audet gave the 190 a final burst that sent it plunging into the ground east of Haardergen.

As soon as the Germans had been spotted, Flight Lieutenant John Edison in the control tower had signalled Norm Keene — 442 Squadron — to return to base. "We're under attack," he told him. North-west of Venlo the Canadians ran into a batch of enemy fighters, Me 109s and FW 190s. Keene chased two of them. He managed to bring one of them down and it hit the ground and exploded.[35]

Flying Officer Len Wilson, who was in the same section, described his own experience:[36]

We had just completed our turn toward base when I spotted a few aircraft on deck flying roughly at right angles to us. I reported them to the section leader and stated that I was going down on them. My Number Two, Flight Lieutenant [Dave] "Tex" Pieri, and I peeled off and came down behind them, gathering speed all the way down. To my astonishment, there were not just a few aircraft, but at least 20. I was in an ideal position as I drew up behind my selected victim, but I hesitated a second too long to clearly identify the aircraft before firing, so that as the opening burst got off, I immediately had to push the nose down to avoid a collision and wound up directly in front of my target.

What to do? To climb would put me in the sights of the entire Staffel. I was too low to dive. All my training made me instinctively break around to port in order to get around behind him for another pass.

A Spitfire can out-turn an FW 190. Unfortunately, this is only true given relatively similar air speeds. Having dived from 10,000 feet and gathered speed on the way down, I must have had 150-180 miles an hour increase in speed over the E/A [enemy aircraft] and therefore could not out-turn him in this circumstance. Halfway around the turn I felt an explosion behind me, the aircraft flick-rolled further to port. I hastily gained control and continued my turns to get on his tail. I looked over my head to the left and saw an FW 190, tell-tale flash of its wing guns firing making it evident he was intent on finishing me off. At the same time he was firing, he was being fired on by a Spitfire flown by my Number Two, "Tex" Pieri. The FW fell away, later claimed by Tex as destroyed. In a flash the sky was empty of aircraft.

Straightening out to look for other targets, I found that the aircraft was extremely difficult to manoeuvre. It could only be flown by putting on full right rudder combined with the left aileron, resulting in the aircraft sluicing through the air with the wings at about a 30 degree left slant. It was virtually impossible to do a turn to the right. I immediately did a left climbing turn to about 5,000 feet, and proceeded to fly in a northerly direction towards base.

Because of the extreme fatigue in my right leg from having to apply full right rudder, it was necessary every now and then to break into a left turning cycle to rest my leg. Hence, I made my way slowly back to base, flying straight, then resting in a turn, flying straight, then rest-ing, all the while looking about for enemy aircraft and hoping I would not encounter any in my crippled condition. Luck was with me.

How was I going to land with the aircraft damage requiring such aberrant behaviour at the controls? Would it affect the stalling speed, or cause me to flick to the left on landing? Nothing to do but go in and trust to luck. Fortunately, as I reduced speed on the approach for landing, the twisting effect on the damaged tail was reduced, and as I pulled off power at the roundout, most of the slipstream torque disappeared and I made a normal landing.

Meanwhile, having destroyed Wilson's assailant, his Number Two, Tex Pieri, spotted a low-flying FW 190 which he attacked, scoring strikes on the cockpit and wing root. It suddenly pulled straight up, stalled, then spun into the ground and exploded. Pieri's engine began to act up, so he turned back to base. But, just as he did so, he saw another FW 190 flying north-east below him at ground level. He couldn't resist attacking it, blasting large pieces out of it. However, oil from the enemy fighter coated his windshield and he was unable to confirm its fate. It was a tough go but by weaving and skidding he was able to make it back to the airfield where he landed safely.

Another 442 Squadron pilot, Flight Lieutenant Donald "Chunky" Gordon, from Wilson's section, was not as lucky. He was flying Al Bathurst's Spitfire because his own was U/S (unserviceable). When the engine started to run rough and the oil pressure dropped, he decided to return to Heesch. But, enroute, he spotted a body of FW 190s flying low in the direction of Eindhoven, and despite his problems, he waded right in. Picking out the closest enemy fighter, he took aim from 200 yards and let go a solid three-second burst. The 109 flicked over on its back and crashed into the ground. Another Focke Wulf loomed straight ahead. Gordon opened fire from 300 yards and saw strikes. The enemy fighter flew on for another few seconds, then nosed into the ground and blew up.

By this time Gordon was near the airfield where the ack-ack gunners were shooting at anything and everything in sight. Suddenly there was an explosion from behind him and shrapnel from a flak burst struck him in the back of his head, neck and back. By this time his engine had begun to seize up so he belly landed, wheels-up, in a field just south of Heesch. Badly banged about, he gingerly climbed out of the cockpit to be greeted by a Dutch woman who slapped him on his aching back, wished him a happy new year and fed him some home-made cookies.

Flight Lieutenant Robert Smith, another member of the flight, was also forced to return to base. His problem was with the drop tank which wasn't feeding properly causing the engine to cut out intermittently. But, like Chunky Gordon, when he spotted FW 190s about to attack Eindhoven, he decided to have a shot at them. Suddenly he found himself in the middle of 20 enemy fighters. Smith dived down taking a wild deflection burst at the one nearest him, then pulled up above the cluster to gain height advantage. Picking out another target, he dived again but was forced to break away as one of the 190s closed in on him.

Smith now rolled down behind another 190 but had to give up when oil spewed over his windshield impairing his vision. He climbed to 800 feet, by which time the oil film had cleared and he could see a Focke Wulf climbing at him on his left. Putting his Spitfire into a diving turn he took the enemy fighter head-on. Both pilots opened fire, though neither scored a hit. Finally, at the last minute, the German broke off to port with only a few feet to spare. Then Smith saw another 190 on the deck and chased it. But this time his fuel gave out. However, he was close enough to base to glide into Heesch dead-stick.

To the north Flight Lieutenant Jack Lumsden's section saw an Me 262 twin-engine jet at 1,800 feet, just below a cloud layer, flying right across the Canadians' flight path. Lumsden swung in behind it, got in a quick burst and saw strikes on the tail before the Messerschmidt disappeared into the safety of the cloud. Trying to find it, Lumsden emerged from the cloud and ran into an FW 190 flying straight toward him. As the two air-craft passed each other, Lumsden swung in behind the enemy fighter, closed in and opened fire. He saw hits on the FW 190 before he lost it in the sun. Lumsden's Number Two, Flying Officer Jacques Cousineau, also saw hits on the 190 before he too lost it in the sun.

Another 442 Squadron section led by Flight Lieutenant Bob Trumley was attacked by an Me 262 head-on. All four Spitfire pilots fired back. Although none of them saw strikes, the Me 262 streamed smoke as it flew past them. They tried to give chase but it was hopeless. The jet easily outpaced them.

When the attack on Heesch began, the pilots of 412 Squad-ron were still in their dispersal. They were quickly scrambled and moments later were in the air giving chase and eventually found themselves in the middle of more than 30 FW 190s. Ten miles west of Venlo, CO Dean Dover and Flying Officer Eric Kelly shared in the destruction of one enemy fighter, while Flight Lieutenants Bruce "Mac" Macpherson, and Joe Doak and Flying Officer Victor Smith accounted for one apiece. Macpherson had spotted a fight between Tempests from Volkel and a group of 190s. Picking out a lone enemy fighter, he chased after it. The enemy pilot tried to make for the refuge of some cloud cover, but Macpherson clobbered the aircraft from astern and could see strikes and fire around the cockpit. He hit it again, but was forced to break off because of flak from his own anti-aircraft gunners. Then, as he turned away, he saw the German pilot take to his parachute.

Vic Smith had become embroiled in a twisting, turning dogfight with a Focke Wulf 190, finally managed to shake off his attacker then found another target below him. The German pilot obviously failed to see him because he maintained straight and level flight, making no attempt at evasive action. Smith got in a solid burst that smashed into the cockpit and wing roots of the enemy fighter, sending the 190 crashing into some woods.

North-east of Helmond, Joe Doak picked out a stray single 190 flying at less than 50 feet and opened fire from less than 200 yards. A single short burst caused the enemy fighter to flick over onto its back and hit the ground.

EINDHOVEN AIRFIELD, Holland

Ed MacKay and the others from 438 Squadron who had driven in from Eindhoven were in time to see the last part of the raid. MacKay described it:[37]

> The scene was incredible, burning aircraft, explosions and fires from piled up jerrycans of 100 per cent octane, 150 grade gas, rockets and bombs blasting away. RAF Regiment Bofors. Black palls of smoke were everywhere. Suddenly the Bofors stopped and I later learned they had simply run out of ammunition.

By 9:30, Gordie Wonnacott, the CO of 414 Typhoon Squadron, was returning from his reconnaissance sweep of the Cologne area. He and his Number Two had been split up by low cloud and intense German anti-aircraft fire, so he flew back alone. As he approached base he could see black smoke rising from the field and dozens of German aircraft milling about. It seems strange that he'd received no alert over the radio transmission. But there is no record of it. Wonnacott waded right into the enemy fighters picking out an Me 109 on which he opened fire from 450 yards. However, the enemy skidded to one side forcing him to break off. But not to worry, there were targets galore. Wonnacott quickly found another Me 109, and took aim. However, one of his cannons packed up, so he confined his attack to his machine-guns. Closing in to ten yards, he saw strikes all along the fuselage of the Messerschmidt, then the enemy pilot jettisoned his cockpit canopy and bailed out.

Wonnacott soon found a fresh target, another 190. The pilot took violent evasive action and pulled up in a loop near the ground. Wonnacott stayed with him, opening fire from 250 yards. Flames burst from the enemy plane but just then Wonnacott was bounced by three FW 190s. He turned into them, fired and saw his bullets strike one of them before all three broke off. With his ammunition gone and one cannon out of action, Wonnacott returned to base where he was credited with three aircraft destroyed and awarded an immediate bar to his Distinguished Flying Cross.

Curiously, the reconnaissance flight of four Typhoons led by Flying Officer Bob Laurence did receive warning of the strike on Eindhoven over the radio and, keeping a sharp lookout, they intercepted some 20 FW 190s from 15 Staffeln of Kommandor Heinz "Pritzl" Bar's JG 3 over Deurne to the east of the field, flying at a height of between 500 and 1,000 feet. In the mêlée that followed, Laurence destroyed two of the German fighters. His combat report graphically describes the engagement:[38]

> ... after considerable manoeuvring, I got on a 190's tail at about 150 yards, closing all the time. He didn't take much evasive action and I gave him a short burst with about five degrees deflection, turning slightly starboard. I saw strikes mostly on the starboard wing, then gave another short burst, getting more strikes on the wings and some on the fuselage. This time the aircraft at 800 feet rocked a little and started towards the ground as if out of control, and at this time I had to break port with an FW 190 on my tail and firing at me. When next I looked in this direction, I saw an enemy pilot descending by parachute.

My Number Two saw at least three or four aircraft go in at
this point and at this time. The fighting continued and I had
one or two short bursts at other aircraft but did not see any
results. As the action broke off, I saw one FW 190 running
away from me and I was able to close from 75 to 100 yards
dead astern. I gave it a short burst, then another burst,
getting strikes both times. The second time the coupe-top
[the cockpit hood] and several other pieces flew off it. It
dropped its nose and went towards the ground; it then rolled
slowly over on its back and I saw it crash into a brick building
and burst into flames.

At that moment another 190 latched onto his tail. He managed to shake it off just as Flying Officer Hugh Fraser, of the
439 Squadron RCAF, closed in on it from 75 yards. Fraser's
combat report relates what happened next: [39]

I gave him a short burst at ten degrees angle off and air
speed about 190-200 mph. Pieces flew off his aircraft; he
caught fire on his back and went straight in at approximately
E6175 [map co-ordinates]. By this time I lost my leader.
Somebody took a squirt at me from 45 degrees angle off,
judging from the holes in my aircraft. At this time I saw four
aircraft hit the ground and one parachute. I was then at about
1,500 feet and saw a long-nosed FW 190 in a shallow dive
underneath me going toward Venlo. I dove after him; when I
was about 100 feet above the ground, I was closing rapidly
and took four short bursts at him. It was line astern shooting
and my last burst was from 50 yards. Pieces flew off his aircraft; I must have severed his elevator controls because he
never levelled off. He went into the deck somewhere near a
large windmill at about E7919 [map co-ordinates]. I had to
break very quickly to avoid hitting the ground at approximately 400 mph. Pieces flew in every direction.

In the same fracas, Flying Officer Sam Angelini was killed. The remaining three pilots, seeing Eindhoven in such a shambles, landed at Volkel instead. They weren't the only ones.

In another action, two more Typhoon pilots, Flight Lieutenant George Clubley and Pilot Officer Don Martyn from 137 Squadron, shared in the destruction of a Heinkel 111. They were returning from an armed recce, during which they shot up a train south of Steinheim and a railway station between Wesel and Emmerich, when they spotted the enemy bomber near Minden below and to their right. This was the first time that Clubley had fired at an enemy aircraft and on his first pass he missed the target altogether. Martyn scored on his first try, as did Clubley on his second attempt. The Heinkel managed to make a well-controlled forced landing in a field but none of the crew were seen to get out. By the time the Typhoon pilots reached Eindhoven the runway was so badly damaged it was obvious landing was out of the question and they were diverted to Volkel.

BRUSSELS-EVERE, Belgium

As soon as Pilot Officer Steve Butte and Sergeant Pilot Doug Lindsay got airborne — the second patrol, behind Dick and Mac Reeves, to take off from Evere that morning — Butte saw a German formation to his left flying in the opposite direction, 300 yards away, which he immediately identified as a mixture of Messerschmidt 109s and Focke Wulf 190s. He ordered Lindsay to drop his jet tank but his own tank refused to jettison. He broke into the enemy formation anyway. He described the subsequent action in his combat report:[40]

> [I] picked the nearest aircraft by closing from 100-200 yards, firing several bursts and observing many strikes. The aircraft crashed in flames .... Next I was on the tail of an FW 190 and closed to approximately 100 yards. I saw strikes, the first one on the starboard wing, then on the port wing, then on the

fuselage. The aircraft continued on a straight course and crashed behind the first row of houses after taking off part of the roof. Then I got behind the tail of an Me 109 and fired several bursts from a range of 175 yards and saw strikes on his wing and fuselage, causing black smoke and pieces to fall off .... One of these pieces hit my drop tank; there was lots of smoke in the area and I could not locate myself. I broke away from the attack at approximately 500 feet and saw the aircraft practically on his back in a steep dive. I had to break away and did not have time to see it crash. I got on the tail of another Me 109 and gave him a short burst from approximately 200 yards when I ran out of ammunition .... I had no more ammunition, so I headed west when I was bounced by two FW 190s. I managed to get on one's tail, but I could only take a picture .... I broke away and flew under some factory smoke and when control gave me the "all clear" I pancaked back at base.

Doug Lindsay had become separated from his leader. He ran across a pair of FW 190s and fired a short burst at them without result. He then latched onto an Me 109 which was streaking toward the airfield. Opening fire, he saw strikes along the fuselage, but by this time he was attacked by several Messerschmidts and lost sight of his victim. He managed to shake them off, then chased after another 109 but again became the target of three more enemy aircraft before he could bring his guns to bear.

Lindsay made a hard climbing turn to port to get clear — the 190s couldn't possibly turn inside that — then he rolled over to attack a Focke Wulf directly below him. Now he had the fighter flown by Unteroffizer Wilhelm Schultz firmly in his sights. His first burst struck the enemy aircraft's belly and long-range tank which Schultz hurriedly jettisoned and broke to the left,

Lindsay still firing at the aircraft. Suddenly flames shot back from the engine and Lindsay watched as the plane crashed in flames in a field near Aalst, striking a tree. Rescuers were later greeted by the gruesome sight of the decapitated pilot amid the wreckage.

Dick and Mac Reeves, the original patrol to get off from Evere that morning, were over the German lines near Weert searching for ground targets when a shout came over the R/T: "There's a beat up going on here!" "Where?" Dick Reeves shouted back. "B-56 [Evere]" was the reply.[41] The pair climbed to 3,000 feet and raced toward the field where they could see that the Germans were indeed beating it up. Fires seemed to be everywhere, mushrooming up as high as 13,000 feet. It was pandemonium.

This did not make it easier for the attackers who, like Leutnant Guenther Bloemertz, an Me 109 pilot with Anton Hackl's Gruppe, had to fly through the dark smoke clouds billowing skyward, as well as over flames sprouting upwards from burning buildings and aircraft.[42]

Dick Reeves shoved the throttle forward to join in the fray then, in what he later described as, "the most frustrating moment of my life," his engine began to vibrate so violently that he was forced to throttle back for fear the engine would shake the Spitfire apart. Mac Reeves throttled back to stay with him, but Dick told him, "Go ahead!"[43]

Mac waded into the midst of what he estimated to be 30 or more German fighters milling about the field. Sighting on an FW 190, he saw his bullets strike the aircraft which began streaming smoke. It rolled over on its back, hit the ground and blew up. Mac then took aim on another Focke Wulf, opened fire from 150 yards seeing strikes on the wings and engine. When smoke started to pour from it, the pilot climbed out on the wing and jumped, his parachute peacefully floating him down into the suburbs of Brussels.

Flying Officer Bill Roddie, who was on his way back to the airfield on foot, having spent the night with the girl he'd met in the Brussels dance hall the night before, looked up to see an aircraft skimming the rooftops. His reaction was: "Jesus, if Wingco Johnnie Johnson catches that idiot, I'll be off the hook as orderly officer."[44] Another aircraft followed in its wake but this time Roddie could see the unmistakable black crosses on the wings. The sound of cannon and machine-gun fire from the direction of the airfield confirmed that an attack of some sort was underway. "Not being one to subscribe to acts of daring the youthful derring do," he later admitted, Roddie took shelter in the nearest doorway.

When things quieted down, Roddie resumed his walk towards the airfield. Suddenly a crewman from the American detachment posted at Evere rushed past him shouting, "Aren't you coming? There are people getting killed, you know!" Roddie yelled right back at him, "Well go and join them, you stupid asshole."

ASCH AIRFIELD, Belgium

In addition to the two victories by their CO, J.C. Meyer, Captain William "Whiz" Whisner and Lieutenant Sandford Moats of the 487th Fighter Squadron each shot down four enemy fighters, Captain Henry Stewart and Lieutenant Alden Rigby each destroyed three and Lieutenants Walker Diamond and Alexander Sears accounted for one apiece.

In his eagerness to get into the fight, Whisner had forgotten to turn on his gun button. "I picked out a 109," he said, "and pressed the trigger. Nothing happened. I reached down and turned on my gun switch and gave him a couple of good bursts."

Whisner was watching as the 109 struck the ground and blew apart when he felt his own P-51 shudder as 20-millimeter cannon shells struck both wings. Breaking hard to starboard and upward, he saw a Messerschmidt only 50 yards behind him still firing. Just in time, another P-51 came to his rescue and his attacker broke off. Although he had also been hit in the oil tank and the left aileron was out of commission, at least he was over friendly ground and saw no reason to go in and land. He turned to the right where a big dog fight was in progress and took aim on an FW 190. After several quick, accurate bursts the enemy pilot tried to bale out but Whisner clobbered him with another burst, sending the 190 in to a dive, straight into the ground where it exploded.

Whisner then spotted several Me 109s in vee-formation, one of which he singled out. After dog-fighting the enemy fighter for five minutes, he got behind him, opened fire and the pilot baled out at 200 feet. But, once again, Whisner opened fire, sending the pilot tumbling to the ground.[45]

No quarter! Whisner noticed some 20 fires burning from crashed planes as he headed for the airfield. He immediately latched on to an Me 109 strafing the north-east end of the strip. The enemy fighter turned into him and the two protagonists made two head-on passes at each other. On the second run Whisner hit the Messerschmidt in the nose and wings and it crashed west of the field. Whisner chased after several other enemy bandits but oil on his windshield so obscured his vision that he was forced to return to the field and land.

Sandford Moats, who also destroyed four enemy fighters that morning, was rescued from being destroyed himself by Lieutenant Dean Houston who, seeing an FW 190 on his tail while Moats was attacking another 190, yelled at Moats to break. The warning saved him.

Likewise Alden Rigby rescued his leader Lieutenant Ray Littge from destruction when he shot down an FW 190 who was on the tail of his Number One. Attacking another FW 190, Rigby's gunsight light went out and he had to shoot blind, "from the hip." But his aim was true, striking the Focke Wulf along the wing roots, and it crashed into some trees. Over the airfield Rigby shot down another 190 that plowed right into the strip. At the same moment an Me 109 turned into him. Rigby fired off the last of his ammunition whereupon the Messerschmidt dived straight into the ground. That was number four for Rigby (destroying three himself and sharing in a fourth).

The other hat-trick winner, Henry Stewart, shot down his first victim right over the airfield. Pulling up, he saw another Me 109 on the deck and quickly dispatched it despite the intense friendly ground fire all around him. Finally he sent a third 109 crashing into the ground.

Whisner's Number Two, Walker Diamond, destroyed one FW 190 and damaged another. Flying at low level, he took on the first Focke-Wulf he saw and closed-in firing steady bursts. He saw strikes on the wings and fuselage, then the 190 crashed into some trees as Walker overshot it. Next, he latched onto another FW and opened fire on it. As the enemy went into a turn, Walker followed, noticing strikes on the engine and tail section. Out of ammunition, he was forced to break away, claiming a damaged.[46]

Flying as J.C. Meyer's wingman, Alex Sears, who destroyed an FW 190, had just taken off when a Messerschmidt came at him head-on. The two made several passes at each other and on the third pass, Sears got in several strikes on the enemy's engine and shot part of the tail section away. The aircraft started to burn then went into a slow spiral and crashed into the ground.

Colonel Norman Holt, commander of the 366th Fighter Group graphically described the battle which he witnessed from the ground:[47]

> The famous all-out raid by the Luftwaffe against our strips
> arrived over our base in force of approximately 50 Me 109s
> and FW 190s. The enemy was engaged immediately by a flight

of eight of our T-bolts that had just taken off and assembled. Jettisoning their bombs, they attacked the enemy planes and kept them from hitting our pitifully unprotected planes on the ground. The entire air circus took place at tree-top level directly over the strip. Roaring engines, spitting machine-guns and flaming planes going down to destruction brought the war right to our doorstep! The onslaught lasted for fully 45 minutes. A couple of our planes, out of ammunition, and low on fuel were forced to drop wheels and land in the midst of it. Alert Nazi pilots veered in on the tails of such juicy targets only to be shot down or scared away by our ack-ack gunners. One squadron commander in his eagerness, ran out and took off in his pyjamas. Sleeping late on his day off, he had leaped out of the sack to get in on the kills. Me 109s and FW 190s were flaming and auguring into the ground within sight of the entire group of officers and men.

Lieutenant John Kennedy of the 391st Fighter Squadron was another pilot who had gone into combat in his sleep wear and who told of his harrowing experience:[48]

I don't know how many planes there were, but I guess there were 50 to 60. We were in the midst of them in seconds — I don't know if I lost Capt. [Lowell B.] Smith or he lost me. With all the aircraft off the deck who could tell? I got on the tail of a 109, which at first I thought to be a Spitfire. This 109 really filled the gunsight and I got off a few rounds when I was hit in the tail. I broke to the right and, of course, those guys followed me still firing away. I got hit again in the right wing and a hell of a fire broke out. I thought about jumping, but changed my mind, because I didn't want to risk jumping through the fire. I broke to the left and flew past a slag pile with the 109s still firing away. Finally two P-51s from the

352nd drove them off and I headed for low cloud. By that time the fire was out and I headed in for a landing. Since my hydraulic fluid had burned away, I had no flaps, so I came in kind of hot. I hit the strip at over 100 mph and then found I didn't have any brakes either. I ran out of runway when the plane was still doing about 30 mph, but it finally came to a halt and I climbed out. When I got back to the tent I realised what a long night it had been. I had flown the mission with my flight suit pulled over my pyjamas.

Kennedy's squadron mate, Lieutenant Bob Brulle, had his own problems trying to land at base:[49]

When I realised I was out of ammo and broke off, I hightailed it west to get out of the area. It happened so fast that I flew right over our field and had all our AA gunners shooting at me. I rocked my wings violently and climbed to 3,000 feet, just below the cloud cover. I felt safe there, since I could duck into the clouds if any enemy aircraft came after me. From there I circled around and had a front seat to the battle below. While circling around and watching the battle, I observed a 109 heading back towards Germany, pursued by two P-51s about 1,000 yards back. As the 109 started to go below my wing, I started to roll over so I could keep an eye on him. He must have seen me, and thinking I was going to dive on him, veered away. This allowed one of the P-51s to turn inside him and get close enough to shoot him down. When there was a lull in the battle I went in and landed. Just as I was turning off the runway, two Me 109s came over. I remember seeing them come right after me, and I shut off my engine and got out of my airplane and was running away from it as they flew over. They strafed an aircraft on the other side of the field.

Then Brulle noticed that the two 109s were being chased by a Mustang which was holding its fire to avoid raking the airfield. The AA gunners now opened fire with all they had. They missed the two 109s but hit the P-51. The pilot dropped his undercarriage gear and landed. Brulle commented later, "I don't know who he was, but I'll bet he was mad!"

Nearly an hour before the fighter-bombers from Specht's Jagdgeschwader 11 assaulted his base at Ophoven Airfield at the same time as the attack was underway at Asch, Flight Lieutenant Tony Gaze, an Australian Flight Commander with 610 Squadron RAF, was leading a four-man patrol which had taken off at 0850. Mission completed, he was leading his flight back to Ophoven, arriving just north of Asch when the Germans began their attack. Gaze dived down to attack, destroying an FW 190 right on the deck after his first bursts of fire missed, the shells exploding in the ground ahead of the enemy fighter. A second burst also missed, but a third found the mark, splattering the 190's fuselage. Its flaps dropped, then the plane nosed over and hit the ground. But Gaze was immediately set upon by two P-51s who mistook his Spitfire for a Messerschmidt 109. Fortunately, they quickly recognised their error before any harm was done.

ST TROND-BRUSTEM AIRFIELD, Belgium

Adding to the losses that JG 2 had sustained on the flight to A-92 Airfield, as well as those over St Trond during the raid itself, were further casualties on the return journey to Merzhauzen. Feldwebel Werner Hohenberg, holder of the German Cross in Gold and a veteran of over 200 operational sorties, who had been shot down in the air fighting over Russia, was hit by AA fire and forced to pancake in a field, when his FW 190 Dora caught fire. Unteroffizier Johann Jager lost his life when his aircraft was hit by anti-aircraft fire, over Lontzen. The final accounting showed that the Geschwader had lost 33 pilots: 23

killed or missing, ten taken prisoner and four wounded. That was nearly 40 per cent of JG 2's total strength — a mortal blow. Those losses were staggering when compared to the negligible damage inflicted on the Americans: only two Thunderbolts destroyed and 14 damaged, all of which were repaired and flying within days. And there was not a single personnel casualty.

HEESCH AIRFIELD, Holland

After scoring his hat-trick shooting down three Messerschmidt 109s, Flying Officer Doug Cameron had returned to the airfield and landed in the hope of hastily refuelling, rearming and taking off again. Instead he was ordered to report to the intelligence officer and present a detailed report of his combat and the general situation. By the time he was finished, the raid was over. Cameron promptly jumped into a jeep and drove off in the general direction of where his last fight had taken place to claim a souvenir. But he was unable to locate the downed aircraft and returned empty handed.

The attack had been a disaster for JG 6. The Geschwader had lost 24 planes and many more damaged, seven of them from ground fire by the RAF Regiment around the airfield. Because most of the aircraft had been airborne, there was little in the way of ground targets and damage was negligible, though the Germans did manage to put a fair-sized hole in the roof of the 411 Squadron dispersal.

EINDHOVEN AIRFIELD, Holland

For the Germans the attack on Eindhoven had been a definite success. The Allied Tactical Air Force had lost an entire squadron of Typhoons on the field along with a substantial number of Spitfires. Casualties totalled 25 men killed and many more wounded. But it had also cost the Udet Jagdgeschwader ten pilots killed or missing and six taken prisoner, a loss of 22 per cent.

As the Germans scampered home away from the airfield, reactions to the raid were mixed. When Flying Officer Ted Smith and the others from 440 Squadron struggled back to their Nissen hut flight shack, they were greeted by Smith's closest buddy, Flying Officer Percy Kerse, who had not been on duty that morning and therefore had enjoyed the show at a safe distance. "Wasn't that great?" he commented enthusiastically. Smith erupted in a rage. "Why you stupid son of a bitch," he lit into his closest friend, which was the beginning of a five-minute diatribe that covered every four-letter word in his vocabulary.

Flight Lieutenant Ernie Savard, leader of one of the squadron's sections, recorded his immediate feelings: [50]

One of the Germans had crashed not far from our location [in the shell hole] and I watched to see if the pilot survived. I had made up my mind that if he left his aircraft and came towards us, I was going to shoot him. After the enemy left, we started back to our dispersal. The damage was terrible. There were aircraft and trucks burning all over the airfield. There were many dead and wounded airmen about. Of our squadron, we only had one aircraft left, and this was because it was hidden by the smoke of others burning on each side.

A squadron of rocket-firing Typhoons were located on the other side of the airfield from us. They had been armed and were facing our side of the field. Some of them were on fire, and this was causing rockets to ignite and fire in our direction. There would be a loud "whoosh," and a rocket would come screaming towards our side of the airfield just above the ground, then hit something and crash with a loud explosion. We reached our dispersal and gathered in the office under the control tower to tell each other of our experiences. While we were talking, there was another loud explosion just outside, and I could see the large plate-glass office window shatter and glass fly around us. Our own bombs, which had been on burning Typhoons just outside, and those alongside gas-filled jerrycans, had started to explode. Pieces of furniture were flying around the office. I wound up with several deep cuts on my face from the flying glass.

Making his way back to dispersal, Andy Lord of 438 Squadron recalled coming across a burnt out Me 109 with a pilot still in it. "I remember saying to the well-cooked body, 'If you had stayed home this morning, you bastard, you'd still be alive.'"[51]

Lord's squadron mate, Ed MacKay, who had not been on duty that morning but had been witness to the last moments of the attack, gave this assessment of the assault:[52]

Some of the attackers were skilled, but others were obviously not. The latter pulled up after shooting instead of escaping at high speed on the deck to avoid flak. They circled almost leisurely to select a target, and one Me 109's pilot at about 1,500 feet, midfield, seemed to be sightseeing. A Spit seemed to casually close in behind him and opened fire; he just drifted into the ground and exploded.

Ed MacKay also reported that a German pilot, who had survived the attack and had been taken prisoner, was brought before Wing Commander Paul Davoud and other senior officers on the station for interrogation. "He was a typical arrogant Nazi bastard who sneered that the German forces would still win the war. He was apparently so obnoxious that someone present muttered that shooting would be too good for him."

With black smoke darkening what had less than an hour earlier been a clear blue wintry New Year's sky, Paul Davoud, surveying the carnage, turned to his successor, Ernie Moncreif, and remarked wryly, "Well Ernie, it's all yours!"[53]

BRUSSELS-EVERE AIRFIELD, Belgium

By the time Flying Officer Bill Roddie reached the field from the doorway in which he had taken shelter, the first sight to greet him was Prince Bernhardt's sky-blue Beechcraft and the VIP passenger Dakota going up in smoke.

When the Spitfires that had been in the air had landed, the airfield was in ruins. Eleven Spitfires were destroyed and another 12 damaged. One airman had been killed and nine wounded. The Canadian pilots had brought down eight enemy planes and damaged several others. The RAF Regiment gunners guarding the field claimed three fighters destroyed and ten damaged. In the opinion of the 127 Wing Commander, Johnnie Johnson, the Germans' shooting was:[54]

> ... atrocious and the circuit at Evere reminded us more of a bunch of beginners on their first solos than pilots of front-line squadrons. Not one Spitfire should have remained undamaged at Evere. The time factor was badly planned, for the basis of the strike should have been a sharp concentrated attack. As it was, the long time spent over the airfield meant that we were able to scramble fighters from secure airfields and divert those already in the air. Tactically the attacks were well planned, but poor flying was their undoing.

BRUSSELS-GRIMBERGEN AIRFIELD, Belgium

For JG 26 and JG 54, the operations to attack this airfield proved to be a disaster. In the case of the former, which had not actually taken part in the attack, 12 aircraft failed to return from anti-aircraft fire. Gruppe III of JG 54 lost ten of its 17 pilots.

Part of the losses to Gruppe III, JG 54, took place on the return trip to Furstenau, when the Germans ran into a flight of Spitfires over Hasselt. Five pilots were killed or missing, including Staffel leader Hauptmann Willi Bottlander. Four others were known to be captured. At least three German planes came down over the densely populated area of Brussels, killing five civilians.

Another pilot shot down was the dyed-in-the-wool Nazi, Stabfeldwebel Steinkamp of JG 54, a veteran of the Russian Front and the summer air battles over France. He had a wing shot off his aircraft, forcing him to bail out. His captors found "his confidence in German victory ... unshakeable." "The faith in the whole German nation was now in the Führer," he told them, "who would find a way out to save Europe from Bolshevism; how and when the Führer knew."[55]

One of the six lost pilots from Gruppe I, JG 26, was Feldwebel Karlheinz Hartmann, who had been with his Staffel for only ten days. Hit by flak over Grimbergen after making his initial strafing run, he reported that he was bailing out. In his excitement, however, he had forgotten to turn his radio on. That was understandable — it was his first combat flight.

ASCH AIRFIELD, Belgium

Just three-quarters of an hour after they had begun their attack the fighter formations of Jagdgeschwader 11 were winging their way home with the Americans hot on their heels. The price that the Germans paid was horrendous: 40 per cent of its entire fighter pilot strength. Twenty-three German planes were destroyed by the Mustangs of the 352nd Fighter Group, four by Thunderbolts of the 366 Fighter Group and one by an RAF Spitfire. Two of the Geschwader's top fighter leaders, its Kommodore Oberstleutnant Gunther Specht and Hauptmann Horst von Fassong (Gruppe III) were killed.

OPHOVEN AIRFIELD, Belgium

American P-47 pilots from the 366th Fighter Group had been the first to spot the Germans headed for Y-32. But they were in no position to do anything about it as Oberstleutnant Gunther

Specht's Jagdgeschwader 11 Focke Wulfs and Messerschmidts bore down on their own airstrip, Y-29.

In fact, the Ophoven assailants were not part of JG 11 at all, though doubtless, in the fighting over the airfield, some of their fighters, given the proximity of the two air bases, might very well have become involved.

Most likely, though, it has never been officially substantiated, the attackers were some of the wayward stragglers from Major Gerhard Michalski's Geschwader 4 which, due to the navigational error on the part of the Ju 88 trailblazer, had become split up, with Gruppen and smaller individual sections left on their own to pick a target at will. It is not illogical to consider Ophoven as one of them. Located in the most southerly area of the 83 Group, 2nd TAF sector, it lay on a direct course 40 miles north-east from Le Culot, the Geschwader's original designated target.

If nothing else, the mix-up at least achieved the element of surprise. And under the circumstances the defenders gave a good account of themselves. The two RAF regiments fired off a total 462 rounds of anti-aircraft ammunition, claiming to have destroyed four Me 109s, and two FW 190s, as well as damaging nine 109s.

In the air, the CO of 41 Squadron, Donald Benham, got a frantic call over the blower that enemy planes were over the field. The controller ordered him to return to base — full throttle! But it was too late, too far. Too many miles separated the squadron from the airstrip. However, this inability to come to the rescue in time was somewhat compensated for by Flight Lieutenant Tony Gaze, of 610 Squadron, an Australian ace with seven victories to his credit, who managed to shoot down an FW 190. When the four-man patrol ran into intense flak from British gunners north of Liege, in taking evasive action, he became separated from the rest of the formation and decided to return to base.

A mile east of Asch, at 2,000 feet, he spotted eight Focke Wulfs in loose formation, flying low, heading north-east. Gaze dived down and zeroed in on the closest 190 from astern. As he closed to within 800 yards, the German pilot caught sight of him, opened his throttle and, hugging the ground, began corkscrewing to try and get away. With the extra speed he picked up in his dive, Gaze narrowed the range to 600 yards and despite intense ground fire all around him, let go a two-second burst but missed, his shells bursting on the ground ahead of the target. He fired again, and once again missed the target. But his third burst did the trick. As the 190 rose over a clump of trees, Gaze's machine-gun and cannon fire splattered its fuselage and belly. Its flaps flopped down, and as Gaze flew over the aircraft, it nosed forward and struck the ground. With friendly ground fire still harassing him, he dodged his way at zero feet as best he could in the direction of Ophoven.

On the ground, 125 Wing got off lightly. Only ten Spitfires were damaged and a fuel dump was set on fire. Three airmen were wounded, one of whom was a corporal with the servicing echelon of 310 Squadron. After being struck by an exploding cannon shell, he was pulled out of the line of fire by two of the unit's pilots, Sergeant Paul Standish and Flight Sergeant Phil Clay, an action that saved his life.

Later, Clay, at personal risk, taxied two Spitfires out of danger despite the hazard of enemy strafing and ammunition from burning aircraft exploding all about him. He then directed the crew of a fire tender in fighting a blaze that saved 200 gallons of high-octane fuel. For his exploits, Clay was promoted to the rank of Warrant Officer and awarded the British Empire Medal for bravery above and beyond the call of duty.

MALDEGEM AIRFIELD, Belgium

By the time Flight Lieutenant Bob Fowler and his gang arrived at Maldegem — in an army truck — the raid was over. Fowler described the chaos he remembered seeing that morning:[56]

Columns of black smoke were rising from the airfield. It was like a scene from Dante. One lone fire-fighting jeep was squirting a forlorn stream of extinguisher fluid on a burning Spitfire. Like the others, it had logged only an hour or two of production testing and ferrying time. Other Spits were burning furiously, and people were being kept back in case one exploded. Fire-fighting equipment was almost non-existent. All that was left of several Spitfires were lumps of charred metal that had been a Merlin engine, a bit of tail section, undercarriage legs with wheels almost burned off, melted propellers, and a few 20-mm cannons. Some Spitfires looked unharmed until one got up close and could see the cannon holes and grooves that had reduced them to attractive junk.

We were surprised to see the ground littered with 13-mm shells and belt links that must have followed along with the 109s and 190s during their strafing runs.

The technical officer drove us up in his jeep, and laughingly told us he didn't think he would be able to do much for our Ansons, and I suggested we have a look at them.

Our two Ansons were a forlorn sight. The tires were flat on both aircraft. [Flight Lieutenant] Bruce White's had a large hole blown through the right wing. I had an old folding Kodak with me and we stood Bruce and Norm [Powell] in the hole while I took a few pictures. I took a picture of a cannon hole in the left side of the fuselage of my Anson where the navigator sat in front of the Gee box. There was no doubt those Ansons were never going to fly again.

Fowler later added this finale to his unforgettable experience that day : "It was a great treat to be able to see 190s and 109s in action so closely, and to have a ringside seat to what was later recognised as a significant event in the history of the air warfare of WW II ... for a long time one of the best-kept secrets of the war ... it was some years before I read any detailed information on the Luftwaffe attack of New Year's Day, 1945."

GHENT, Belgium

After 40 minutes over the target, a badly mauled and thoroughly dispirited Gruppe II of Geschwader 1 had started home to Drope Airfield. The morning outing had been a disastrous one for Jagdgeschwader 1 which all told had lost 24 pilots — 12 killed, six taken prisoner, one wounded and five missing. While losses to the Allies in numbers of aircraft were substantial, pilot casualties were relatively light — on the airfield at St Denis-Westram alone, some 25 Spitfires, an American Flying Fortress and a British Stirling bomber were destroyed but only two Polish pilots had been killed.

Most significantly as far as the Germans were concerned was the loss of some of their most experienced pilots. Among those killed were: the Gruppe II leader Hauptmann Hans-Georg Hackbarth, Feldwebel Paul Mayr, Leutnant Ernst von Johannides, Feldwebel Harry Klints and Unteroffizier Karl Hahn. Having lost a third of his pilot strength, JG 1 Kommodore Oberstleutnant Herbert Ihlefeld made no secret of his bitterness and disgust over the damage to his Gerschwader through the ill-conceived, hastily prepared Operation Bodenplatte — a total waste to no good purpose.

VOLKEL AIRFIELD, Holland

In all, the Tempest pilots had scored eight German fighters destroyed, one probably shot down and four damaged. Together with the fighting at Heesch, Jagdgeschwader 6's abortive attempt to attack Vokel had resulted in the loss of 32 fighters destroyed and many more damaged. But even more significant than the quantity of casualties was the quality. Among them:

the Geschwader Kommodore Oberstleutnant Johann Kogler and Hauptmann Ewald Trost, commander of Gruppe I, were shot down and taken prisoner; commander of Gruppe III, Major Helmut Kuhle, and Staffel leader Hauptmann Norbert Katz were both killed. These were the calibre of casualties the German Fighter Command could ill afford.

BRUSSELS-MELSBROEK AIRFIELD, Belgium

It was carnage on both sides. German Focke Wulf 190 and Messerschmidt 109 fighters seemed to be everywhere, darting in and out and across the field, climbing and diving, spitting fire in all directions, picking off targets at will. There was a plethora of sitting ducks: Mitchells, Mosquitoes, Spitfires and Wellingtons, a smattering of B-17 Flying Fortresses, B-24 Liberators and P-47 Thunderbolts as well as a flight of harmless old Handley Page Harrow transports from the Sparrow Squadron.

There was no relief from the air. Melsbroek's Spitfires were either out on a distant mission or nailed to the ground by the attack. The airfield had to fend for itself. Anti-aircraft defences were limited — six guns from one RAF Regiment squadron battery had been relocated for anti-flying bomb defence. One flight only had Bren guns at its disposal. Individuals pitched in as best they could with revolvers and any firearms they could lay there hands on. Squadron Leader "Chunky" Chown, the 139 Wing Engineering Officer, blasted away at the marauders with a double-barrelled shotgun.

All the same these somewhat anaemic ground defences took their toll. On his fifth pass over the field after destroying at least five aircraft, Gruppe IV JG 27 leader Hauptmann Hans-Heinz Dudeck's FW 190 was so riddled with fire he was forced to bail out, but his parachute snagged on the tail of the aircraft, tearing it before he shook loose. His fall was broken when he tumbled into the branches of a tree, badly injuring him but also saving his life. Rescued by British soldiers, he was taken prisoner. Fahnrich Otto Theissen shared a similar fate though he was able to get down all in one piece but was severely burned. He too was taken into custody. Unteroffizier Gerhard Ohlenschlager from Geschwader 54 also fell victim to the ground fire. He ploughed his shot-up Messerschmidt into the centre of the field and climbed out of the cockpit, only to spend the rest of the war in captivity.

It was lucky for Flight Lieutenant Hugh Tudor and Flying Officer Ian Ewing that the latter had forgotten his pipe; otherwise they would have been strapped in the seats of their Mosquito. When the raid was over and they surveyed the damage, Tudor's leather flying helmet, which was hanging over the control column, had two bullet holes in it and his parachute was shredded. The aircraft was a complete write-off.

When Wing Commander Mike Shaw arrived at his office after the Germans had gone, it was to find that a bullet had pierced the window and embedded itself on the other side of his desk. Had he been sitting at it during the raid, the bullet would have gone right through his head.

When the 35 Mitchells from 139 Wing, which were in the air and had been spared sure destruction on the field, finished their mission bombing the Dasburg road centre, they were diverted to Epinoy Airfield. It was not until late afternoon that the field had been cleared up enough for them to land back at their own base.

METZ-FRESCATY AIRFIELD, France

The crunch of anti-aircraft fire explosions splotching the clear blue morning sky and the sight of a cluster of single-seater aircraft swooping across the field, skimming the treetops startled ground crews and pilots alike out of their complacency. At first the Messerschmidts of the Pik As (Ace of Spades) Jagdgeschwader 53, what was left of it, were mistaken for Spitfires. One observer pointed out, "They're in loose formation. The Limeys like to fly like that!" Two crewmen, Sergeants George Wasson and John Lehnert of the 386th Fighter Squadron, standing near a shell hole, chatting idly, while enjoying a smoke, mistook them for American Mustangs. "Look at those goddam P-51s buzzing the field, the crazy bastards," Wasson yelled. "P-51s my ass," Lehnert shouted back as gunfire suddenly erupted, "They're fucking Germans! Watch out!" Both dived for the shelter of the shell hole.[57]

Others took whatever cover they could, leaping into slit trenches, ditches, foxholes, furrows, ground depressions, anything handy without thought to the consequences. Sergeant Dave Hutchins of the 388th Fighter Squadron was seated on one of the outdoor latrines taking his time over his regular morning dump while scanning the *Stars and Stripes* when he heard the rattle of machine-gun fire. Caught with his pants down and literally "scared shitless," he dived right into "it" without hesitation. The CO of the 386th Fighter Squadron, Major George Brooking, found himself in a similar situation: squatting on the can in the officers' toilet tent. When he heard the sound of gunfire he looked out the tent flap to see a flight of Me 109s, all 16 of which appeared to be aiming straight at him. Brooking promptly swan-dived into a snow bank, with his pants dangling around his ankles — not a pretty sight, but a lot better, and a whole less fetid, than that of the turd-covered Sergeant Hutchins.

Most people recall their twenty-first birthday with fond memories. In the case of Corporal Irving Wassermann of the 387th Fighter Squadron, it was a particular anniversary he could never forget. Wasserman was towing a pair of trailers each loaded with a dozen 500-pound bombs, unaware that anything was amiss. The noise of his truck engine drowned out the sound of the attacking enemy aircraft. But, when he saw bullets splashing in the snow in front of him, he quickly jumped from his vehicle and plunged into a foxhole adjacent to the bomb dump. His coming of age proved to be his lucky day. The Messerschmidt fire missed the bomb dump and Wassermann later discovered a shell casing on the driver's seat of his truck.

Captain Tom Stanton's "alert" Thunderbolt at the end of the runway presented the first and foremost target for the attackers. Before he could do anything about it, an Me 109 took aim and drilled his fire directly at the P-47. Fortunately for Stanton, in his overzealousness, the enemy pilot missed the aircraft, splattering his cannon fire all around the machine but not a single strike on it. Stanton's "missing" wingman, Flight Lieutenant Sam Lutz, who was too late to join him at the end of the runway, sought shelter behind a steamroller. From there he snapped off a couple of frustrated, random shots with his Colt .45 automatic at the enemy fighter which was so low, "I could have reached out and touched the German pilot." A 650-calibre cannon shell from the anti-aircraft defence gunners struck the pilot in one eye and sent the Messerschmidt smashing into the runway. The body of the pilot was thrown from the shattered wreck, hurtled along the tarmac, bouncing up and down until it rolled to a stop. But this macabre sight failed to stop a couple of ground gunners from running out and pulling the flying boots off the battered, inert body to keep as souvenirs.

Another Me 109 that hit the deck as the result of being peppered by anti-aircraft fire was even more grisly. As the machine broke apart the pilot was decapitated, both his legs chopped off above the knee, and the rest of him mutilated beyond recognition. Even that didn't deter one ghoulish souvenir hunter who, undeterred by the gruesome sight of the carved-up carcass, calmly unfastened the wristwatch from the corpse and pocketed it.

By comparison, the fate of Luftwaffe Oberfeldwebel Stefen Kohl, who was flying his first mission since being hospitalised back in August, was lucky. As he crossed the airfield perimeter from the south-east, the engine of his Me 109 was riddled by machine-gun fire from the ground. Kohl managed to climb to 1,200 feet and bail out over the small French hamlet of Marly.

He was captured and taken to the airfield to be held in custody before being turned over to Army Intelligence for interrogation and eventually to a POW camp. His jailers in the Y-34 guard-house found him "cocky and insolent." He refused to allow them to photograph him until "he'd combed his hair and shined his boots." They were also surprised to discover that he spoke English fluently.

Though no pilots were lost in the shoot-up, one was injured and three of the ground crew were wounded. Second Lieutenant Carl Riggs, who had been one of those left behind from the 388th Fighter Squadron's morning sortie, was injured when a 109, hit by a volley of bullets which killed the pilot, hit the run-way and did pinwheels into a hangar where Riggs had taken ref-uge. Staff Sergeant Robert Gabarine of the 386th Fighter Squad-ron was on the wing of a P-47, refuelling it, when a bullet creased his skull and knocked him to the ground unconscious. Staff Sergeant Kirby Garner was hit in the arm while servicing another 386th Thunderbolt. Corporal Lee Welden of the 388th was working in the cockpit of a bombed-up Thunder-bolt when a bullet pierced his thigh and set fire to the aircraft. Welden was trapped, unable to extricate himself from the aircraft. Fortunately, one his crewmates, Corporal Emanuel Catanuto, rushed to his rescue. Fighting his way through the smoke and flames, he pulled Welden out of the cockpit, dragging him 30 yards away from the P-47 seconds before it exploded. For his bravery Catanuto received the Soldier's Medal to add to the Bronze Star and Silver Star he had won two weeks previously for attacking a German gun position and killing seven of the enemy. At the time, he had been serving with the 45th Infan-try Division before transferring to the Air Corps.

Three other acts of heroism that morning earned two of the ground crew of the 386th Fighter Squadron the Soldier's Medal as well. When one of the Thunderbolts parked next to another bombed-up P-47 was set ablaze, Staff Sergeant John Lawless and Sergeant Olin Holcomb, in the face of concentrated enemy strafing, grabbed fire extinguishers and put out the flames, preventing a serious explosion which could have spread to other aircraft parked on the field.

When a fuel tanker, hooked up to the P-47 under his charge, caught fire, crew chief Staff Sergeant Gordon Hurt, with the help of two others, got the aircraft started and taxied it out of range of the burning fuel truck.

When the 388th Fighter Squadron's "unwanted" spare, First Lieutenant Lavern Alcorn, eventually arrived back at the Frescaty Airfield and lined up on the runway for a landing, his aircraft was suddenly bracketed by exploding flak from his own anti-aircraft gunners. He began a series of violent evasive manoeuvres which the ground gunners took for a display of aerobatics, then, finally recognising the P-47 as one of "ours" abruptly stopped shooting at it. By this time, the raid was over anyway, ending as quickly as it had begun. The Germans had disappeared, leaving in their wake the smouldering wreckage of 22 destroyed and seven damaged "Hells Hawks" Thunderbolts, as well as a couple of dozen trucks, fuel tankers and other vehicles burning and smoking. Alcorn jettisoned both his 500-pound bombs and chased off in the direction he calculated the Germans had fled for home. But no luck! And, by this time the returning 365 Fighter Group squadrons (the 387th and 388th) were even more frustrated at arriving too late.

Over and above the casualties incurred by Gruppe III from P-47s which bounced the Messerschmidts before they reached the target area, during the raid itself, Gruppen II and IV of the Geschwader each lost seven pilots (five killed and two taken prisoner) and each had a pilot wounded. By comparison, not a single American pilot was lost, nor were any airborne aircraft damaged.

Two days later, 386th Fighter Squadron CO Major George Brooking had the group's German prisoner Oberfeldwebel

Stefan Kohl brought to his office for questioning. He found that his imprisonment had in no way mollified the Luftwaffe Oberfeldwebel's Teutonic arrogance or militancy. Time for the American major to make his point. Brooking pointed at a row of spanking new, shining P-47 Thunderbolt replacements lined up awaiting inspection. "What do you think about that?" he asked Kohl. The prisoner stared at the floor. Some of the cockiness went out of him but none of the Nazi defiance. "That," he replied slowly, deliberately, "is the only reason you are winning."

GILZE-REIJEN AIRFIELD, Holland

Near Eindhoven, Flight Lieutenant Dave Mercer of 268 Squadron chased three FW 190s away from the field. As he closed in on one them which still had its bomb aboard, he pressed the trigger and there was nothing but a hiss of air; he had run out of ammunition. He pulled up alongside the 190 and when the pilot turned to look at him, Mercer responded with the V-for-Victory sign. The enemy pilot pulled away and dropped his bomb harmlessly into an open field. "He probably never realised how near he had been to getting the chop," Mercer reported later.

Mercer's next problem was that he was short on fuel. He had to throttle back "low on revs and lean mixture." It was hardly conducive to the situation in which he now found himself.[58]

> I nearly got clobbered by four American Mustangs who probably had heard of the troubles and were coming for a look-see .... They were the Mustangs with the Packard engine, all silver, and me being an Allison Mustang, all camouflaged for low level, they must have thought I was an Me 109. I had to do a lot of wing waggling and showing of the roundels [the military identifying mark] before they left me alone.

HAUS DER FLIEGER, BERLIN, Germany

While his Staffeln were being decimated over and around the Allied tactical airfields across Belgium, France and Holland, Hermann Goering was in a state of euphoria under the illusion that his Jagdgerschwadern would by this time have wiped out his enemy's tactical air forces on the ground. Bodenplatte, for which he had given the final authorisation the previous day, had won him back favour with Hitler — at least temporarily. Having breakfasted in sumptuous comfort and splendour in his luxurious private train parked nearby, the Reichsmarschall entered Luftwaffe Headquarters where he issued a proclamation that oozed with such smug pride and satisfaction that it must have turned the stomach of those German fighter pilots returning from their missions:[59]

> Comrades of the Luftwaffe!
>
> A year, heavy with fateful tests, has come to a close. In the teeth of all opposition and in spite of all our needs and worries, the year found us more than ever ready to fight steadfastly to do our duty. On the threshold of a new year, we turn our gaze, full of trust and hope, to the future. At the present time, we see the first fruits of the hard and dogged work of the reconstruction of the Luftwaffe to maturity. With your new Geschwader, which have again risen, with exemplary paratroops, zealous flak gunners ... our air force will continue to prove that it will continue in the old tried-and-true ways. We bow our heads in homage and proudly mourn our dead, who at the front and at home, laid down their lives for Germany. Their sacrifice fills us with glowing faith.

Endnotes

1 John Edison, conversations, 1984.
2 Robert Bracken, *Spitfire: The Canadians,* p. 122.

3 Norman Franks, *The Battle of the Airfields,* p. 51.

4 Franks, p. 52.

5 Franks, p. 56.

6 Ken Langmuir, interview, June 15, 1997.

7 Eric Downer, interview, May 1, 1996.

8 Franks, p. 95.

9 Danny S. Parker, *To Win the Winter Sky,* p. 423.

10 Dick DeBruin, correspondence, October 24, 1996.

11 Parker, p. 389.

12 Franks, p. 121.

13 Franks, pp. 121-22.

14 Franks, p. 123.

15 Franks, p. 77.

16 Franks, p. 78.

17 Bob Fowler, correspondence, June 10, 1996.

18 Franks, p. 112.

19 Bill Baggs, interview, November 9, 1997.

20 Andy Lord, correspondence, May 6, 1996.

21 Ted Smith, interview, May 15, 1996.

22 Ernie Savard, correspondence, June 1, 1996.

23 Ted Smith, interview, May 15, 1996.

24 Jim Prendergast, interviews and correspondences, June 1996 to September 1997.

25 Gordon Hill, correspondence, July 26, 1996.

26 Franks, p. 60.

27 Franks, p. 60.

28 Franks, p. 55.

29 J.E. Johnson, *Wing Leader,* p. 271.

30 Parker, p. 389.

31 Parker, p. 387.

32 Parker, p. 387.

33 Franks, p. 41.

34 Bill Baggs, interview, October 11, 1997.

35 John Edison, interviews, 1994.

36 Len Wilson, *Invasion without Tears,* pp. 162-65.

37 Ed MacKay, correspondence, March 1, 1996.

38 Hugh A. Halliday, *Typhoon and Tempest: The Canadian Story,* p. 106.

39 Halliday, pp. 106-07.

40 Parker, pp. 424-25.

41 Dick Reeves, interview, July 11, 1996.

42 Franks, p. 99.

43 Dick Rreeves, interview, July 11, 1996.

44 Bill Roddie, correspondence, July 8, 1996.

45 Franks, p. 133.

46 Franks, p. 135.

47 Parker, p. 389.

48 Parker, p. 390.

49 Parker, p. 388.

50 Ernie Savard, correspondence, June 1, 1986.

51 Andy Lord, correspondence, May 6, 1996.

52 Ed MacKay, correspondence, March 1, 1996.

53 Johnnie Johnson, speech to the Canadian Air Force Association.

54 Johnson, p. 272.

55 Parker, pp. 203-04.

56 Bob Fowler, correspondence, May 1, 1996.

57 Franks, p. 111.

58 Franks, p. 42.

59 Parker, p. 450.

CHAPTER 6

RESPONSE

In the chaos created by Bodenplatte on those fields most heavily hit, there were fires to be extinguished, wounded to be attended to, dead to be buried and wreckage to be cleared. But the premium was still to get on with the war, to put the Allied planes back in the air and give back as good as they got.

January 1, 1945

1000 Hours
EINDHOVEN AIRFIELD, Holland

At 83 Group Headquarters, Air Vice Marshal Harry Broadhurst had no way of telling to what extent or even which of his airfields and his fighters and fighter-bomber squadrons had sustained damage. But he was determined that, whatever the loss was, to give the Germans the immediate impression that it was a lot less than what it really amounted to. His boss, Air Marshal Sir Arthur "Mary" Coningham, agreed with him. Broadhurst immediately signalled all his wing leaders to get airborne as soon as possible and once in the air to use every last wing call sign over the R/T to show the Luftwaffe that 2nd TAF was still very much alive and flying.

Eindhoven, by far the hardest hit of all the tactical airfields and indeed the Luftwaffe's most successful attack by far, was left in a shambles. Flight Lieutenant Ed MacKay of 438 RCAF Typhoon Squadron, gave this graphic description:[1]

There certainly was a gigantic mess to be cleaned up. A group of us inspected various shot-down aircraft. One was an FW 190. It looked like the pilot hadn't pulled out from a strafing attack soon enough. It had mushed into the ground and shot across the field. It was surprisingly intact, cowlings and hood had sprung; the pilot's body was some distance away. We turned him over and it seemed every bone had been smashed and half his face was missing. I remember marvelling at the compact exposed innards around and behind the 190's engine, and the neat intricate electric circuitry.

I visited sick quarters which was like the front-line casualty stations in the movies — blood on the floors, personnel attending bullet, shrapnel and burn wounds. Pete Wilson [the CO of

438 Squadron] was lying on a table, his legs dangling over the edge. A towel was stuffed in a gaping stomach wound, and he was dying. I held his hand and called his name. His eyes moved, and he seemed to acknowledge me, but they glazed over in a stare, and I think he died right then. He had been CO for only one day.

At some time during the day, I saw corpses sewn up in blankets lined up behind sick quarters; one was very small, the remains of an airman who was beside a refuelling bowser when it was hit.

I was assigned as one of the officers in charge of the burial party for the Germans in a local cemetery. I had very mixed feelings. The enemy was entitled to a respectful burial, as I would expect them to do for us, but I was disgusted to find that someone had taken the trouble to get a covering Nazi swastika flag for the burial. To me it was totally out of place and gave solemn recognition to an evil symbol, forced on Europe by a murderous, totally ruthless gang of cut-throats.

Another gripping account came from the 143 RCAF Typhoon Wing medical report:[2]

Sick quarters were busy [on that] first day of the New Year. Luckily there were few patients in sick quarters, and when it became evident that we would receive many casualties from the drome after the enemy had wished us Happy New Year, they were told to dress and get out, no more no less. Shortly after the guns had stopped, the wounded started coming in. Some walked, others were brought in three tonners, 15 hundred weights, bowsers, anything ... and in a very few minutes the floors of our large ward and the corridors were literally covered with an anonymous mass of gaping wounds and bloody uniforms. One airman in the corner was screaming and waving in the air two mangled hands that hardly seemed attached at all to the arms. The rest of the wounded seemed surprised to find themselves there; they were silent and patient, waiting for someone to take care of them. One chap who had trouble with varicose veins looked at his shattered leg and said, "They sure fixed my veins for me." He died the next day. Another, whose arm was almost severed at the shoulder, was saying, "If they put me to sleep and I wake up without arms, I shall go crazy." Such sights may be common in army sick quarters, but 143 Wing was not accustomed to desolation. To us, it seemed particularly ugly.

Pain was alleviated, wounds were dressed summarily, and the wounded evacuated as quickly as possible in the midst of explosions that shattered our windows and managed to produce a few more cuts. The staff worked hard. The drivers were right on the bit. We got help from the outside, and every patient had left within an hour and a half. In that time, we handled 63 patients and evacuated 49.

In the afternoon, the mess was cleaned up and the dead prepared for burial — these included four enemy pilots. The next few days we were still busy, but in a different manner, trying to clarify the confusion that reigned in our reports, finding out where patients had to go, what, in detail, was the matter with them, how they were getting along. There were also many broken windows to repair and repainting to be done. We definitely did not think much of Hitler's talent as an interior decorator.

A fact worthy of note. On January 1, four airmen were on sick parade; this was to take place at 10 o'clock, and, of course was cancelled. We never saw those blokes again ... how sick were they? The next few days we coped with the aftermath. Many small injuries were treated .... We also tried to quiet the unstable minds and found our equipment meagre when it came to dealing with "shattered nerves." The psychiatrist was (and still is) busy.

1030 Hours
VOLKEL AIRFIELD, Belgium

First off the ground, once Broadhurst gave the order to "get them back in the air," were nine Tempests of 80 Squadron led by their CO, Squadron Leader Bob Spurdle, on an armed recce over the Paderborn-Bielefeld area. Around 1130 hours north-west of Munster, while returning to base, Canadian Flying Officer Johnny Garland spotted a "bogie" flying north-east on the deck. He half-rolled and dived down after it. As he levelled out he saw another aircraft some distance ahead of the first one he'd spotted. He was close enough now to identify them as long-nosed Focke Wulf 190D-9s. Closing in on the rearmost Dora he fired a short burst from 200 yards that blasted pieces off the fuselage. A second burst ripped into the wing roots and set the belly tank on fire. Then he overshot, but as he whipped by, he saw the entire aircraft catch fire and crash into some woods. He then went after the second enemy plane.

As it banked to the left he opened fire and with two perfect deflection shots sent it diving down on fire into a field where it bounced several times, the wings breaking off, and smashed into some trees.

1043 Hours
ASCH AIRFIELD, Belgium

Like his 83 Group counterpart, General Elwood "Pete" Quesada, commander of the 9th Tactical Air Command of the 9th USAF, wanted as many of his planes in the air as quickly as possible following the raid to show the Germans that damage to his squadrons had been negligible — which in fact it was. The 366th Fighter Group responded immediately by sending out seven

Thunderbolts of the 389th Fighter Squadron, led by First Lieutenant James Taylor, to dive-bomb targets in the vicinity of Lashed where they destroyed a Tiger tank and damaged four trucks.

1100 Hours
BRUSSELS-EVERE AIRFIELD, Belgium

With the runway finally cleared of the three shot-up Spitfires of 416 Squadron abandoned by Warrant Officer Lou Jean and Flying Officer Len Commerford and Eric Downer, Squadron Leader Danny Brown of 421 Squadron RCAF took off with eight of his Spitfire XVIs — two of which aborted shortly after getting airborne — to go looking for trouble. The remainder had to settle for beating up a few ground targets, a train, some trucks and a factory. But the exercise achieved its purpose. The Germans were getting an earful from the R/T chatter they were listening in on and knew that the Canadians were in the air and raring to go.

Later what was left of 416 Squadron reconnoitred the Bruhl-Mayen area searching for enemy aircraft but without result.

VOLKEL AIRFIELD, Holland

Simultaneously four Typhoons of 175 Squadron were sent out to attack the marshalling yards in the Munster-Rhine region. A pair of Australians, Flying Officer Tom Hall and Pilot Officer Will Speedy were forced to turn back. Hall's aircraft took a hit in the port fuel tank from ground fire while the Sabre engine of Hall's Typhoon started to run rough. Both made it home safely to B-80. En route Speedy strafed a German staff car which literally leaped off the road and ended on its side in a ditch.

Back at the field, for Pilot Officer Ron Pottinger, the unused spare Tempest pilot with 3 Squadron, it seemed that his expired operations tour was never going to end. Now he found himself on the roster for a patrol after lunch. That one "last" flight was to have ironic consequences.

1112 Hours
ASCH AIRFIELD, Belgium

Over Scheid, eight Thunderbolts of the 390th Fighter Squadron led by First Lieutenant Cecil Brotton Jr. ran into such intense and accurate light flak that their attempt at bombing trucks in the area was unsuccessful and had to be abandoned. However, 21 minutes later another eight "Jugs" from the 391st, led by Lieutenant William Johnson, damaged ten of some 30 tanks in the battle zone.

1130 Hours
ANTWERP-DEURNE AIRFIELD, Belgium

With the ice that had kept them grounded finally cleared from the runway at B-70, the Typhoon fighter-bombers of 145 Wing, which had escaped from the abortive attack by Major Erich Leie's Jagdgeschwader 77 with a minimum of damage, were at last able to take to the air. Leading off was 197 Squadron headed up by Flight Lieutenant Robert Curwen, followed five minutes later by A Flight of 193 Squadron led by Flight Lieutenant Jimmy Simpson. Next, 257 Squadron led by Flight Lieutenant Stan Eaton, 263 Squadron skippered by Ronnie Sheward and 266 Squadron under the leadership of Squadron Leader John Deall, took off in quick succession. By 1155 hours the entire wing was airborne, on its way to selected ground targets.

Curwen's pilots attacked the German occupied village of Mauween, wiping it off the map. But although Simpson's flight — less one pilot who had to drop out with engine trouble — dropped 14 bombs aimed at a bridge at Vianen, it failed to score a single hit. Eaton's Typhoons had better luck. Despite the flak they encountered during their low-level bombing attack against the bridge near Beesch on the Utrecht road, only one aircraft was slightly damaged from the ground fire and they blew a gaping hole in the target. Sheward's 263 Squadron scored 56 direct rocket hits on more than 20 barges east of Dordrecht, while Deall's pilots also successfully struck at barges and blew up an ammunition warehouse in the same neighbourhood.

At noon, 74 "Tiger" Squadron led by Flight Lieutenant Donald Usher and 345 Free French Squadron commanded by Capitaine Jacques Lemaire from 145 Spitfire Wing, took off to fly fighter escort to a group of 9th USAF B-26 Marauder medium-bombers. Their purpose was to plaster targets south of Trier and cut off the German escape routes for Marshal von Rundstedt, who led the German forces during the Battle of the Bulge, from what had, by this time, become known as the "Rundstedt Pocket."

1200 Hours
HEESCH AIRFIELD, Holland

Led by Squadron Leader John Newell, 411 Squadron Spitfires flew a sweep over Münster and Osnabruck, but it proved uneventful. Not a single enemy aircraft was to be found. But as soon as CO Dean Dover got his 412 Squadron off the ground, the controller, Flight Lieutenant John Edison, radioed that enemy aircraft were in the vicinity of Venlo, which at the time he feared might be the signal for a second German air strike. It turned out to be something less than that. Halfway to Venlo to investigate, Dover spotted a Focke Wulf 190 on the deck headed north-east. He dived down and chased after it from behind, closing to a distance of less than 100 yards — so close he couldn't miss. He didn't. His cannon and machine-gun fire peppered the enemy plane's tail. Meanwhile, his Number Two, Flying Officer Eric Kelly, let go a three-second burst from 300 yards narrowing the range to 75. The 190 burst into flames and crashed into a wood where it exploded.

Nor had Flying Officer Wilfred Banks been idle. When he saw a twin-engine Junkers 88 beneath him hugging the ground, he flipped over onto his back and swept in behind it. His initial burst struck the port engine and smoke began to stream from it.

His second salvo set the aircraft on fire. It crashed into a field and blew up. Just to round out the foray, Dover led his 12 Spitfires in a strafing attack on a train south of Hamm.

1215 Hours
BRUSSELS-MELSBROEK AIRFIELD, Belgium

Flight Lieutenant Edward Dutt of 16 Squadron took off on a photographic reconnaissance of German airfields in the Ruhr canal area around Dortmund. On reaching his destination he was intercepted by several FW 190s but they did not seem too anxious to mix it up. After a brief skirmish, although the Germans held the advantage of numbers, they broke off and headed north-east, leaving Dutt free to complete his mission.

1230 Hours
PLANTLUNNE AIRFIELD, Germany

When he landed his flak-damaged Messerschmidt, Walter "Count" Krupinski was elated over the performance of his Gruppe III (JG 26) in the attack on Evere. They had shot down at least three Canadian Spitfires and left the field in a shambles, fires all over the place. And of the 29 of his 109s that had taken off, only four pilots had been lost and one wounded. It was quite a feat. As far as he was concerned, Bodenplatte was a success. He summoned his surviving pilots for a gala lunch, starting with several rounds of schnapps before tucking in to the victory meal. But his unit was about the only one in the Luftwaffe that New Year's Day with any reason to rejoice, and things were not about to get a whole lot better before it was over.

1235 Hours
VOLKEL AIRFIELD, Belgium

Shortly after lunch 12 Tempests from Squadron Commander Spike Umbers' 486 New Zealand Squadron were sent aloft on an armed recce, two of which had to turn back with engine trouble. The remaining ten encountered more than 50 FW 190s over the Paderborn area around 1235 hours. But as soon as the Tempests gave chase, the German aircraft turned tail, dived low and disappeared. The New Zealanders had to take solace in beating up a railway signal box instead.

0100 Hours
EINDHOVEN AIRFIELD, Holland

The field had been devastated beyond recognition as an operational fighter-bomber-reconnaissance aircraft base, but by lunchtime it had been sufficiently cleared to open again for business. Two raids by rocket-firing Typhoons from 124 Wing were ordered out simultaneously. Six aircraft from 181 Squadron led by Flight Lieutenant Len Boucher and another six led by Flight Lieutenant Bert Tatham took off one after the other. Boucher's aircraft directed their attention to trains around Euskirchen, while Tatham's pilots concentrated on firing their rockets at transport in the same area.

Less than an hour later, Australian Flight Lieutenant Johnny Stubbs led another six Typhoons on a strike against road transport in the St Vith area. Despite heavy ground fire the flight returned to base without damage to any of the aircraft.

0135 Hours
GILZE-REIJEN AIRFIELD, Holland and
CHIEVRES AIRFIELD, France

Flight Lieutenant Bill Baggs and five of his mates with 164 Squadron took off from Gilze to join the rest of 123 Wing at Chievres. Halfway there, their Typhoons were mistaken for FW 190s by a flight of American Mustangs from one of the local fighter squadrons which rushed them. Angrily Baggs fired off his rockets at the P-51s but it failed to dissuade them. Three of the Tiffies were shot down. On arrival at the Belgium airfield the Typhoon pilots encountered one of the Mustang pilots who was regaling his buddies with how he had got the better of a pair of 190s. Baggs begged to differ — in no uncertain terms! After his initial outburst and the Mustang's pilot's horror at what he had done, both pilots squared off at the bar. *C'est la guerre.* This case of mistaken identity was not an isolated one by any means. The FW 190 and the Typhoon resembled each other, particularly in profile, and especially from a distance or where visibility was impaired by atmospheric conditions.

0200 Hours
OPHOVEN AIRFIELD, Belgium

Another case of mistaken identity led to no harm. Four Spitfires from 610 Squadron led by Flight Lieutenant Jack Sheppard were patrolling the Malmedy area. The warning came over the R/T that FW 190s were over their base. Was it another attack? They took no chances but immediately wheeled around back to the airfield where, on close inspection, the Focke Wulfs turned out to be Typhoons — the same Typhoons from 164 Squadron, three of which had already been shot down by Mustangs.

0215 Hours
ANTWERP-DEURNE AIRFIELD, Belgium

Squadron Leader Rastus Erasmus led eight of his 193 Squadron's bomb-carrying Typhoons on a mission to attack a busy crossroads south of Mauween during which Flying Officer Charlie Hall's aircraft was the only casualty. It took a cannon shell which exploded in the starboard main tank. However, he managed to coax his machine safely back to base.

Meanwhile Flight Lieutenant Robert Curwen, leading 197 Squadron, attacked targets around Arlborg, while at Kerzersveer, Jack Deall's 266 Squadron pilots set a factory on fire with their cannons and rockets. As both units returned to base, Flying Officer Arthur Proctor of 263 Squadron led eight Typhoons on an assault against a church spire near the town of Hedel, on the north side of the Meuse River. The Germans had established an observation post there and were causing grief to ground forces in the district. The Typhoons scored 16 hits on the steeple, knocking it out of commission for which they later received a "thank you" signal from their grateful khaki-clad comrades-in-arms.

0221 Hours
ASCH AIRFIELD, Belgium

Soon after lunch, pilots of the 391st Fighter Squadron found themselves over Herschied on a free-for-all mission against ground targets. Led by Major Sheldon Brinson, with their 500-pound bombs and machine-guns, the Thunderbolts destroyed eight trucks outside the town, blasted five others and damaged four light tanks. Later they strafed German soldiers they found marching along a road.

0230 Hours
VOLKEL AIRFIELD, Holland

Tempest 3 Squadron Pilot Officer Ron Pottinger, with three others, took off on the flight which was to mark the oft-postponed end of his tour of operations. The patrol was uneventful, not another aircraft, friendly or unfriendly, to be seen anywhere. But on the return flight at 8,000 feet over Haltern, the Tempests ran into flak, heavy and accurate. Pottinger's aircraft received several hits in the engine. With oil spewing everywhere and the temperature reaching the danger point, he took to his parachute, drifting down into a wood alongside some railway tracks. Stripping off his parachute and looking about for a place to hide, he was spotted by some German children and eventually picked up by an army patrol. Taken to a nearby railway signal box he was locked up in a room below it. Later his captors marched him to Dulmen where he ended up in the town hall jail.

Some days afterwards, the Germans moved him to Essen where he was handed over to intelligence for interrogation. The enemy was anxious to learn of the results of the Bodenplatte raid on Volkel. It was not hard to identify which base he belonged to — Volkel was the only one where Tempests were stationed. Not quite sure whether they ever believed him or not, Pottinger deliberately played down the raid, assuring them that damage had been negligible. He was then assigned full prisoner-of-war status and despatched by cattle car to Barth via Berlin where he spent several uncomfortable and terrifying nights on the receiving end of RAF air raids on the German capital. Pottinger never did reach Barth. Due to the swift advance of the Allied armies, he ended up in a POW camp at Luckenwald instead.

0230 Hours
HEESCH AIRFIELD, Holland

Flight Commander Jake Lee of 401 Squadron was determined to show the "bloody Huns" that the Canadians resented their intrusion into their airfields by retaliating in kind. He led his section of four Spitfires right into the Rhine Airfield circuit, the home of Gruppen I and II of the Jagdgeschwader 27 as well as Gruppe III of JG 1 which had taken such a shellacking at the hands of the Poles over the St Denis-Westram airstrip.

But, just east of Munster, the acting CO of the squadron, Flight Lieutenant Johnny MacKay, called up to tell him to take his section down and have a go at two trains steaming out of the town of Rhine. As he dived down, he saw an Me 262 directly under him flying in the direction of the town. As he chased the jet, followed by his section, it led them right into the airfield circuit, where they had wanted to be in the first place — under a convenient cover of a dozen or so Me 109s and FW 190s. But the odds of three to one did not deter the Canadians in the slightest. Far from it.

Lee sighted on the nearest Messerschmidt and let go a barrage of cannon and machine-gun fire. His burst struck the enemy aircraft's cockpit and it nosed-dived right into the ground. He then took aim on a second 109, and saw his shells strike the port side of the machine before it too flipped over on its back and went straight in.

Meanwhile Lee's Number Two, Flying Officer Don Church, who had latched on to an FW 190, snapped off a sharp burst that struck home forcing the Focke Wulf to break away. He then got behind another 190 letting off two volleys from 400 and 300 yards that sent black smoke streaming from the engine and forcing the pilot to bail out right over the airfield.

Pilot Officer Dan Horseborough, flying the Number Three position in the section, also scored. Attacking an Me 109, his fire hit the hydraulic system causing one of the wheels to flop down. Then the aircraft rolled over on its back and crashed into the field.

Adding to his hat-trick he'd performed earlier in the day, Flight Lieutenant Johnny MacKay, the acting CO, chased the Me 262 which had led Lee's section into the hornet's nest over Rhine Airfield. He and Flight Sergeant Ken Woodill both got in "several good squirts" before MacKay's cannons packed up, by which time the jet had easily pulled away from its assailants. MacKay and Woodill shared a "damaged" between them.

It had been another banner day for 401 Squadron RCAF, its greatest since June 7, 1944 over the Normandy beachhead. This day's tally totalled nine enemy aircraft destroyed, one

probably destroyed and three damaged. It was a great start for
the New Year!

0300 Hours
ASCH AIRFIELD, Belgium

The targets for the eight 39th Fighter Squadron Thunderbolts
led by First Lieutenant Clair Cullinan were vehicles and buildings around Lanzerath. The American pilots successfully damaged a dozen trucks, knocked out two tanks and demolished a
building.

Simultaneously, Thunderbolt fighters from the 389th and
390th Fighter Squadrons escorted six A-26 Invader medium-
bombers against targets around Mont Le Ban near Namur, Belgium. However, haze over the target prevented the A-26s from
dropping their bombs and the fighters from strafing the area.
One of the P-47s took a hit from the heavy flak in the area
forcing the pilot to bail out.

0320 Hours
HEESCH AIRFIELD, Holland

There was no holding down 412 Squadron this day, particularly its CO Dean Dover who, before lunch, had shared in
shooting down an FW 190 with Flying Officer Eric Kelly. Now
after the noon day meal, he was at it again, leading a patrol to
Osnabruck, the squadron's third for the day, eight miles west
of Gutersloh Airfield, home of the Udet Geschwader that had
enjoyed such a success over Eindhoven that morning. At a
height of 12,000 feet heading south-east, Dover spotted two
Messerschmidt 109s on the deck. From 400 yards he opened
fire on the one to his right, winging it on the left of the body
of the plane. As the enemy pilot began a turn to port, Dover
shortened his range to 50 yards and fired a burst that clobbered

the wings and fuselage. The 109 flipped over on its back, hit the ground, and exploded.

Dover's Number Two, Flight Lieutenant Jack Swan, meanwhile, had a Messerschmidt firmly in his sights and let go a burst that struck the enemy fighter in both wing roots. The 109 flicked to starboard then nosed into the ground.

But 412 also suffered its only loss of the day when an Me 109 set Joe Doak's Spitfire on fire and sent it crashing to earth in flames, killing him.

0345 Hours
EINDHOVEN AIRFIELD, Holland

Though fires still smouldered and the field remained littered with wreckage, the Typhoons continued to put up a vigorous show of might right up until dusk. Led by Flying Officer Kenneth Brain, 136 Squadron raided targets to the north. Pilot Officer Edward Jarvis led a section of 181 Squadron aircraft to blast the railway lines between Wesseling and Dorsten. Another section of Tiffie pilots, one from 247 Squadron led by Flight Lieutenant Edward Magee, fired their rockets into a factory on the outskirts of Veen. Pilot Officer Fred Skelly, one of those 438 Squadron RCAF pilots who'd had to abandon his aircraft when the Bodenplatte raid started that morning, was at last able to take to the air to lead six Typhoons on an armed recce to the east of the field. Flight Lieutenant Johnny Carr, who had been in the CO's jeep with "Bing" Crosby when the Germans attacked, had another close call. Near Duren, his section of four aircraft was set upon by American Thunderbolts. Fortunately, before they opened fire, they recognised what they had mistaken to be Focke Wulf 190s as Typhoons.

Endnotes

1 Ed MacKay, correspondence, March 1, 1996.

2 Hugh A. Halliday, *Typhoon and Tempest: The Canadian Story,* pp. 107-10.

Surveying the scene at Eindhoven on January 2, 1945. Aircraft
ramains are visible in the foreground and airmen wonder about.
(Department of Defence)

CHAPTER 7

THE SCORE

Measured in terms of planes destroyed and damaged, Bodenplatte resulted in an even shit kicking for both sides. Statisticians and historians, pundits and theorists and the like, then and now, taking into account inaccurate and, in some cases, exaggerated claims (for propaganda purposes), generally agree that both attackers and attacked suffered something in the vicinity of 300 aircraft lost. That is not an unrealistic estimate, all things considered. It is, however, only a superficial appraisal. Allied losses were for the most part unmanned aircraft parked on the ground, while German casualties were piloted fighters in the air. The result was that while the multiple carnage left the Allied tactical air forces fractured but unbowed, it had broken the back of the Luftwaffe.

POST MORTEM

Attack on Dutch and Belgian Airfields

A MAJOR SUCCESS FOR OUR FIGHTERS

Berliner Morgenpost

This air effort had no great influence on the battle, certainly no interference was caused to the Allied fighter-bomber offensive, and alternative methods of attack were sought and put into practice on New Year's Day ....

Over the targets the organisation broke down to some extent; shooting and flying was reported as erratic in some respects, and one head-on collision occurred ....

In view of losses, it is illogical to suppose that other such costly attempts will be made. The [German] High command, however, has now given abundant proof that logic is no longer necessarily the feature of German air force operational policy, then there is no guarantee that similar attempts will not be made .... [But] he failed to check our fighter-bombers in the air over the battle area ... he failed to neutralise their effort by attacking them on the ground .... It remains to be seen how long it will be before he admits his incapacity to interfere with the Allied offensive at all.

Report from Supreme Headquarters Allied Expeditionary Force,
The Battle of the Airfields

New Year's Day '45 — The Execution Order from the Bunker — 304 Machines failed to return — 59 Geschwadern commanders sacrificed to the murderous Allied air defence.

The German Press

Although good weather prevailed and initial surprise was achieved, this operation became a victory for the Allied air forces .... The most competent German authority, General Galland, has since described this day's operation by the German Air Force as "The final dagger thrust into the back of the Luftwaffe."

Report by Air Marshal Sir Arthur Coningham,
2nd Tactical Air Force Commander

Operation Baseplate [sic] amounted to a total defeat. The home defence formations equipped with the standard type of fighter never recovered from the blow. The subsequent operations were insignificant seen against the situation as a whole and offered no further threat to the domination of the enemy air forces.

The gaining of a dubious advantage at the cost of 151 fighter pilots killed or missing, all within a period of four hours, can only be described as nonsensical.

Werner Girbig,
Six Months to Oblivion

This determined attempt to strike a crippling blow at the tactical air forces had no appreciable affect except possibly on the enemy, who lost a large number of his most experienced pilots with all the consequences that that implied.

Hilary St G. Saunders,
The Fight is Won: Royal Air Force 1939-45, Vol. III

... the damage they wrought was not enough to change the course of the Luftwaffe's fate.

Danny S. Parker,
To Win the Winter Sky

It brought home to me with great force and not for the first time, that in a battle of this nature there is nothing the AOC can do about it. He is absolutely dependent on the organisation, training and morale of his chaps, particularly the junior commanders and controllers.

A low-level attack under the radar cover and virtually without warning, leaves no time for the senior commanders to do anything but depend on the reaction from the sharp end and I think my chaps reacted splendidly.

Their [the enemy's] losses were crippling and this time we could count what was shot down by picking up our wreckage and not by claims in the air.

Report of Air Vice Marshal Harry Broadhurst,
Air Officer Commanding 83 Group of the 2nd TAF

... the Luftwaffe had failed in its bid to deliver a knockout blow. The raids were a desperate act, the last throw of a gambler's dice. All that they had achieved, like the December offensive in the Ardennes, was to briefly delay the Allies' preparations to break into Germany.

Monty Berger (Chief Intelligence Officer,
126 Wing RCAF) and Brian Jeffrey Street,
Invasions Without Tears

PROFIT and LOSS

ANTWERP-DUERNE AIRFIELD (B-70), Belgium

Bodenplatte marked 77 "Red Hearts" Jagdgeschwader's last major operation of the war. Starting out on its foray to attack Deurne Airfield with 100 fighters, arraying itself as one of the most formidable of all the Luftwaffe formations that early morning, for all the damage it achieved, it might just as well have stayed at home. Only 30 planes got anywhere near the target. Five pilots were killed, four were taken prisoner and two went missing in action. While this casualty figure seemed light compared to some of the other Geschwadern, the raid on the Antwerp Airfield resulted in pitifully little gain. A Dakota and a Flying Fortress were damaged. One of 266 Squadron's Typhoons was destroyed and a few others took a mild beating. Two Typhoons from 257 Squadron got spattered and 197 Squadron lost three aircraft from the strafing. It was nothing to get too terribly excited about.

On the minus side, German pilots killed were: Gefreite Helmut Kofler, Unteroffizier Rolf Brabant, Leutnant Hans-Jurgen Schumacker (who belly landed his Messerchmidt 109 on the field) and Leutnant Heinrich Hackler, all of whom bought it in and around the target area. Leutnant Heinrich Munninger was killed when hit by ack-ack fire near Tilburg on his way home.

Gefreite Erwin Mannweiler, Unteroffizieren Johann Twietmeyer and Alfred Hoffschmidt (who crashed near Eschweiler after his engine packed up), and Leutnant Heinz Abendroth who was shot down by German flak on the outward leg near Maeseych, were taken prisoner. Missing in action were Oberleutnant Karl-Heinz Bartels and Feldwebel Paul Tanck.

By contrast the only personnel casualty at Deurne Airfield was RAF Corporal John Ford, who got hit in the mouth with a piece of flying shrapnel. A few stitches soon had him talking — and smiling — again.

ASCH AIRFIELD (Y-29), Belgium

This raid amounted to the most spectacular Allied Tactical Air Forces' victory of the entire Bodenplatte operation that morning, while for Jagdgeschwader 11, it spelled total disaster.

To begin with, among the 42 German pilot casualties (32 in air-to-air combat — the rest from ground fire and other causes) sustained in the half-hour clash with the American 352nd and 366th Fighter Groups, resulting from the attack on the US Belgian base, were a pair of sharpshooters the Luftwaffe could ill afford to lose: the Geschwader Kommodore himself, the one-eyed Oberstleutnant Gunther Specht, and the fiery Hauptmann Horst-Gunther von Fassong, the CO of Gruppe III, an ace with 100 victories to his credit. Both got the chop. Also killed in the raid were Felwebelen Peter Reschke, Harald Schartz and Herbert Kraschinski; Unteroffizieren Ernest Noreisch, Hermann Barion and Kurt Nussle; Oberleutnant August Engel; Oberfeldwebel Karl-Heinz Sistenich; and Gefreite Gerhardt Bohm. Missing, presumed dead, were Unteroffizieren Max Milkreiter, Walter Gattner and Sophus Schmidt; Fahnrichen Gunther Hoffmann, Heinrich Wiethoff and Herbert Huss; Leutnanten Alwin Doppler and Gerhard Newmann, Feldwebelen Franz Meindl, Alfred Temple and Xaver Giese; and Major Gunter Vowinkel. Luftwaffe pilots taken prisoner were Oberleutnant Hans Fiedler and Feldwebel Karl Hiller.

The enemy deaths were not without their macabre side. Major Dick DeBruin, the 352nd Fighter Group support officer assisted the Army Graves Commission team in searching the area. In a field less than a mile from Y-29 they located an Me 109 completely destroyed by fire. DeBruin later recalled: "It was not something I cared to observe. The pilot's torso was lying on the ground with the head and limbs severed and spread over the area. I kept thinking if he had only been able to stay on the ground that day, he'd be home alive."

In contrast to the Geschwader 11 demise, the 352nd and 366th Fighter Groups' scoreboard lit up with a total of 32 victories in the air without a single casualty! The only loss to the units were a few P-51s clobbered on the ground by the strafing. But these merely amounted to "brush" fires that were easily and quickly extinguished.

The Mustang pilots of the 487th Fighter Squadron of the 352nd Fighter Group had a field day, accounting for 23 German aircraft destroyed. Captain William "Whiz" Whisner and Lieutenant Sandford Moats each shot down four of the enemy, while Captain Henry M. Stewart and Lieutenant Alden Rigby both scored hat-tricks. The CO, Lieutenant Colonel J.C. Meyer, shot down two Focke Wulf 190s to bring his total of kills in the air to 24, the highest of any American pilot in the European Theatre. Lieutenant Ray Littge duplicated the feat with a pair of victories as well. Major William Halton and Lieutenants Walker Diamond, Dean Houston, Nelson Jesup and Alex Sears each shot down one of the enemy marauders to complete the squadron's total success.

Between them, the Thunderbolts of the 390th and 391st Fighter Squadrons of the 366th Fighter Group added another nine victories to the morning's tally. Captain Lowell B. Smith and Lieutenants Bob Brulle, Currie Davis, John Feeney, Joe Lackey, Melvin Paisley and Flight Officer David Johnson Jr. of the 390th racked up a score of seven German planes blown out of the air, Paisley accounting for three of them himself. At the same time Lieutenants John Bathurst and Donald Holt of the 391st each shot down a Messerschmidt 109.

Running up a score of 32 aircraft destroyed in the air was even more remarkable in face of the fact that the American pilots had to wrestle with the danger of flak from their own antiaircraft gunners defending the field who were unable to distinguish friend from foe, under the circumstances.

When word reached HQ of the morning's sensational success, Asch Airfield soon became inundated with VIP brass hats on hand to congratulate the fighter pilots. Among them were Lieutenant General Carl "Tooey" Spaatz, commander of the

United States Strategic Air Forces, Major General Hoyt
Vandenberg, commander of the 9th US Air Force and Brigadier
General Elwood "Pete" Quesada, CO of 9th Tactical Air Command who had given J.C. Meyer permission to mount the early
morning patrol that won the day.

For J.C.'s "Bluenosed Bastards of Bodney," it represented
an outstanding achievement of aerial combat unmatched in air
fighting in so short a time in such a confined air-duelling
space. For this notable accomplishment, the 478th Fighter
Squadron was awarded he United States Distinguished Unit
Citation, the only squadron in Jimmy Doolittle's entire 8th
USAF to be so honoured. It reflected in no small measure
Meyer's prescience in anticipating — "think like the enemy" —
retaliatory German attacks on Allied tactical airfields.

Colonel Norman Holt, commander of the 366th Fighter
Group, commented caustically: "I hope at least one of the bastards got back home to tell the story. They'd think twice before
trying it again." Indeed they had!

When Major Jurgen Harder, a former Gruppe commander
with JG 53, took over the command of Geschwader 11 after
Gunther Specht was killed, he was horrified to find how little
was still left of the once proud unit he had inherited. Almost
40 per cent of the pilot strength committed to Bodenplatte
were dead or captured.

BRUSSELS-EVERE (B-56) and BRUSSELS-GRIMBERGEN (B-60) AIRFIELDS, Belgium

There were pluses and minuses. The twin attacks on B-56
and B-60 by Oberstleutnant Pips Priller's "Abbeville Boys,"
Jagdgeschwader 26 proved triumphant on the one hand and
catastrophic on the other. At Evere Gruppen II and III led by
Major Anton Hackl could gloat over the scene of chaos and carnage they had left in their smouldering wake. They were under

the impression that they had netted at least 120 enemy aircraft destroyed on the ground, among them 60 to 65 fighters of various types, 32 bombers a number of transports, and damage to motor vehicles, fuel tankers, hangars and other buildings. That in their exuberance in the heat of the moment the Germans had, understandably, overestimated their claims in no way detracted from their success. Accumulated damage and destruction to Evere had been severe.

The collective machine-gun and cannon firepower of the two JG 26 Gruppen effectively turned those aircraft conveniently parked on either side of the field wing-tip to wing-tip — as if to invite destruction — as well as those others waiting to take off, into a blazing pyre of scrap metal. It was a veritable turkey shoot! Serviceable fighter strength for 416 Squadron was reduced to four aircraft. 421 Squadron, which did not even get off the ground, lost five of its fighters from the strafing. In all, 11 of the 127 Wing Spitfires set on fire were completely written off, while 12 others were damaged almost beyond repair. The VIP luxury Dakota transport was set ablaze, as was Prince Bernhardt's precious sky-blue Beechcraft. Of 11 motor transports hit by enemy fire, one was totally destroyed and a hangar, housing a variety of twin-engine airplanes, was set on fire. Remarkably, for all the clobbering the field sustained during the 45 minutes the raid lasted, there was only one ground fatality. Leading Aircraftsman Robert Medford was killed while 11 other airmen were wounded by the gunfire.

Smoke over the field billowing from the conflagrations became so dense that at times it impaired the aim of attackers like Oberleutnant Adolf Glunz who made nine runs and managed to set the hangar on fire, and Major Anton Hackl who completed seven passes over the target. Incredibly neither pilot was hit by anti-aircraft fire from the Royal Air Force Regiment flak gunners who fired off 2,600 rounds of Bren gun ammunition and 350 40-mm shells claiming seven German aircraft destroyed and two damaged.

In the air, the Canadians held the edge though it in no way redressed the balance in terms of material damage. For one pilot killed — Flight Lieutenant Dave Harling — six German aircraft fell to RCAF guns: Pilot Officer Steve Butte accounted for three; Flying Officer "Mac" Reeves and Sergeant Pilot Doug Lindsay both dispatched a pair apiece; and Harling destroyed an Me 109 before he himself was shot down.

There was no question that at Evere the Luftwaffe had scored a singularly audacious and brilliant triumph, so much so that Gruppen II and III Kommodores Major Anton Hackl and Hauptmann Walter "Count" Krupinski found the loss of 20 pilots — killed, missing or taken prisoner — totally acceptable under the circumstances. Before even reaching the target, four pilots had been lost to anti-aircraft fire, all of them killed. In the target area, among the other victims to become casualties was Unteroffizier Wilhelm Schmitz whom Doug Lindsay nailed with a three-second burst after the latter's second pass across the airfield. With the pilot either dead or wounded, Schmitz's 190 Dora continued flying for another 20 miles until it crashed into a tree near Aalst where he came to a grisly end. Later his decapitated body was found shrouded in his parachute amid the wreckage.

Five other casualties were identified: Gefreite Willi Kunz and Leutnant Gottfried Meyer, both killed, the latter after crashing onto the field. Gefreite Hans-Karl Goetz was shot down and taken prisoner. Having survived the strafing attacks, two pilots were lost on the way back to Germany. Unteroffizier Ernst Lamperhoff and Feldwebel Erich Ahrens were struck by flak over Beveland in Holland, successfully bailing out to become prisoners of war.

These losses aside, by all measurements the raid on Evere had been a success for Priller's Geschwader despite his reservations over the entire idea and his own lack of actual participation in the attack itself. Echoing these sentiments, the noted German historian, Werner Girbig, put it this way: "In the final analysis, even 26 Wing's success and its relatively 'light' casualties could not conceal the fact that all in all, Operation Baseplate [sic] was a failure."

The attack against Grimbergen Airfield was quite a different story. The raid by Gruppe I of JG 26, led by Major Karl Borris, supported by Oberstleutnant Hans Dortenmann's Gruppe III from Jagdgeschwader 54, began and ended in utter disaster. Before reaching the enemy lines, three of the Gruppe I pilots and another from JG 24 fell victim to their own anti-aircraft gunners. Each of them managed to crash-land safely, one severely wounded, but all had been taken out of action. Worse followed. As the formations crossed the Belgian border, five JG 54 pilots were shot down by Spitfires flown by Poles from 308 Squadron. Over the Scheldt River another of their confrères was hit by enemy flak and managed to bail only to be taken prisoner.

Over the "non-operational" airfield itself, five pilots from the combined Gruppen were lost to the RAF Regiment flak batteries who fired off salvos of 230 anti-aircraft shells. In all, it was a misadventure for Karl Borris's Gruppe I, to say the least. Of the 17 FW 190 Doras that set out on the mission, only 11 returned to Furstenau, and eight of those were badly shot up from ground fire. These included Oberleutnant Alfred Heckmann, Leutnant Karl-Heinz Ossenkop, Feldwebelen Wolfgang Franz, Walter Kereber and Walter Haeger, and Unteroffizieren Gunther Kaebler, Gerhard Reichow and Karl Zeidler.

Oberstleutnant Hans Dortenmann's Gruppe III from JG 54 fared even worst; it was virtually slaughtered. Only seven of the 17 aircraft that had taken off on the mission returned. Some of these losses occurred on the return flight to Furstenau when the FW 190s ran into a group of Spitfires. Those killed were

Hauptmann Willi Bottlander, a Staffel commander, Offizier Walter Eckert, Unteroffizier Aloysious von Hooven and Leutnant Jurgen Ratzlaff. Three of the aircraft crashed into the built-up section of Brussels, killing five civilians.

The Luftwaffe had paid a heavy price for the damage it inflicted on Grimbergen. A B-17 Flying Fortress and a Dakota transport had been set on fire. A Mustang fighter had been destroyed. Two hangars were demolished. Several barrack blocks and other buildings suffered damage. Twelve motor transports and two fuel tankers had been destroyed. Casualties included one airman killed and two wounded.

BRUSSELS-MELSBROEK AIRFIELD (B-58), Belgium

The attack on Melsbroek by Gruppen I and II of JG 27 led by Hauptmannen Eberhard Schade and Gerhard Hoyer, respectively, and Gruppe IV of JG 54 under the command of Major Rudolf Klemm rivalled that of the havoc heaped on Evere and then some. They had achieved complete surprise but the distinct difference was that they enjoyed impunity from any interference from the air.

In just over 30 minutes, the German fighters left the airfield wreathed in smoke and flame. Thirty-four aircraft were destroyed on the ground and another five damaged. Sixty-nine Squadron lost 14 of its twin-engine night-reconnaissance Wellingtons. Of the three squadrons making up the 139 Mitchell Wing, 98 Squadron had one of the twin-engine medium-bombers destroyed and two damaged; 180 Squadron, three destroyed and three damaged; 320 Squadron, two destroyed. Sixteen Squadron lost three Spitfires while 140 Squadron had six of its Mosquitoes wiped out. Seven of the Handley Page Harrow transports from 271 Squadron's "Sparrow Flight" (code name) were blasted apart.

Although no Allied pilots were lost or even injured, five airmen were killed and 25 wounded. But the cost to the Germans had also been heavy. Of the more than 60 aircraft which set out on the foray, half of them never made it back. Before the formation even reached the target, JG 27 had already lost five of its pilots. Unteroffizieren Heinrich Braun and Heinrich Frickmann, along with Feldwebel Alfred Mannchen were shot down by friendly flak before reaching the front lines. Over Holland near Breda, enemy flak claimed two more victims: Leutnant Heinrich Weiss whose Messerschmidt smashed into the bank of the Wahl River, and Unteroffizier Karlheinz Berndt who crash-landed his 109 into a field nearby.

Over the target, in addition to the losses of Hauptmann Hans-Heinz Dudeck, Fahnrich Otto Theissen and Unteroffizier Gerhard Ohlenschlager (JG 54), Leutnant Joachim von Stechow, Feldwebel Gert Gehel and Unteroffizieren Karl Rehak and Werner Kopp were all killed when brought down by ground fire. After making four passes over the field, Unteroffizier Johannes Hartlein lost his compass and had to head back home on dead reckoning. Over Thielen in Belgium, his aircraft was so badly clobbered by flak he was forced to bail out and was taken prisoner by the British.

JG 54, which had lost four fighters during the attack, also suffered casualties on the way home. Some pilots became lost or disoriented and were shot down by ground fire from both sides.

EINDHOVEN AIRFIELD (B-78), Holland

Though it only lasted 23 minutes, the attack on this Dutch airfield, home to a Spitfire reconnaissance and two Typhoon fighter-bomber wings, by the Focke Wulf 190s and Messerschmidt 109s of Luftwaffe ace (202 kills) Oberstleutnant Heinz "Pritzl" Bar's JG 3 "Udet" amounted to the most calamitous, devastating raid of the entire Bodenplatte operation. In the words of one observer, "It was as if the sky was bursting apart at the seams!"

Aircraft were being shot up in the air and on the ground, fuel, bomb and rocket dumps exploded, buildings bombed and strafed, hangars set on fire and motor vehicles and fuel trucks wrecked and left burning. Smoke and flames were everywhere. The thunder of bombs and rockets exploding mingling with the rattle and thump-thump of machine-gun and cannon fire, the blasts from the Bofors ground defence guns, the whining and whirring of aircraft swooping and swerving, and the explosions of planes crashing into the ground or being blown to bits in the air, added a deadly cacophony to the already frightening spectacle of the field under relentless attack.

A hundred and forty-four planes were destroyed on the ground and another 84 were damaged. These included some 40 Typhoons, 28 Spitfires, 11 Wellington bombers, several DC-3 Dakotas and Mitchells, two Ansons, two Austers as well as a damaged B-17 Flying Fortress undergoing repairs.

The operational squadrons were left in shattered shape. A crippled 124 Wing could only muster 24 Typhoon fighter-bombers; 137 Squadron had 11 operational aircraft serviceable, 181 Squadron eight, 247 only five and 182 Squadron none whatsoever. Likewise, 143 Wing also took a beating; hardest hit was 483 Squadron with only two of its Typhoons left on strength, both badly damaged by gunfire. 440 Squadron lost at least eight of its aircraft. 39 Reconnaissance Wing suffered heavily also with the equivalent of an entire squadron of Spitfires destroyed or damaged.

More Allied pilots were lost at Eindhoven than in any other attack on the tactical airfields that morning. Five Canadians were among the six casualties. Those killed included Flight Lieutenant Pete Wilson, and Flying Officers Ron Keller and Sam Angelini. Flying Officer Ed Flanagan survived to be hospitalised with leg and facial wounds. Flight Lieutenant Jim Prendergast was treated for a head injury from a bullet that creased the back of his skull. Two British pilots were killed:

Flight Lieutenant Harold "Gibby" Gibbons and Flight Sergeant Len Burrows.

The Luftwaffe triumph over B-78 cost the Udet Geschwader dearly. Out of a total fighter strength of over 70 aircraft that set out on the foray, 22 pilots were killed, went missing or were taken prisoner with at least another dozen returning to base wounded. Among the most severely injured were Unteroffizier Alfred Dors and Oberfeldwebel Robert Reiser.

One of the first to die was Oberfahnrich Uwe Nauman whose Messerschmidt received a direct hit from one of the Bofors guns that sent it crashing onto the field where it blew up. Almost simultaneously Feldwebel Gerhard Leipholz was shot down by "Gibby" Gibbons before the latter was himself killed. Leipholz's Me 109 dived headlong into the airfield and exploded. Elsewhere in the vicinity, Oberleutnant Graf von Treuberg met his death at the hands of Squadron Leader Gordie Wonnacott, one of three German fighters the Typhoon pilot brought down that morning. At the time, Treuberg was posted as Missing in Action, but his body was never found and he was later presumed dead . Others killed in and around the airfield area were Feldwebel Theodore Schmitt, Gefreite Rudolf Wieschoff, Leutnant Hans Jun, Unteroffizieren Erich Busch and Hans-Joachim Grell.

Unteroffizier Horst Schone, Oberleutnant Siegfried Reuther and Unteroffizier Alois Schmidt were listed as Missing in Action. Six pilots ended up in Allied prison camps. Before even reaching the target, Feldwebel Paul Schmidt was forced to break formation when his Me 109 developed engine trouble. Near Venlo he was attacked by a Spitfire. Forced to bail out, he was quickly taken prisoner. On his approach to the field Obergefriete Friedrich Tazreiter's Me 109 was riddled with flak. Badly injured, he was nevertheless able to bail out right into the waiting arms of Canadian troops who took him into custody. Unteroffizier Helmut Reinecke zeroed in on a Typhoon parked on the runway noticing strikes all round the aircraft. But at that moment, his Messerschmidt absorbed a volley of ground-fire shells, causing him to lose control of the machine. Too low to bail out, he successfully crash-landed in an open field adjacent to the airfield where he was immediately picked up.

Since this was Offizierwebel Friedrich Hameister's first sortie with JG 3 he was determined to prove himself worthy of the assignment. He did just that, although his success was short-lived. Despite blinding smoke over the target, he managed to penetrate it sufficiently to set fire to a fuel tanker and a twin-engine aircraft. On his return to base, he encountered a Spitfire in the process of finishing off an Me 109. The pilot was so preoccupied with what he was doing that he never even saw Hameister sneak up from behind and underneath and take careful aim. With a sharp, short burst, Hameister dispatched the enemy to his doom. But, just then, another Spitfire latched onto the tail of his Messerschmidt, setting it on fire. Miraculously, Hameister managed to belly land his burning aircraft in a farm field without further mishap or injury to himself. After aimlessly wandering about the countryside for the rest of the day, he was captured early next morning half asleep, huddled against a hay stack.

Having destroyed two of 39 Wing's Spitfires on the ground, Unteroffizier Gerhardt Schmidt broke off his attack to return to base along with two other JG 3 Focke Wulf 190 pilots. En route they ran afoul of the four 439 Squadron Typhoons returning from their weather reconnaissance led by Flying Officer Bob Laurence. During the mêlée Schmidt shot down Flying Officer Sam Angelini, whose mangled aircraft and body were discovered two days later near Rips. But Schmidt's own aircraft was so badly damaged in the exchange, he had to crash-land his 190 20 miles east of Eindhoven, not as close to his own lines as he had hoped. He was still in enemy territory. Climbing out of the cockpit he faced a pair of British Tommies with carbines levelled at him. Without ceremony they marched him to an interrogation centre, where he spent several days before being officially classified as a bona fide prisoner of war. He was then shipped to a detention camp where he spent the rest of the WW II unpleasantness.

During the same encounter, Laurence shot down Feldwebel Walter Rutowski, a novice on his first fighter mission who had proved his mettle by completing four strafing runs over Eindhoven Airfield. Rutowski managed to bail out of his stricken machine, peacefully wafting down into captivity by parachute after only a single kick at the can. But it was a commendable one all the same.

Ground personnel casualties at Eindhoven, all sustained within less than half an hour, were grim and gruesome. Over 40 officers and enlisted men were killed and another 145 wounded, some so critically they were beyond recovery or repair.

It was some consolation at least that the Allied pilots had shot down nine enemy planes in the air, seven of them destroyed by Canadians. Squadron Leader Gordie Wonnacott bagged two Me 109s and a 190, a hat-trick that earned him an immediate bar to his Distinguished Flying Cross. Flying Officers Hugh Fraser and Bob Laurence scored a brace of Focke Wulfs apiece, while Flying Officer Ian Woloschuk accounted for another 190. Three RAF pilots shared in the destruction of a Heinkel 111 bomber between them, with Flight Lieutenant George Clubley, Pilot Officer Don Martyn and Flying Officer Jim Cole all in on the kill.

From the ground, the RAF Regiment's three squadrons of anti-aircraft gunners fired off a total of 2,750 rounds of ammunition with which they destroyed six of the marauders.

Although, by noon, rescue salvage and maintenance crews had cleared the field of enough debris and destruction to allow take-offs and landings on a limited scale, it was not until mid-January that the field was once again fully up to strength and totally operational. Leading Aircraftsman Desmond Shepherd, armourer with 137 Squadron, provided this epitaph to the morning's devastation:

After the raid, at the bottom of the field where the Canadians were, thick black smoke columns were rising and explosions, including one big one that sent a mushroom cloud up to a great height, added to a very noisy morning.

Shortly after this, as I was watching, several large formations of USAF medium-bombers passed overhead towards the German positions. The leading plane broke away and started circling Eindhoven, then a British plane flew up towards it, firing a flare. The leading plane then rejoined its formation and resumed leading them towards the German lines. I've often wondered if the leader thought he was over his target!

Some days before the raid, a four-engined USAF bomber, badly shot up, force-landed on the airfield and an American ground crew came and worked hard for many days repairing it and even changed its engines. After the raid I saw the American crew chief standing with his men, scratching his head, looking at the burnt-out piece of twisted metal that was once their pride and joy. One of our Erks [ground crew] stepped forward and said, "Well, Chief, you really have something to repair now!"

Later, [I visited] the sickbay for treatment to my knee .... Many wounded were also there so I came out and dressed my own wound. It healed well but I still have the scar.

GHENT and ST DENIS-WESTRAM AIRFIELD (B-61), Belgium

Oberstleutnant Herbert Ihlefeld's direst premonitions had been inexorably vindicated. His predilection that Bodenplatte was a futile, wasteful, poorly conceived, impulsively contrived, concept that could only end in failure and disaster had been justified even beyond his worst fears. The deadly duels fought in the air above the Ghent fighter base against the Poles cost his Oseau Jagdgeschwader 19 pilots (plus another six: three before the formation even reached the target, and three pilots shot down in the attack on Maldegem Airfield). Among them were five of JG 1's most experienced fighter pilots: Gruppe II leader Hauptmann Hans-Georg Hackbarth, Feldwebel Paul Mayr, Leutnant Ernst von Johannides, Feldwebel Harry Klints, and Unteroffizier Karl Hahn, all of whom were killed. Seven other fatalities were Unteroffizier Reinhold Schober, Feldwebel Wilhelm Krauter (while attacking Maldegem), Unteroffizier Paul Wunderlich who was brought down by anti-aircraft fire over the Scheldt, and Unteroffizieren Egon Comtesse, Heinz Bohmer and Heinz Jurgan Killian who all lost their lives to their own flak gunners.

Taken prisoner were Unteroffizieren Edgar Ardner, Alfred Fritzsche and Fritz Hoffmann. This marked the third time Hoffman had been shot down, first over Falaise and then over Paris. This time he was forced to parachute down into enemy territory where he was badly battered about by Belgian civilians before being rescued by British troops who took him into captivity — and safety.

It was a high price to pay for strafing 25 Spitfires parked on the ground wing-tip to wing-tip belonging to 302, 316 and 317 Squadrons. Some of them were destroyed, others a bit shot-up. There was also accidental damage to a B-17 Flying Fortress when a Focke Wulf 190, that had been nailed by one of the airborne Spitfires, plowed into it. A Stirling bomber burned up and two enemy pilots were killed.

By contrast, the Poles' scorecard was impressive. Between them, 308 and 317 Squadrons claimed 12 FW 190s destroyed, two probably destroyed and five damaged. The defenders lost two pilots. Flight Lieutenant Walclaw Chojnacki (308) and Flight Lieutenant Tadeusz Powierza (308) were killed.

Four of the Polish pilots shot down two enemy planes apiece: Flight Sergeant Josef Stanowski, claiming as his victims the veterans Hauptmann Hans-Georg Hackbarth and Unteroffizier

Karl Hahn; Flight Lieutenant Bronislaw Mach (who also damaged an FW 190); Warrant Officer Stanislaw Bednarcyzk; and Sergeant Stanislaw Breyner. Others, scoring single victories, included Flight Lieutenant Ignacy Ozsweski, Flying Officer Tadeusz Szlenkier (Harry Klints's executioner), Pilot Officer Andrezj, Dromlewicz and Waclaw Chojnacki. With the exception of Breyner, all were members of 308 Squadron.

Breyner's 317 Squadron mates accounted for six FW 190s destroyed — Squadron Leader Marian Chelmecki, the squadron CO who shot down Fritz Hoffmann; Flight Lieutenants Czeslaw Mroczyk and Roman Hrycak; Warrant Officers Stanislaw Piesik and Zeonbieuz Wdowczynski; and Sergeant Kelnis Hubert. In addition, Hubert and Flight Lieutenant Zbigniew Zimgrodski each claimed an enemy machine probably shot down, while Piesik, Zimgrodski and Sergeant Seg Wanowski were credited with damaging three others.

The Polish triumph over the Luftwaffe on that frigid New Year's Day in 1945 has never been forgotten by the grateful citizenry of the small village of St Denis-Westram. A street was renamed "Polish Wing," and every year a remembrance service is held in the church where mass was being observed in celebration of the first New Year's in five in which the Belgians had been free of the Nazi occupation, when the Germans attacked the airfield.

GILZE-REIJEN AIRFIELD (B-77), Holland

If the performance of individual Bodenplatte air raids on the Allied tactical fighter fields had been rated on a scale of one to ten, the attack on Gilze-Reijen would have barely drawn a three.

Although 16 Messerschmidt 109s, a medley of small detachments from JG 3 (an extemporaneous participation on their part) and JG 27 (both of whose main targets were Eindhoven and Melsbroek respectively) strafed the airstrip and a few Arado

234 jet bombers dropped anti-personnel bombs on the field, the assault could at best be classified as a diversionary foray — and a highly unsuccessful one at that. To say it was poorly co-ordinated would be putting it mildly

The two RAF Regiment squadrons which fired off 803 rounds between them had a clear shot at the disorganised ma-rauders, bringing down an A 234 jet and claiming two Me 109s destroyed and another three damaged. During the fracas, Flight Lieutenant John Lyke from 268 Squadron, returning from a tactical reconnaissance patrol, had his Mustang shot up on landing by a 109 before the ground gunners brought down the enemy aircraft.

Other damage to the field was just as negligible. One of 164 Squadron's Typhoons was destroyed and another damaged. An Anson perforated by machine-gun fire was soon patched up in time to be flown to England. Seven airmen on the field were slightly injured. A truck convoy carrying ground crew person-nel from 35 Wing on their way to join the aircrews that had already moved, or were about to move, to Chievres was shot up by Messerschmidts during which two of the airmen passengers were wounded, neither seriously.

In the air, Flight Lieutenant Ed Packwood from 2 Squad-ron shot down a Messerschmidt 109 while his section leader, Flight Lieutenant Jim Young, destroyed a Ju 188. According to the records, the German casualties among the Me 109 pilots from Jagdgeschwader 27 might possibly have been Unteroffizier Peter-Michael Gisevius, Obergefreite Erich Heyman, Unteroffizier Heinrich Fickmann and Feldwebel Alfred Mannchen, killed; Unteroffizier Heinrich Maus was wounded.

HEESCH AIRFIELD (B-88), Holland

For the totally unprepared Canadians of 126 Wing, it was an unadulterated triumph. For the wayward Focke Wulf and

Messerschmidt pilots of Jagdgeschwader 6, it was an unmitigated disaster.

The score could not have been more one-sided. The Germans lost a third of their attacking force — 24 FW 190s and Me 109s destroyed and another seven damaged. The Allies lost three Spitfires shot down, from which two of the pilots walked away, one with only minor injuries. Now for the really bad news — for the Luftwaffe. Included in their demise were ten officer casualties, among them three Staffel leaders, an unprecedented loss of experienced command-calibre talent for only one Geschwader in a single sortie. Three of the senior leaders were lost: the JG Kommodore Oberstleutnant Johann Kogler and Hauptmann Ewald Trost, CO of Gruppe I who were shot down and made prisoners of war, while Gruppe III Kommodore, Major Helmut Kuhle, crashed to his death when clobbered by anti-aircraft fire. Of the three Staffel leaders two were killed: Hauptmann Norbert Katz (Staffel 5) and Oberleutnant Lothar Gerlach (Staffel 9), while Hauptmann Wilhelm Kindler (Staffel 11) was taken prisoner.

The Canadian pilots' scorecard was imposing: 18 enemy aircraft destroyed and seven probably destroyed. Leading the parade was 401 Squadron with Flying Officer Doug Cameron and Flight Lieutenant Johnny MacKay destroying three enemy aircraft each, Cameron a trio of Me 109s, MacKay two 109s and an FW190, for which he received an immediate bar to his Distinguished Flying Cross.

Flight Lieutenant Dick Audet of 411 Squadron added a pair of FW 190s to the five enemy planes he had shot down two days earlier to rank him as an ace. Flight Lieutenant Bruce "Mac" Macpherson of 412 Squadron also posted a tandem kill, shooting down two Me 109s, while Flight Lieutenant Joe Doak and Flying Officer Victor Smith each destroyed a Messerschmidt.

442 Squadron chalked up a pair of twin scores: Flight Lieutenant Dave "Tex" Pieri, a couple of 190s destroyed and two

others probably destroyed; Flight Lieutenant Chunky Gordon who, before he was shot down himself, sent two 109 pilots to their graves and probably delivered the death sentence to one other. Flight Lieutenant Robert Smith also of 442 Squadron was credited with shooting down an Me 109 and probably destroying another, while Flight Lieutenant Norm Keene put an FW 190 away and jointly, with Flight Lieutenant Jack Lumsden, claimed another as a probable. Also credited with a probable was Flying Officer Jacques Cousineau (an FW 190). A quartet made up of Flight Lieutenant Bob Trumley, Flying Officer Bill Dunne, Flight Lieutenant John Dick and Pilot Officer Ed Baker scored a probable on an Me 262 though with the getaway power the jet enjoyed a "damage" might have been a more accurate claim.

Two members of the squadron were shot down in the morning's fighting. Flying Officer Dave Brigden was killed instantly when his Spitfire crashed into a field. Flying Officer Len Wilson was more fortunate. Although badly shot up in a contretemps with a 190, he managed to belly land his stricken aircraft and walked away uninjured.

Between the two RAF Regiment squadrons guarding the field the gunners who gasped in amazement that they'd "never seen so many bloody Huns all at once in the same place," fired off a total of 344 rounds claiming six of the enemy destroyed and 12 others damaged.

Damage to the airfield was so negligible it was hardly worth mentioning: a fair-size hole blown through the roof of the 411 Squadron dispersal hut. The Germans might just as well have saved their ammunition.

LE CULOT AIRFIELD (A-89), Belgium

It was the raid that never took place.

The Americans had no idea how lucky they were. The 36th, 363rd and 373rd Fighter Groups of the 29th Tactical Air Force lay dormant. More than 100 Thunderbolt fighters, as well as contingents of Mitchell medium-bombers, crowded the field, almost side by side, with no attempt to camouflage or disperse them. Without a single aircraft in the air, and their defences entirely dependent on the anti-aircraft gunners, they were blissfully unaware of the carnage that might have occurred had Major Gerhard Michalski's Jagdgeschwader 4 found the target.

Except for two casualties from flak, the formation of some 60 FW 190s and ME 109s of the Geschwader remained intact since take-off. It was still very much a force with which to be reckoned, until their Ju 88 pathfinder was shot down leaving the JG so disoriented it never got close to the Belgian fighter base.

Although A-89 escaped unscathed, its would-be attackers were beset with calamity. In disarray, the German fighter formation split up into various groups and, to all intents, ceased to operate as a cohesive unit. Instead they became embroiled in a number of individual attacks on other airfields as well as ground assaults on self-chosen targets.

At St Trond-Brustem, which they had mistaken for Le Culot, what remained of Major Max Schroder's Gruppe II pilots were fortunate to lose only one of their members. However, in the donnybrook at Melsbroek, in which Hauptmann Max Laube's Gruppe IV became accidentally involved, four pilots were shot down. Both Feldwebel Karl Berg and Obergefreite Horst Gruner were killed. While blasting away at a string of Flying Fortresses, Obergefreite Hans Peschel, a stray from Hauptmann Wilhelm Steinmann's Gruppe I, was hit by anti-aircraft fire. He managed to climb his FW 190 to 1,600 feet before jumping out and was taken prisoner only 200 yards from the airstrip. Obergefreite Arnulf Russow made two strafing runs over the airfield before being nailed by ground fire, crash-landing at Ulbeek. Unteroffizier Lothar Schmidt never made it as far as Melsbroek with his Gruppe IV comrades. His aircraft was hit by flak forcing him to belly land near Butgenbach in the Ardennes. Schmidt and Russow both ended up as prisoners of war.

Others from JG 4, scattered from Bastogne to Brussels, became totally disoriented and got lost trying to get back to their own lines, some over Aachen, others through southern Holland. Feldwebel Franz Schneider, Unteroffizieren Erich Keller and Hans-Gustav Diercks were all shot down and killed by flak. Others reported killed, some doubtless in the fighting over Ophoven into which some of the errant Geschwader 4 pilots had stumbled, were: Obergefreite Franz Sharr, Unteroffizieren Werner Zetschke, Heinz Richter, Willi Breves, Erich Guldenpfenning, Walter Huber (who crashed at Babenhausen Airfield), Hermann Holtkotter, Gefreiten Karl Noppener and Kurt Lack and Leutnant Elmer Ecker. Leutnant Gottfried Morio was seriously injured.

Of the 60 aircraft that took part in the ill-fated mission, half did not return. JG 4 had lost 17 pilots, killed or missing, and six more captured after being shot down. Hauptmann Georg Schroder's ten Sturmgruppe II Messerschmidts had been virtually wiped out. Michalski's threat to his pilots before take-off that "if the mission is not carried out with determination and success you will be sent out again to complete the job," had become a logistical impossibility.

MALDEGEM AIRFIELD (B-65), Belgium

Gruppe II of Jagdgeschwader 1 was dishing out destruction but paying a fearful price for their successes at St Denis-Westram. Several miles to the south-east the Focke Wulf 190 and Messerschmidt 109 pilots of Gruppen I and III were enjoying a relatively easy time of it in their brief attack on the Maldegem fighter base. The 135 Fighter Wing squadrons had been transferred to another airfield some days earlier, taking the airfield defences with them, reducing B-65 to the status of a maintenance depot. In a matter of minutes the raiders polished off 11 of the 17 Spitfires parked on the line waiting to be repaired. And they also did a number on the two Ansons, whose crews had sought refuge on the field the night before, after getting lost. That very minute, they were rudely awakened out of a sound sleep in the Cornet d'Or Hotel in Bruges by the pounding of cannon fire.

There was little interference from the ground, only sporadic fire from the two 20-mm cannon and Vickers machine-guns the fighter wing had left behind, and pot-shots from some rifles and handguns. Still, it was just enough to down three German fighters and scare them off from further attacks. Leutnant Anton Guha and Feldwebel Wilhelm Wichard, who was on his first operational sortie with less than 30 hours flying time on Messerschmidts, crash-landed close to the field and were taken prisoner. And Feldwebel Wilhelm Krauter was killed when his aircraft was damaged by the anti-aircraft fire and piled into the Scheldt on the flight home. At Maldegem there wasn't a single field casualty.

By its faulty nature the attack could hardly be termed a victory on anybody's part, but neither was it a failure. Perhaps, in fairness to both protagonists, it should be called a draw.

METZ-FRESCATY AIRFIELD (Y-34), France

The dogged determination displayed by the defenders spoke volumes. Through their extraordinary exertions they prevented what would have been a cakewalk for the Luftwaffe. It was a stout achievement — a feat they accomplished all by themselves. For, despite lack of air support from their own fighters, who were elsewhere in the air or still on the ground, and the bellyaching by the ack-ack crews that the attackers were too low for them to take proper aim, the gunners in the field accounted for 14 enemy fighters shot down and many more damaged. That remarkable effort in the face of fierce enemy fire thwarted what otherwise might have been a much costlier loss in equipment by the 365th Fighter Group.

While the price paid could hardly be called insignificant — 12 of 386th Fighter Squadron's Thunderbolts destroyed, seven damaged; nine of 387th's P-47s set on fire and another damaged; one of the 388th's fighters completely written off along with three others badly shot about — it was still far from critical. Not a single American pilot received a scratch and the aircraft were easily replaceable. By comparison, casualties suffered by the Germans in both men and machines, measured not only in terms of the losses sustained by the two attacking Gruppen from JG 53 during the raid itself, but also against those resulting from the entire sortie from take-off to landing, dealt Oberstleutnant Helmut Bennemann's entire Jagdgeschwader a devastating blow.

Before the raid even got down to serious business, Gruppe III had been taken out of the picture after losing nine Messerschmidts when attacked by a group of P-47s between Kaiserslautern and Pirmasens. Remarkably, all the pilots were able to take to their parachutes. Among them was Unteroffizier Karl Goller who hit the silk after ramming a Thunderbolt and, incredibly, landed with only minor injuries. Also lucky was Hauptmann Karl Luckenback who also bailed out safely after the engine of his brand new Me 109 "blew up around my ears."

The JG suffered yet another casualty before the remaining Gruppen reached Frescaty Airfield. Near Waldweisdorf, Gefreite Alfred Michel, a freshly graduated trainee pilot, on his first and, as it turned out, last fighter mission ended his brief career by being taken a prisoner of war after his engine packed up forcing him to pancake into a meadow close to a clump of trees.

The first two Messerschmidts to open fire on the target were both demolished by the ground defences, both of the pilots — assumed to be Feldwebeln Werner Kaschek and Otto Benz — killed before their aircraft slammed into the ground. Three others, all from Gruppe IV, were also killed outright: Feldwebelen Ernst Nachotsky and Ernst Off and Unteroffizier Herbert Maxis. Their scattered remains were only discovered some time later; in the case of Maxis, he was found a month after the raid — near Saarlouis. In fact, the bodies of five pilots from the same Gruppe — among them Kaschek and Benz — were never found, their fate remaining unresolved to this day. Another fatality was Feldwebel Johannes Muller who died in an American hospital the next day from severe burns.

Three of the other raiders following in the wake of those who met their demise were more fortunate. Unteroffizier Horst Pechchardscheck never even got to press the firing button before ack-ack fire took his plane out of action. Though wounded, with his Me 109 badly crippled and the engine intermittently sputtering, he somehow managed to coax his disabled machine back to the Gruppe IV home base of St Echterdingen.

First to open fire was Oberfeldwebel Kurt Opitz. Leading his Schwarm of four fighters — a box formation of two pairs abreast of each other — Opitz's guns set three Thunderbolts on fire before he felt a resounding thump and saw smoke billowing from the engine hood. He pulled up smartly and bailed out. Neither Unteroffizier Rudolf Konitzer nor Oberfeldwebel Stefan Kohl got a chance to bring their guns to bear before the ground defences put their 109s out of commission. However, both pilots survived the unnerving experience, Konitzer crash-landing in a field south of the airfield and Kohl bailing out into captivity.

Attackers and defenders alike witnessed more destruction and devastation than they were ever likely to see again. Although the raid lasted no longer than ten minutes, to those on the ground manning the defences, and others huddling in ditches, foxholes and crevices, or clutching the ground in terror, it seemed more like a lifetime. That apocalyptic hell reached a climax at the sight of one of the marauding Messerschmidts taking a direct hit only a few feet above the runway at midfield. Exploding into a fiery ball of flame, it nearly struck the Group Headquarters building as it hurtled past, spewing flaming gasoline that set a transport ablaze before it crashed into some trees at the edge of a field, a heap of burning metal spewing debris in all directions. The victim was never properly identified, but according to investigators the pilot could have been either Feldwebel Werner Kaschek or Oberleutnant Otto Benz (two of the five whose fate was never resolved).

For all their success in virtually wiping out more than three score American Thunderbolts (to no real avail), the Ace of Spades Jagdgeschwader had taken a fearful pasting. By day's end its fighter strength had been reduced by nearly 60 per cent; only 30 Messerschmidts remained serviceable. Nor had the Geschwader Kommodore been granted immunity. During the battle Helmut Bennemann picked up a few scars to remind him of the futility of Operation Bodenplatte. His Me 109 didn't escape damage either. The plane's tail resembled a sieve. To add misery to injury, the next day JG 53 lost the services of its gifted commander of Gruppe IV, Hauptmann Friedrich Muer, who was killed in combat with an American P-47.

OPHOVEN AIRFIELD (Y-32), Belgium

How to fairly and properly assess an absolute fiasco? Ophoven was not on the Bodenplatte hit list, not even as a secondary target. Nor did it stand in the way. It quite innocently happened to be in the wrong place at the wrong time, an unsuspecting victim of circumstances that the wayward JG 4 FW

190 pilots of Major Max Schroder's Gruppe II blundered onto wholly by chance. As well, in all probability, some of the JG 11 fighters assigned to attack nearby Asch Airfield, spilled over by chance.

At the outset, the protagonists had one thing in common; both attackers and defenders were taken completely by surprise. This worked in favour of the defenders. For the cost of only seven Spitfires damaged and three airmen wounded, the RAF Regiment anti-aircraft gunners shot down four Messerschmidts and damaged two others as well as bringing down two FW 190s. Add to the score a Focke Wulf destroyed by Flight Lieutenant Tony Gaze (presumably one of JG 4 Gruppe II's pilots). The winner by acclaim — Ophoven!

ST TROND-BRUSTEM AIRFIELD (A-92), Belgium

This engagement was hardly worth the candle, to put it mildly. For less than a dozen of Brigadier General Richard Nugent's 29th Tactical Air Force P-47s of the 48th and 407th USAF Fighter Groups destroyed, the A-92 mission, by the redoubtable Richthofen Jagdgeschwader 2, cost the JG 40 per cent of its fighter strength, a whipping from which it never recovered. Going into the attack already short by some 15 aircraft lost from flak en route to the target, by the time the brief ten minute attack was over, a total of 21 pilots had been killed or were missing in action, nine had been taken prisoner and two more — Unteroffizier Herbert Korber and Feldwebel Joseph Peschak — were badly injured. In addition, the supporting SG 4 lost four of its pilots. Among the total of the 36 casualties sustained were five highly expensive losses in the shape of veteran fighter leaders Hauptmann Georg Schroder, JG 2 Gruppe II commander, a veteran of 108 missions; SG 4 Gruppe III commander Oberstleutnant Albert Druschel, who had flown over 800 missions chiefly on the Russian Front where he had made a name for himself attacking ground targets; and three Staffel leaders from the Schlackgerschwader: Oberfeldwebel Hans Schmieder who bailed out and was taken prisoner near Aachen, as well as Feldwebelen Richard Heinz and Rudolf Fye, both of whom were killed near Maasmechelen.

St Trond got away with murder. For all the chaos to the Luftwaffe attackers it had created, it escaped without a single personnel casualty.

URSEL AIRFIELD (B-67), Belgium

In the absence of the 12 Spitfires that German Intelligence had led Oberstleutnant Herbert Ihlefeld's Oseau Jagdgeschwader 1 to believe occupied the field, but which in reality had returned to England the day before, the four remaining FW 190s of Oberleutnent Hans-Gottfried Meinhof's No 4 Staffel had to settle for the destruction of four stationary crippled aircraft under repair: the twin-engine Mosquito, the B-17 Flying Fortress and the two four-engine Lancaster bombers. It was hardly a decisive score, but better than nothing at all.

At Ursel there were no casualties but in addition to the loss of Unteroffizier Alfred Fritzsche, who was shot down just prior to the attack on the field, the Gruppe I Staffel also lost its leader. Hans-Gottfried Meinhof was killed on the return flight to Twenthe when his Focke Wulf was hit by Allied anti-aircraft fire over Breda.

VOLKEL AIRFIELD (B-80), Holland

The meticulously planned attack on B-80 to which all 70 pilots of Oberstleutnant Johann Kogler's Jagdgeschwader 6 had looked forward so eagerly and with such confidence, turned out to be a complete failure. After the navigational error on the part of the Ju 88 pathfinder, the formation ended up scattered all over Holland. Only a handful, including a Messerschmidt 262 jet, ever found the intended target. Except for a few Tempests perforated by gunfire, damage to the airfield was negligible.

The three RAF Regiment anti-aircraft squadrons, which were overjoyed at what they called "a wonderful tonic after months of no action," shot down five of the enemy raiders. 486 Squadron, which was in the air at the time, destroyed five German fighters, probably destroyed another and damaged two more, though not all of them over the airfield. Among the JG 6, probable victims included the Geschwader Kommodore Johann Kogler, Gruppe I and III Kommodores Hauptmann Ewald Trost and Major Helmut Kuhle and Staffel leader Hauptmann Norbert Katz. Also killed or missing in action were Leutnant Karl Grabmair, Feldwebel Helmut Grislawski, Unteroffizieren Karl-Heinz Riedel and Paul Scheider and Leutnant Hans Wulff, prisoner of war.

WOENSDRECHT AIRFIELD (B-79), Holland

This was a big zero all around! By the time the RAF Regiment ack-ack gunners fired off an exasperated 44 rounds of ammunition and three Spitfires from 127 Squadron led by Flight Lieutenant Arthur Covington, along with another hastily gathered flight from Squadron Leader Jan Tvelte's 332 Squadron had been scrambled, it was all too late. By then the Me 109s from JG 77s Gruppe I that had buzzed the airfield — the only feasible description — had flown the coop and were well on their way home to Dortmund, well out of reach. There were no pluses here, but no minuses either.

CHAPTER 8

KAPUT

Bodenplatte had torn the guts out of the Luftwaffe. Of the 269 pilots reported killed, missing in action, wounded, taken prisoner or crashed (as opposed to Allied losses of nine pilots killed and two wounded), two were Jagdgeschwader Kommodores, 14 were Gruppe commanders and 64 were Staffel leaders. This loss of leadership, combined with the corrosion of pilot and aircraft fighter strength, so severely crippled the German fighter air arm that it was nothing short of a miracle that it was able to continue to conduct operations. Somehow the Luftwaffe was able to cope with the task of defending against RAF and USAF bombing raids on German cities, factories and other targets, as well as to interfere with Allied tactical air operations over the battlefield capably and with determination. But not for long.

Exactly two weeks after the low-level attack against the Allied airfields, the Luftwaffe suffered another disastrous blow. On January 14, 1945, "Black Sunday," Allied fighters shot down 184 German aircraft, a feat that all but put the German air arm right out of business. This wasn't just the beginning of the end for the Luftwaffe; it *was* the end, period.

Disintegration of what had once been the most powerful aerial armada the world had ever known came quickly. On the day following the "Black Sunday" debacle, a date on which the OKW High Command issued the statement that "the initiative has passed to the enemy," Adolf Hitler, resigned to the fact that the Wacht Am Rhein Ardennes offensive was now beyond redemption, packed up his belongings and abandoned Der Adlershorst to return to the Reichschancellory in Berlin. Two days afterwards, convinced that after the disaster of Bodenplatte the Luftwaffe could no longer protect Germany from the Allied heavy bombing raids, he ordered half his fighter forces transferred to the Russian Front where the final offensive had opened, threatening to engulf eastern Germany within a fortnight. To no one's surprise, Generalmajor Dietrich Peltz was relieved of his command of the Jagdkorps 11, which to all intents, now ceased to exist anyway.

Exactly two weeks later, on January 22, 1945, in what would become notorious as the "Mutiny of the Aces," a delegation of the most prominent German fighter leaders presented themselves at the Haus de Flieger (Luftwaffe Headquarters) in Berlin, demanding an audience with Hermann Goering. Among them were Oberst Hermann Graf (212 victories), Oberst Gunther Lutzow (108), Oberst Gustav Roedel (98), Oberst Johannes "Macky" Steinhoff (175 — including six as an Me 262 pilot), and Oberst Hannes Trautloft (57 victories).

As spokesman for the group, Lutzow presented a written list of their grievances to the Reichsmarschall and his Chief of Air Staff, General Karl Koller. High on the list of complaints was the dismissal of Generalleutnant Adolf Galland as chief of the fighter arm whom the delegates regarded "as an outstanding personality and leader" and the repeated allegations of cowardice levelled at the fighter pilots by Goering. The appointment of General Dietrich Peltz as head of 11 Jagdkorps for which the deputation held responsible for the current losses of over 700 pilots also came under fire. The dossier pulled no punches. In sum, it accused Goering of misadministration of the Luftwaffe and misguided use of its deployment.

Goering was furious. "Are you accusing me of having built a weak Luftwaffe?" he challenged the gathering. Lutzow decided to stick his neck out — all the way out. What did he have to lose now? "On the contrary Reichsmarschall," he replied emphatically. "You built a strong air force for the early victories in Poland and France in 1940. But since then, you have been asleep!" That did it. Goering went almost blind with rage. This was treason! "You are a ring of mutineers," he ranted. "I'll have the lot of you shot!" With that, he stomped out of the room.[1]

It was pure bombast bordering on the melodramatic. In reality Goering had lost all authority. Nobody was shot, but the Reichsmarschall was able to make sure that the key fighter figures never held another command. Lutzow, Trautloft and the others were relegated to obscure positions though, as matters turned out, their fighting days were far from over.

Reinstatement of Adolf Galland, the central figure of all Luftwaffe fighter operations throughout the war from start to finish, as General de Jagdflieger, was quite out of the question, of course. But in the early morning hours of March 31, 1945, with the end of the war in Europe just over a month away, under Galland's command, twin-engine Messerschmidt 262 jet fighters of Jagdverband 44 took off from their base at Munich-Rhine Airfield in close formation on their first operational flight. It proved to be uneventful except that in landing at Munich proper 42 minutes later, it had established a record of having covered a distance of 300 miles in so short a period of time.

The jet-powered JV 44 was a model of Luftwaffe fighter pilot strength. Galland had lured most of the top aces into the fold, including "exiles" Lutzow and Trautloft. Others were Oberst Guenther Barkhorn (JV 44), Major Karl-Heinz Schnell (JV 44), Major Erich Hohagen (JV 44) and Hauptmann Walter "Count" Krupinski, to name just a few. Oberst Johannes "Macky" Steinhoff took charge of converting the pilots from piston to jet-engine aircraft. The cast of the "Squadron of Experts" was star-studded indeed, boasting one Generalleutnant, two Obersts, one Oberleutnant, three Majors, eight Leutnants and an equal number of officers of junior rank.

Even with their super-fast machines, however, the task of the world's first jet fighter squadron pilots was no piece of cake. Constant patrols of American Mustang and Thunderbolt fighters hovered overhead waiting to pounce on the Me 262s as they took off and landed. This situation was so critical that on alighting, the aircraft had to be hastily towed off the field and dispersed over the surrounding countryside where they were completely camouflaged. Returning them to the airfield for take-off was also a hairy, harried, hurried experience, often under fire. Between times, Marauder medium-bombers plastered the runways with bombs. Thousands of labourers had to be conscripted to keep a landing space open between craters.

In the closing days of the war, there was some small consolation for the jet pilots at least. Their fighters were rearmed with extra firepower: R4M rockets slung under the wings in two racks of 24 rockets. A single hit by one of the missiles was sufficient to blow a multi-engine bomber to smithereens. But it was all too late to have any real significance.

On April 26, the day after American and Russian troops joined hands at Torgau on the River Elbe, Galland flew his last mission of the war. A week later, most fighting on the Western Front had come to a halt. Next morning at Salzburg Airfield, to which JV 44 had been hurriedly transferred days earlier, Galland and his pilots stood watching American Thunderbolts circling above them like buzzards waiting for the field to capitulate so that they could take possession and try out the now uncamouflaged Me 262 jet fighters that had caused them so much grief. However, in their overzealous anticipation, they had failed to anticipate that final act of defiance by their defeated adversary. As the clanging and rattling of a pair of General Jacob Devers' 6th Army Group tanks, lumbering their way through the perimeter defences at the north end of the field, reverberated across the tarmac, in Alf Galland's own words: "there was no other possibility left; our jet fighters went up in flames." [2] That was a foreshadow of the ultimate fate of what remained of the rest of the once-proud Luftwaffe. Like the phoenix, emblem of death and resurrection, it had risen from its own funeral pyre only to flounder, fail and finally fall to a fiery finale. Kaput! Ashes to ashes!

Endnotes

1 Danny S. Parker, *To Win the Winter Sky,* p. 496.

2 Adolf Galland, *The First and the Last,* p. 279.

EPILOGUE

OVER AND OUT

For someone who had been as severely clobbered in the Luftwaffe attack on B-78 airfield while preparing to take off in his Typhoon fighter-bomber on New Year's Day morning as Flying Officer Ed Flanagan of 440 Squadron RCAF, his speedy recovery from his wounds was truly remarkable. After little more than a month in the military hospitals in Eindhoven, Holland and Swindon, England his face and leg injuries had sufficiently healed for the doctors to pronounce him fit enough to be discharged and released on convalescent leave.

Four days later, after a 30-day enforced postponement, on the beautifully clear winter's day of February 10, Ed and his fiancée, Leading Aircraftswoman Renee Taylor, were finally married at Colgar Parish Church near Huddersfield in Yorkshire. Following the wedding ceremony, as the bride and groom emerged from the church entrance, they were greeted by the sight of snow that had blanketed the countryside while they were exchanging vows. Best man Dick Watson, Ed's squadron buddy and survivor of the Bodenplatte shoot-out, declared it "a sign of good luck." It surely was. The blissful romance lasted 50 years until Ed's death in 1995.

Although rations were still scarce in late wartime Britain, the wedding guests did not lack for food or refreshment. Renee had made sure of that. By scrounging ration coupons from family, friends and neighbours, she had ensured an abundance of both. The enthusiasm to contribute to the occasion had, in fact, caught on like wildfire. So much so that the local grocer, completely carried away in his zeal to fashion a suitably tiered wedding cake for the event, was briefly jailed by the local constabulary for having dealt in black market ingredients to create his masterpiece. Cheers! Was there ever a toast to the happiness of newly-weds quite so novel or well meant?

BODENPLATTE SCOREBOARD

Under Attack	From
B-70 ANTWERP-DEURNE	DORTMUND, BONNINGHARDT and DUSSELDORF-LOHAUSEN
115 Fighter Wing RAF	**Jagdgeschwader 77 "Red Hearts"**
74 Squadron Spitfire IX	Gruppe I Me 109 G-14
145 Squadron Spitfire IX	Gruppe II Me 109 K-4
329 Squadron Spitfire IX	Gruppe III Me 109 K-4
329 Squadron Spitfire IX	
341 Squadron Spitfire IX	
146 Fighter Wing RAF	Four pilots MIA, six pilots killed, four pilots POW.
193 Squadron Typhoon IB	
197 Squadron Typhoon IB	
257 Squadron Typhoon IB	
261 Squadron Typhoon IB	
266 Squadron Typhoon IB	

Three Typhoons destroyed, several damaged; one DC-3 Dakota, one B-17 Flying Fortress damaged. One airman wounded.

Raid Rating xx
Defence Effective ++

Under Attack	From
Y-29 ASCH	DARMSTADT-GREISHEIM, ZEILLHAUSEN and GROSS-OSTHEIM
352nd Fighter Group USAF	
487 Fighter Squadron P-51 Mustangs	
366th Fighter Group USAF	**Jagdgeschwader 11**
390 Fighter Squadron	Gruppe I FW 190 A-8
391 Fighter Squadron	Gruppe II Me 109 G-14/K-4
	Gruppe III FW 190-A
32 Victories air-to-air; seven ack-ack, four Mustangs slightly damaged.	Seven MIA, 23 killed and 2 POWs.

Raid Rating x
Defence Effective ++++

Under Attack	From
B-56 BRUSSELS-EVERE	NORDHORN and PLANTLUNNE
127 Fighter Wing RCAF	**Jagdgeschwader 26 "Schlageter"**
403 Squadron Spitfire XVI	Gruppe II FW 190 D-9
416 Squadron Spitfire XVI	Gruppe III Me 109 G-14/K-4
11 Spitfires destroyed, 12 severely damaged, VIP Dakota and Prince Bernhardt's Beechcraft set on fire, 11 motor transports destroyed, one hangar damaged. One airman killed, 11 wounded, one pilot killed. Six German fighters shot down in the air, 7 by ack-ack.	20 pilots lost, killed MIA or POW.

Raid Rating xxxx
Defence Effective +++

Under Attack	From

B-60 BRUSSELS-GRIMBERGEN

Non-operational RAF Fighter Field

One B-17 Flying Fortress destroyed and one set on fire, one P-51 Mustang destroyed; and 2 hangars, 12 motor transports and 2 fuel tankers demolished. One airman killed, 2 wounded.

FURSTENAU

Jagdgeschwader 26
Gruppe I FW 190 D-9

Jagdgeschwader 54
Gruppe III FW 190 D-9

Five aircraft destroyed by ack-ack fire over the airfield. Total losses: 13 pilots, 8 aircraft returned badly shot up.

Raid Rating xx
Defence Effective ++

Under Attack	From

B-58 BRUSSELS-MELSBROEK

34 Reconnaissance Wing RAF
16 Squadron Spitfire XII
69 Squadron Wellington XIII
140 Squadron Mosquito XVI

139 Medium Bomber Wing RAF
90 Squadron Mitchell II
180 Squadron Mitchell II
320 Squadron Mitchell II

271 Squadron Harrow Transport

14 Wellingtons, 7 Harrows, 6 Mitchells, 6 Mosquitos, 3 Spitfires destroyed; 5 Mitchells damaged. Five airmen killed, 25 wounded.

RHINE-MAIN

Jagdgeschwader 27
Gruppe I Me 109 G-14/K-4

VORDEN

Jagdgeschwader 54
Gruppe IV FW 190 A-8/A-8

30 out of 60 planes that set out never made it back. Over target, JG 27 lost 6 pilots killed, one POW. JG 54 lost five pilots.

Raid Rating xxxx
Defence Effective +++

Under Attack	From
B-78 EINDHOVEN	**PADERBORN, LIPPSPSINGE and GUTERSLOH**
39 Reconnaissance Wing RCAF	
400 Squadron Spitfire IX	**Jagdgeschwader 3 "Udet"**
404 Squadron Spitfire IX	Gruppe I Me 109 G-10/G-14
430 Squadron Spitfire IX	Gruppe III Me 109 G-14/K-4
124 Wing RAF	Gruppe IV FW 190 A-8
131 Squadron Typhoon IB	
181 Squadron Typhoon IB	Out of an attacking force of 70
182 Squadron Typhoon IB	fighters, 22 pilots were killed, MIA
247 Squadron Typhoon 1B	or POW. A dozen others returned to
143 Wing RCAF	base badly shot up, some severely
168 Squadron Typhoon IB	wounded.
438 Squadron Typhoon IB	
439 Squadron Typhoon IB	
440 Squadron Typhoon IB	

184 aircraft destroyed, 84 damaged including 40 Typhoons, 20 Spitfires, 11 Wellingtons, several DC-3 Dakotas and Mitchells, 2 Ansons, 2 Austers and a B-17 Flying Fortress. 5 pilots were killed and 2 wounded. Ground casualties totalled 145, 40 killed among them.

Raid Rating xxxx
Defence Effective +++

Under Attack	From
B-61 ST DENIS-WESTRAM	**RHINE-MAIN**
131 Wing RAF (Polish)	**Jagdgeschwader 1 "Oseau"**
302 Squadron Spitfire IX/XVI	Gruppe II FW 190 A-8
308 Squadron Spitfire IX	
317 Squadron Spitfire IX	19 pilots killed, 3 before reaching target; 2 POW.

25 Spitfires, one Stirling, one B-17 Flying Fortress destroyed. Two pilots killed.

Raid Rating xxx
Defence Effective +++

Under Attack	From
B-77 GILZE-REIJEN	LIPPSPSINGE

35 Reconnaissance Wing RAF

2 Squadron Mustang II, Spitfire XIV
164 Squadron Typhoon IB
268 Squadron Mustang IA/II

One Typhoon destroyed, another
damaged; one Anson and a Mustang
shot up. Seven airmen wounded.

Jagdgeschwader 3

Gruppe III Me 109 G-14/K-4

HESEPE

Jagdgeschwader 27

Gruppe III Me 109 F-4

MUNSTER-HANDORF

Einsatzastaffel

Gruppe III (76) Arado 234

Three Me 109s destroyed, another 3
damaged, one Ju 188 destroyed, one
Ar 234 shot down.

Raid Rating x
Defence Effective ++

Under Attack	From
B-88 HEESCH	DELMENHORST and BISSEL

126 Wing RCAF

401 Squadron Spitfire IX
402 Squadron Spitfire IX
411 Squadron Spitfire IX
412 Squadron Spitfire IX
442 Squadron Spitfire IX

Three Spitfires shot down — no
casualties. One Building damaged.

Jagdgeschwader 6

Gruppe I FW 190 A-8
Gruppe III Me 109 G-10/G-14

24 aircraft destroyed, 7 damaged.

Raid Rating x
Defence Effective ++++

Under Attack	From
A-89 LE CULOT	DARMSTADT-GREISHEIM, BABENHAUSEN and RHINE-MAIN
36th Fighter Group USAF	
363rd Fighter Group	**Jagdgeschwader 4**
P-47 Thunderbolts	Gruppe I Me 109 G-14/K-4
373 Fighter Group	Gruppe II FW 190 A-8
P-47 Thunderbolts	Gruppe III Me 109 G-14/K-4
No attack! No action!	Geschwader disoriented when trailblazer shot down. Gruppen dispersed to find other targets.

Raid Rating 0
Defence Effective 0

Under Attack	From
B-65 MALDEGEM	TWENTHE and RHINE-MAIN
RAF Maintenance Depot	**Jagdgeschwader 1**
17 Spitfires	Gruppe I FW 190 A-8
2 Ansons	Gruppe III Me 109 G-14
11 Spitfires destroyed. Both Ansons severely damaged.	Three Me 109s shot down. One pilot POW.

Raid Rating xxx
Defence Effective ++

Under Attack	From
Y-34 METZ-FRESTACY	MALMSHEIM, KIRRLACH and ST ECHTERDINGEN
365th Fighter Group USAF	**Jagdgeschwader 53 "Ace of Hearts"**
386th Fighter Squadron P-47 Thunderbolt	Gruppe I Me 109 G-14/K-4
387th Fighter Squadron P-47 Thunderbolt	Gruppe III Me 109 G-14
388th Fighter Squadron P-47 Thunderbolt	Gruppe IV Me 109 G-14
22 Thunderbolts destroyed, 11 damaged.	Gruppe III taken out of action before reaching target with loss of 9 Me 109s; 14 aircraft shot down and several more damaged in target area. Geschwader strength reduced by 60 per cent. Only 30 fighters left serviceable, most badly damaged.

Raid Rating xxx
Defence Effective ++++

Under Attack	From
Y-32 OPHOVEN	BABENHAUSEN
125 Fighter Wing RAF	**Jagdgeschwader 4**
41 Squadron Spitfire XIV	Gruppe II FW 190 A-8
130 Squadron Spitfire XIV	
350 Squadron Spitfire XIV	ZEILLHAUSEN
610 Squadron Spitfire XIV	**Jagdgeschwader 11**
	Gruppe II Me 109 G-14/K-4
Seven Spitfires damaged, 3 airmen wounded.	Three FW 190s and 4 Me 109s destroyed, 2 109s damaged.

Raid Rating xx
Defence Effective ++

Under Attack	From

A-92 ST TROND-BRUSTEM

48th Fighter Group USAF

492 Fighter Squadron P-47 Thunderbolt
493 Fighter Squadron P-47 Thunderbolt
494 Fighter Squadron P-47 Thunderbolt

404th Fighter Group USAF

506 Fighter Squadron P-47 Thunderbolt
507 Fighter Squadron P-47 Thunderbolt
508 Fighter Squadron P-47 Thunderbolt

Less than a dozen P-47s destroyed.

MERZHAUZEN, NIDDA and ALDERNSTADT

Jagdgeschwader 2
"Richthofen"
Gruppe I FW 190 A-87/A-9
Gruppe II Me 109 G-14/K-14
Gruppe III FW 190 D-9

COLOGNE-WAHN

Schlacktgerschwader 4
Gruppe III FW 190 F-8

15 JG 2 aircraft lost en route to target. 21 more pilots lost, killed, MIA, or POW. Two others injured. SG 4 lost 4 pilots.

Raid Rating x
Defence Effective +++

Under Attack	From

B-67 URSEL

No. 424 RAF Rearmament and Refuelling Unit

One Mosquito, a B-17 Flying Fortress and 2 Lancasters, all under repair, destroyed.

TWENTHE

Jagdgeschwader 1
Gruppe I FW 190 A-8

Two FW 190s destroyed, both pilots killed, one before reaching target, the other on the way home.

Raid Rating xx
Defence Effective ++

Under Attack	From
B-80 VOLKEL	DELMENHORST, QUACKENBRUCK, VECHTA and BISSEL
121 Wing RAF	
174 Squadron Typhoon IB	**Jagdgeschwader 6**
175 Squadron Typhoon IB	Gruppe I FW 190 A-8
184 Squadron Typhoon IB	Gruppe II FW 190 A-8
122 Wing RAF	Gruppe III Me 109 G-10/G-14
3 Squadron Tempest V	Six pilots killed or missing. One POW.
56 Squadron Tempest V	Two aircraft damaged by ack-ack.
80 Squadron Tempest V	
274 Squadron Tempest V	
486 Squadron Tempest V	

Several Tempests perforated by gunfire.

Raid Rating xx
Defence Effective ++

Under Attack	From
B-79 WOENSDRECHT	DORTMUND
132 Wing RAF	**Jagdgeschwader 77**
66 Squadron Spitfire XVI	Gruppe I Me 109 G-14
127 Squadron Spitfire XVI	
322 Squadron Spitfire IX	No result.
331 Squadron Spitfire IX	
332 Squadron Spitfire IX	

No result.

Raid Rating 0
Defence Effective 0

BIBLIOGRAPHY

Allen, Colonel Robert S. *Lucky Forward,* New York: The Vanguard Press Inc., 1947

Baumbach, Werner. *The Life and Death of the Luftwaffe,* New York: Coward-McCann, Inc., 1960.

Berger, Monty and Street, Brian Jeffrey. *Invasions Without Tears: The Story of Canada's Top-Scoring Spitfire Wing in Europe During the Second World War,* Toronto: Random House of Canada, 1994.

Bishop, Arthur. *Courage in the Air, Canada's Military Heritage,* Volume 1, Whitby, Ont.: McGraw-Hill Ryerson, 1992.

Bloemertz, Gunther. *Heaven Next Stop,* London: William Kimber Ltd., 1953.

Bracken, Robert. *Spitfire: The Canadians,* Erin, Ont.: Boston Mills Press, 1995.

Calvocoressi, Peter and Wint, Guy. *Total War: The Causes and Courses of the Second World War,* New York: Pantheon Books, 1972.

Carter, Kit C. and Mueller, Robert. *The Army Air Forces in WWII 1941-1945,* Maxwell, Ala: Albert F. Simpson Historical Research Center, 1973.

Churchill, Winston S. *Triumph and Tragedy, The Second World War,* Boston: Houghton Mufflin Company, 1953.

Clostermann, Pierre. *The Big Show,* London: Chatto and Windus, 1951.

Franks, Norman L. *The Battle of the Airfields,* London: Grub Street, 1994.

Frischauer, Willi. *The Rise and Fall of Hermann Goering,* New York: Ballantine Books, 1951.

Galland, Adolf. *The First and the Last,* New York: Henry Hill and Company Inc., 1954.

— *The Luftwaffe at War,* London: Ian Allen, 1972.

Gerbig, Werner. *Six Months to Oblivion,* New York: Hippocrene Books, 1975.

Greenhous, Brereton, Stephen J. Harris, William C. Johnston and G.P. Rawling. *The Crucible of War 1939-1945,* Toronto: University of Toronto Press, 1994.

Halliday, Hugh A. *Typhoon and Tempest: The Canadian Story,* Toronto: Canav Books, 1992.

Hart, Liddel B.H. *History of World War II,* New York: G. Putnam's Sons, 1970.

Heilmann, Willi. *Alert in the West,* London: William Kimber Ltd., 1953.

Jablonski, Edward. *Flying Fortress,* Garden City, NY: Doubleday & Company Inc., 1965.

Johnson, Charles, R. *History of the Hell Hawks,* Aneheim: Dabney, 1975.

Johnson, J.E. *Full Circle,* New York: Ballantine Books, 1964.

— *Wing Leader,* New York: Ballantine Books, 1957.

Killen, John. *A History of the Luftwaffe 1915-1945,* New York: Berkley Medallion Books, 1967.

Mason, Herbert Molloy. *The Rise of the Luftwaffe: Forging the Secret German Air Weapon, 1918-1940,* New York: Dial Press, 1973.

McIntosh, Dave. *High Blue Battle,* Toronto: Stoddart Publishing Co. Limited, 1990.

Parker, Danny S. *To Win the Winter Skies: The Air War Over the Ardennes 1944-1945,* Conshohocken, Penn: Combined Books Inc., 1994.

Payne, Robert. *The Life and Death of Adolf Hitler,* New York: Praeger Publishers, 1973.

Rawlings, John D.R. *Fighter Squadrons of the RAF and Their Aircraft,* London: Macdonald & Janes, 1969

Sims, Edward. *American Aces of WW II,* London: Macdonald Ltd., 1958.

Smith, J. Richard. *Focke-Wulf,* New York: Arco Publishing Company, Inc., 1973.

Shore, C.F. *2nd Tactical Air Force,* London: Osprey Ltd., 1970.

Saunders, Hilary St George. *Royal Air Force, 1939-1945: The Fight Is Won,* Volume III, London: Her Majesty's Stationery Office, 1954.

Toliver, Col. Ralph F. and Trevor J. Constable. *Horrido,* New York: Bantam Books, 1979.

The R.C.A.F. Overseas: The Sixth Year, Volume 3, Toronto: Oxford University Press, 1949.

Ziegler, Frank (Tr.). *The Luftwaffe War Diaries,* Garden City, N.Y.: Doubleday, 1968.

INDEX